AIB Latin America

**Series Editor**
Leonardo Liberman
Libens Research and Development
Santiago, Chile

The AIB-LAT book series is an initiative from the Latin American chapter of the Academy of International Business. The series publishes books that bring together theory, academic research and research-driven practice in the field of International Business (IB) from, and within, the Latin American region. The AIB-LAT Book Series is a significant outlet of research-driven knowledge on IB and multinational company (MNC) behavior in the region. The AIB-LAT series invites scientific research and theory that deals with strategies, structures and decision-making processes of MNCs in Latin America; cross-border activities of enterprises such as intra-company trade, investments, finance, technology transfer, people management and innovation; interactions between MNC enterprises and other relevant actors in Latin-America: organizations, institutions, markets, governments, and indigenous stakeholders. The series also deals with research on the impact of, and interaction between, the different Latin American cultural, economic, legal, and political settings on activities, strategies, structures and decision-making processes of MNCs. Other topics of interest are cross-country comparative studies of businesses, business processes, contexts and organizational behavior in Latin America and the development of strategic export alliances, and mergers and acquisitions in the Latin American context. The AIB-LAT book series will serve to inform scholars and practitioners about the current developments of IB theories and research in the region and also awake the interest of IB scholars to further advance the knowledge and understanding of IB and MNC behavior in Latin America.

More information about this series at
http://www.palgrave.com/gp/series/14760

# Contents

# Notes on Contributors

**Simone R. Barakat** is an Assistant Professor at the graduate program in Hospitality at University Anhembi Morumbi. She holds a PhD and a Master's Degree in Management from the School of Economics, Management and Accounting, University of São Paulo (FEA-USP). She was a visiting researcher at the Darden School of Business, University of Virginia. Her current research focuses on Stakeholder Theory, Sustainability, Corporate Social Responsibility and Organizational Capabilities. Simone has published in academic journals such as *Management Decision*, *Journal of Cleaner Production* and *Organization and Environment*, and in Conference Proceedings such as AoM, EGOS and AIB-LAT.

**Constanza Bianchi** has a PhD in Management and MSc in Marketing from Queen's University, Canada. Currently, Constanza is Professor of Marketing and co-Director of the PhD in Management program at the School of Business, Universidad Adolfo Ibanez, Chile. She is also Adjunct Professor at Queensland University of Technology, Brisbane, Australia. Her research interests focus on international marketing, internationalization of services, and tourism competitiveness of Latin American destinations. She has investigated topics such as failure and success of retail internationalization, drivers and barriers of SME internationalization commitment and performance (particularly for emerging market firms), the role of technology on international market performance, tourism competitiveness, destination attractiveness and branding, and consumer engagement in social media. Constanza's research has appeared in a range of journals including the *Journal of Business Research*, *International Marketing Review*, *International Business Review* and *Tourism Management* among others.

**Catherine Bradley** earned her Master's Degree in Political Science at Northeastern University. During her time at Northeastern she focused on international relations, comparative politics, institutional frameworks, and European politics. She currently serves as a research associate for Lieberman Consulting.

**Nicholas J. Cid** is a senior revenue management analyst at the global headquarters of The Hertz Corporation, a Fortune 500 company (ranked #335 in the latest, 2018 ranking) and one of the largest, worldwide, airport general-use, vehicle rental companies that operates in more than 150 countries around the globe. Nicholas Cid has a demonstrated history of working in the leisure, travel and tourism industry. His fields of expertise include event planning, customer service, data analysis, demand forecasting, strategic planning and business development. He holds an MBA Degree from the Lutgert College of Business at Florida Gulf Coast University.

**Diego Bonaldo Coelho** is an Assistant Professor at Escola Superior de Propaganda e Marketing (ESPM), São Paulo, Brazil, and is Associate Professor at the Graduate Program on Public Management and International Cooperation of the Federal University of Paraiba (PGPCI/UFPB), Paraiba, Brazil. Diego also works as a consultant and professor at FIA Business School and lectures at Fundação Dom Cabral (FDC) and at São Paulo School of Economics FGV (EESP/FGV). He is the coordinator of the ESPM's Multinationals Observatory. Currently, his research interests are: internationalization of Brazilian companies; trade policies and support for internationalization; international business; global value chains; corporate diplomacy; technology and innovation; and regional development.

**Angela da Rocha** is Associate Professor of Marketing and International Business and Coordinator of NUPIN – Center for International Business Research at the IAG Business School, the Pontifical Catholic University of Rio de Janeiro. She is a former Professor of Marketing and International Business at the Coppead Graduate School of Business, the Federal University of Rio de Janeiro, where she served twice as Dean. She holds a PhD in Business Administration from the IESE Business School. She is a member of CIMaR—Consortium for International Marketing Research—and is a senior researcher of the Brazilian National Council for Scientific and Technological Research (CNPq). She has published extensively in Brazilian and international journals including *International Business Review, Journal of Business Research, Journal of International Entrepreneurship, International Marketing Review, Entrepreneurship Theory and Practice, Entrepreneurship & Regional Development, International*

*Journal of Retail and Distribution Management* and *Journal of International Business Studies*. She has published several books in Brazil and chapters in international and Brazilian books.

**Jorge Ferreira da Silva** is Professor of Strategy at the Pontifical Catholic University of Rio de Janeiro (PUC-Rio). He has served for several years as President of ANPAD, the Brazilian Academy of Management. He is also a senior researcher in the area of Business Administration in the ranking of the National Council for Scientific and Technological Research (CNPq). Dr Da Silva has published in national and international journals, such as the *Journal of Business Research, Journal of International Entrepreneurship, International Journal of Hospitality Management, Latin American Business Review* and *Brazilian Administration Review*. Prior to his academic career, Dr. da Silva was a Vice-President of leading Brazilian firms in the Information Technology area. He is an electrical engineer and holds a PhD in Industrial Engineering from PUC-Rio.

**Luis Alfonso Dau** is Associate Professor of International Business and Strategy at the D'Amore-McKim School of Business, Northeastern University. His research and teaching interests include global strategy, emerging market firms, institutional changes, pro-market reforms, business groups, family firms, firm performance, international corporate social responsibility, sustainability, formal and informal entrepreneurship, and culture. He is also a John Dunning Visiting Fellow at Henley Business School, University of Reading.

**Keysa Manuela Cunha de Mascena** is an Assistant Professor at the Graduate Program in Business Administration at the University of Fortaleza (UNIFOR), Brazil. She holds a PhD and a Master's Degree in Management from the School of Economics, Administration and Accounting at the University of São Paulo (FEA/USP), Brazil. She was a Visiting Researcher at the University of the Basque Country (UPV/EHU), Bilbao, Spain. She is engaged in research groups at UNIFOR, USP and UPV/EHU and presented papers in international conferences and published in journals. She is interested in topics related to business for society, stakeholder theory, corporate social responsibility and performance.

**Bruno de Oliveira Carvalho** is Professor of Production and Mechanical Engineering at Unifanor | Wyden (Brazil). He received his Master's Degree at University of Fortaleza (Brazil). Since 2009, he has worked as a program management officer at Ford Motor Company. He founded the Automotive Engineering Center at Unifanor | Wyden, where he coordinates undergraduate courses related to the automobile industry.

**Jason A. Hoop** holds an MBA Degree from the Lutgert College of Business at Florida Gulf Coast University (FGCU) and is the Marketing Director of Hoop Dental. He currently is a Doctor of Dental Medicine Candidate. He also holds a BSc Degree in biotechnology and served as the Senate President of the Student Government at FGCU, Chapter President of FGCU's Global Medical Brigades, Alumni Relations Graduate Assistant, and Chapter President of the Sigma Phi Epsilon Florida Chapter. He also worked for Algenols Biofuels Inc. as a biochemistry and physiology intern and worked in the field of analytical chemistry.

**David Kimber C.** is Assistant Professor of Marketing and Master of Science in Marketing Program Director at the School of Business and Economics, Universidad de los Andes, Chile. He is also PhD candidate at Universidad de Navarra, Spain. He received his Commercial Engineering Degree in 1994, his MBA (1999) and MSc in Management (2012) all from Universidad Católica de Chile. He is a member of AEJMC. His research interests are international sales/marketing management, consumer behavior, communication and advertising.

**Beatriz Kury** received her PhD in International Business from the IAG Business School, Pontifical Catholic University of Rio de Janeiro, Brazil. She is presently a Research Associate at NUPIN—Center for International Business Research at the same university. She is presently engaged in research projects mainly related to service firms' internationalization and to export promotion. Since May 2016, Beatriz integrates the technical team of PEIEX—a capacity building EPP led by Apex-Brasil, the Brazilian Trade and Investment Promotion Agency, and implemented in inexperienced exporters in the State of Rio de Janeiro by PUC-Rio. Other than her academic background, Beatriz has more than 20 years' experience built up at institutions of different sizes, industry sectors and corporate cultures where she occupied mainly senior management positions. Her research interests combine internationalization of clusters and firms, and export promotion activities.

**Leonardo Liberman** is a Senior Researcher at Libens Research and Development. He recently worked as an Associate Professor at the Business Faculty at Universidad de los Andes in Santiago, Chile, and previously at the School of Management at Queensland University of Technology and as the Director of the International Graduate Program at Stockholm School of Economics in Sweden. He also was the director of the International MBA program at Universidad Adolfo Ibañez. Before pursuing his academic career, Leonardo was the HR Principal of two international companies and worked as instructor in several executive management courses at iCARE, Santiago, Chile. Professor Liberman has published in several peer-reviewed scientific journals and has led a number of research projects, conferences and private consultancies at local and international levels. Leonardo was one of the founding members of AIB-LAT and its first Chapter Chair.

**Elizabeth M. Moore** is a Visiting Assistant Professor in International Business & Strategy at the D'Amore-McKim School of Business and the Global Resilience Institute, Northeastern University. She recently finished her PhD in International Relations. Her research and teaching interests center on formal and informal entrepreneurship, corporate social responsibility, institutional changes, institutional disruptions, transnational institutions, pro-market reforms, firm performance, emerging market firms, and international organizations.

**William Newburry** is Chair of the Department of International Business and the Ryder Eminent Scholar of Global Business at Florida International University. He also serves as a Non-Resident Senior Research Fellow at the China Europe International Business School (CEIBS) Center for Emerging Market Studies. His research focuses on how multinational corporations manage and relate to subsidiaries and other local stakeholders when they invest in foreign countries, particularly in terms of issues related to corporate reputation. Bill has published 40+ articles in top-tier, peer-reviewed journals, along with another 20 articles in edited books. He recently coauthored *Emerging Market Multinationals: Managing Operational Challenges for Sustained International Growth* (2016, Cambridge University Press), and has coedited two additional books. Bill was Chapter Chair of the Academy of International Business Latin America (AIB-LAT) Chapter from 2012–2018, and serves as Series Editor for *Research in Global Strategic Management.*

**Mário Henrique Ogasavara** is Professor of International Business at Escola Superior de Propaganda e Marketing (ESPM), São Paulo (Brazil), in the Graduate Program in International Management. He received his PhD Degree in Management at the University of Tsukuba (Japan). He was a Visiting Professor at the Deggendorf Institute of Technology (Germany) and joined the Department of Japanese Studies as a post-doctoral fellow at the National University of Singapore. He served as a Track-Chair of "FDI and Internationalization" at the AIB-LAT conference (2017–2018), Co-Chair of the track "MNE Strategy and Organization" at the 2015 EIBA Conference, and Guest-Editor of a Special Issue of *Journal of Business Research*. Currently, he is an Avocational Letter at Steinbeis University (Germany) and Associate Coordinator of Asian Studies

Program (ProAsia—University of São Paulo, Brazil). He is also the Chair of the Academic Division of Strategy (ANPAD—Brazilian Academy of Management) and the Regional Coordinator (Brazil) of the Society for Global Business and Economic Development (SGBED). His primary research interests include internationalization strategy, the performance of multinational corporations, entry mode, joint ventures, and Asian and Brazilian companies.

**Moacir de Miranda Oliveira Jr.** is Full Professor and Head of the Business Administration Department at USP—University of São Paulo. Moacir is currently the Chief Editor of *INMR—Innovation & Management Review* (Emerald). He is a member of the Executive Committee of the Academy of International Business—Latin America Chapter, Director for Latin America of GLORAD—Center for Global R&D & Innovation and member of the Board of the EMI—Emerging Markets Institute of Cornell University. As a consultant in the field of strategy, innovation and international business, he has been working for major Brazilian companies and for the government over the past 25 years.

**David M. Peterson** is a customer success manager at FieldEdge, a private company that develops and delivers software for the service industry in the United States and internationally. He has won personal sales awards and works in the company's award-winning customer success team, which recently won the Stevie Award, the worldwide Oscar for customer service that has been awarded to companies such as DHL, Delta Airlines and Vizio. He has experience in business development, operations management, team leadership and development, strategic planning/implementation, personnel management and sales. He holds an MBA Degree from the Lutgert College of Business at Florida Gulf Coast University.

**Javier Pinto Garay** is professor of Business Ethics at the School of Business and Economics, Universidad de los Andes, Chile. He has published several articles and chapters on Theory of Work and Virtue Ethics in Business. He is currently working on virtue ethics applied to employee compensation and fiduciary responsibilities of managers. Professor Pinto-Garay holds a BSc Degree in Philosophy (Universidad de los Andes), an MSc Degree in Human Resource Management and Organizational Behavior (Universidad Católica de Chile) and a PhD Degree in Philosophy (University of Navarra).

**Daniel Rottig** is an Associate Professor of International Business and Strategic Management in the Management Department of the Lutgert College of Business at Florida Gulf Coast University in the United States. He has published extensively in the areas of institutional and cultural environments of multinational corporations, the performance determinants of international mergers and acquisitions, and emerging markets. He has received several awards and award nominations for his scholarly work from the world's leading academic associations and publishers in the field of international business and management, including the Academy of International Business, the Academy of Management and Emerald Publishing. He is a passionate educator whose goal is to help students and executives understand the global business environment and how to strategically manage firms in international markets. He has taught in the undergraduate, graduate, executive and doctoral programs at several universities in the United States, Australia, Asia, the Middle East and Latin America. He is actively involved in the academic community and currently serves as the Editor of the Academy of International Business Insights.

**Greici Sarturi** is a Professor of Business Administration at the Federal University of Santa Maria (UFSM), Brazil. She holds a PhD Degree in Business Administration from the School of Economics, Administration and Accounting—University of São Paulo (FEA-USP) and a Master's Degree in Business Administration from the Federal University of Santa Maria. She was a visiting scholar at the University of Texas at Arlington. Her research interests are in the area of Corporate Strategy and Stakeholder Theory. She is a researcher engaged in the Stakeholders & Networks Research Group and Leader of the Group of Extension and Research in Organizational Strategy (GEPEO).

# List of Figures

# List of Tables

# 1

# Building a Whole from the Parts: Environmental, Firm and Individual-Level Factors

**William Newburry, Leonardo Liberman, and Moacir de Miranda Oliveira Jr.**

Since the chapter's approval at the 2008 Academy of International Business (AIB) annual meeting in Milan, the AIB Latin America Chapter (AIB-LAT) has continually grown. Back in 2008, AIB-LAT had 27 members coming from Brazil, Chile, Colombia, Mexico and the United States. The founding members were: Alexandre Faria, Ana Lucia Guedes, Andrés Castro Figueroa, Angela da Rocha, Belmiro N. Joao, Christian Felzensztein, Chile Dirk Boehe, Eva Stal, Francisco Castañeda González, Frederico Turolla, Jaime Alonso Gomez, Jairo Laser Procianoy, Jorge Carneiro, Leonardo Liberman, Luciano Barin Cruz, Luiz Alberto

W. Newburry (✉)
Department of International Business, Florida International University, Miami, FL, USA
e-mail: newburry@fiu.edu

L. Liberman
Libens Research and Development, Santiago, Chile

M. de M. Oliveira Jr.
Business Administration Department, University of São Paulo, São Paulo, Brazil
e-mail: mirandaoliveira@usp.br



W. Newburry et al. (eds.), *Contemporary Influences on International Business in Latin America*, AIB Latin America, https://doi.org/10.1007/978-3-319-98340-0_1

Campos, Ma. Teresa de la Garza Carranza, Marcela Anzola, Marcelo Andrés Machado, María Teresa Fleury, Miguel Olivas-Luján, Paulo R. S. Terra, Sandra Milena Santamaria, Sascha Furst, Sergio Garcilazo, Victor Almeida and Zandra Balbinot. Since then, AIB-LAT has held several conferences, meetings and academic activities that have evolved each year in both the breadth and depth of its activities.

The chapter held its Fifth and Sixth Annual Conferences in 2015 and 2016, respectively. The Fifth Annual Conference occurred in Santiago, Chile in January 2015 on the topic of Internationalization of Family and Entrepreneurial Businesses in Latin America. The Sixth Annual Conference was held in São Paulo, Brazil in February 2016 on the topic of Innovation Environments and Global Value Chains in Latin America. Together these topics of family and entrepreneurial business along with innovation and global value chains capture a much broader overarching theme within international business in Latin America: the multiple levels of influence on international business occurring at the environmental, firm and individual levels. The content of these two conferences captured these levels of analysis well across the spectrum of international business in Latin America. Several exemplars of these papers that focus on each influence level are contained in the following chapters in this volume.

Prior to overviewing the specific works in the volume, we think it appropriate to overview some figures concerning the AIB-LAT conferences to illustrate the current state of the organization. First, given that the organization is largely defined in terms of geography, it is relevant to look at the participants from the region. Figures 1.1 and 1.2 illustrate the number of authors from the two conferences located in Latin America based on their institutional affiliations. As can be seen, 81 out of the 122 program authors (66%) in Santiago had Latin American affiliations. Similarly, 187 out of 240 program authors (78%) in São Paulo were associated with Latin American institutions. Both conferences also had a significant number of participants from the United States (18 and 30, respectively), with 23 additional participants for each conference scattered from around the world, with Europe, Asia, Australia and the Middle East represented. Overall, these statistics suggest that

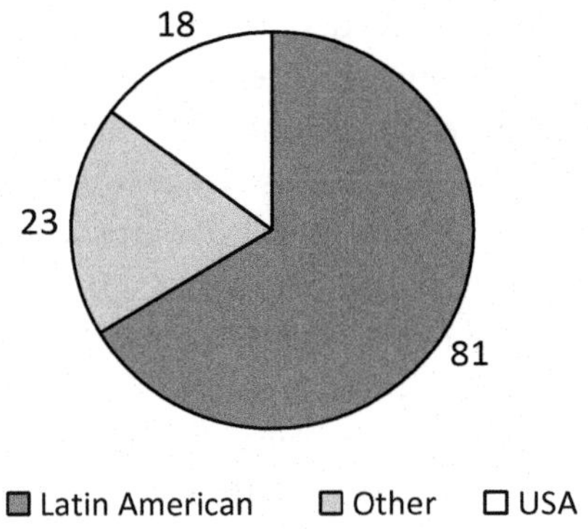


**Fig. 1.1** AIB-LAT Santiago author affiliations

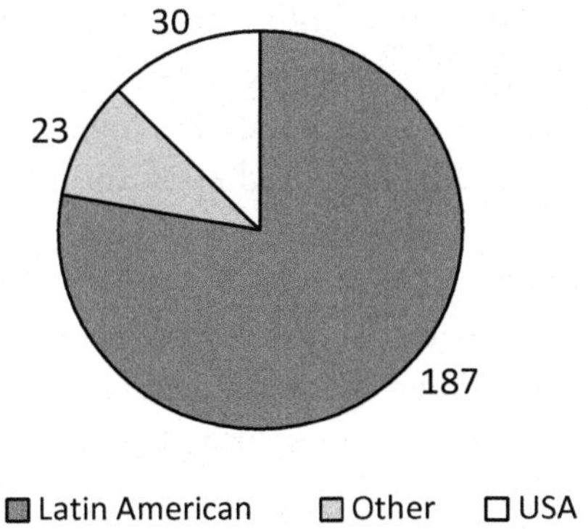


**Fig. 1.2** AIB-LAT São Paulo author affiliations

the conference is fulfilling its primary mission within the broader Academy of International Business organization of serving authors in the region, while also providing outreach to scholars in other areas of the world—particularly those interested in pursuing scholarship focused on Latin America.

A second component of the degree to which the conferences were Latin American in nature concerns the content of the papers presented. While the AIB-LAT conference does not limit itself to papers exclusively about Latin America, but also receives works within the broader area of international business along with those that cross regions, Latin America is nonetheless a key focus of the conference. In Santiago, 58% of the presented manuscripts directly concerned the Latin American context. In São Paulo, 56% focused directly on Latin America. As such, this demonstrates the strong Latin American focus of the conference, while also suggesting a dual, broader, international business focus as well.

Third, given that AIB-LAT is a chapter of the Academy of International Business, it is also interesting to consider the works that involve international collaborations involving authors from several countries. In Santiago, 23% of the manuscripts involved international collaborations. In São Paulo, 19% had authors from multiple countries. As such, in both conferences, the vast majority of works involved authors from a single country. This may be logical in terms of the logistical challenges of collaborating across borders, but is nonetheless an area which the chapter hopes to build upon in the future.

Finally, it is worth noting the gender of authors submitting papers for the two conferences. In Santiago, 34% of authors were female and in São Paulo, 36%. These percentages mirror a general pattern of greater male participation in academic activities in the region, and in most emerging markets globally.

Having reviewed the participants of the conference, we now turn to a discussion of the specific works in this volume, which cover a wide range of topics related to international business in the Latin American context.

## Environmental-Level Factors

The work of Diego Bonaldo Coelho and Moacir de Miranda Oliveira Jr. (Chap. 2) examines the role of government, through governmental policies, in the aid of internationalization efforts by Brazilian mechanical and capital goods companies. Furthermore, the internetworking relationships between the Brazilian Trade and Investment Promotion

Agency (Apex-Brazil) and the Brazilian Association of Machinery and Equipment Manufacturers (Abimaq), which aids in international strategy development and facilities government support through various measures, is examined. After the selection of 104 unique cases, data analysis revealed that government instruments were not relevant, on average, for internationalization. However, the study finds a small group of companies, within the larger sample, where the government's efforts were seen as relevant, thus meriting future research and presenting challenges for Brazilian business institutions. In this light, understanding that international competition is not a matter of choice but a necessity, this study carries a weight of significance as internationalization is an emerging subject for emerging market government agendas.

The comparative case study of Luis Alfonso Dau, Elizabeth M. Moore, and Catherine Bradley (Chap. 3) extends literature on the impact of reforms on firm performance by examining the dissimilar paths to pro-market reforms taken in Argentina and Chile. In addition, this study attempts to strengthen the tie between the political economy and international business literature through the impact that regime type has on institutional stability and how regime types in turn affect the relationship between reforms and firm performance. While this study does not settle the debate between which political economy is most conducive for economic development, it does, however, note that authoritarian regimes offer merit, as precursors to democratic ones, provided they are enlightened. Another implication of this study is that government type and institutional stability impact firm performance, which is a significant finding within the scope of the international business literature. Though this study does not answer the central issues surrounding development, it does add to the literature by highlighting some of the overlooked merits various political structures offer in support of development.

The study by Simone R. Barakat, Greici Sarturi and Keysa Manuela Cunha de Mascena (Chap. 4) analyzes the trajectory of a particular cluster in Brazil by describing the stages of evolution, focusing specifically on their attempts to develop export activities. While there is substantial literature on cluster lifecycles, this research looks more closely at the issue of cluster decline. The results show how local firms and supporting institutions fail to take advantage of the typical benefits of being within a cluster, largely in part due to the inability to cooperate; whereas the key assets that determine viability are mostly firm-based, with the capital market also contributing. Thus, this study promotes a new cycle of innovation in order to avoid facing stagnation or decline in a globalized market.

The work of Daniel Rottig, Jason A. Hoop, Nicholas J. Cid and David M. Peterson (Chap. 5) examines how multinational corporations can successfully enter the emerging market of Brazil. The authors contend that given formal barriers to trade and investment, along with reliance on informal institutions in economic activities and corruption, Brazil constitutes a challenging market to enter and foreign companies face considerable liabilities for their foreignness. Based on a qualitative approach, the authors study the formal and informal institutional challenges in Brazil and sketch out external and internal strategies that companies can consider to gain and maintain legitimacy in this emerging market.

The work entitled "Internationalization and the tale of the Cabo Frio Beachwear Cluster" by Beatriz Kury, Angela da Rocha and Jorge Ferreira da Silva (Chap. 6) investigates the association between the country's development stage and the level of corporate social disclosure of firms. Moreover, in contrast to existing literature, this research contributes to the corporate social disclosure (CSD) topic by analyzing the phenomenon on the country level rather than the firm level. With a sample of 144 countries, the data confirms that there is a relationship between a country's stage of development and CSD. Countries within the first stages of development present lower levels of disclosure, middle stages are associated with average levels, and advanced countries with high levels. Thus, the associations explain the extent to which a society strengthens its institutions, considering institutional issues and stakeholder pressures, and signal that practices related to corporate social responsibility (CSR) and CSD are vital.

## Firm-Level Factors

At a firm level, the study by Constanza Bianchi (Chap. 7) examines factors, on both the firm and managerial levels, that may enhance or deter export activities for emerging-market, family-owned small and medium sized enterprises (SMEs). Additionally, this research identifies managerial capabilities that differentiate exporters from non-exporters. The findings show that there are three major barriers to exporting activities: lack of financial resources, problems in selecting a reliable foreign distributor and limited government support. Furthermore, a high level of proactive commitment is crucial for managers; otherwise stagnation, setbacks or failure may occur. Thus, this research is important because it includes noteworthy practical suggestions to better assist future SME export activities. It provides a positive outlook with regard to internationalization of the Chilean export industry.

Additionally, the work of Bruno de Oliveira Carvalho and Mário Henrique Ogasavara (Chap. 8) analyzes the acculturation process in a cross-border acquisition of a domestic firm by a foreign multinational company. The authors submit that cross-border mergers and acquisitions are characterized by a dual process: adapting to the unfamiliar national culture and to a new organizational culture. Using a case analysis approach, the study finds that managers of the acquired company perceive the acculturation process as an integration and assimilation and that this leads to increased strain. The authors propose an in-depth analysis and framework to deal with the adverse effects of acculturation.

## Individual-Level Factors

Leonardo Liberman and David Kimber C. (Chap. 9) explore the influence of some personal characteristics of employees on their service performance at the international level. Using a subsample of employees subject to regular intercultural contacts, they explore the relationship between ethnocentric traits, cultural intelligence, emotional intelligence and service performance. This study's relevance is rooted in its practical implications, such that employers may now be able to better understand which cultural environments are most conducive for different people.

In Chap. 10, Leonardo Liberman, David Kimber C. and Javier Pinto Garay assess the effects that self-efficacy, optimism and curiosity have on work performance in international employees. The influences of these traits are examined on a wide array of behaviors when coping with challenging situations in intercultural interactions. The results show that self-efficacy and curiosity are directly associated with the international performance of employees. Those who showed a general positive perception about their capacity to perform their job exhibited higher performance in relation to their duties. Therefore, this study increases our understanding of the relationship between traits and performance of people working internationally.

# 2

# Public Instruments to Support Internationalization: The Case of Brazil Machinery Solutions

Diego Bonaldo Coelho
and Moacir de Miranda Oliveira Jr.

## Introduction

The emergence of a global economic reality has shown enterprises that international competition is not a matter of choice, but a necessity (Porter 1986). Although most companies still concentrate their activities in domestic markets, it is possible to anticipate the elimination of the domestic-international dichotomy, which makes the competence of being internationally competitive one of the contemporary business requirements, both for the mere survival of enterprises and for the growth and expansion of their business (Ricupero and Barreto 2007). In this context, internationalization assumes the most typical contemporary

D. B. Coelho (✉)
Escola Superior de Propaganda e Marketing, São Paulo, Brazil
e-mail: diego.coelho@espm.br

M. de M. Oliveira Jr.
Business Administration Department, University of São Paulo,
São Paulo, Brazil
e-mail: mirandaoliveira@usp.br



W. Newburry et al. (eds.), *Contemporary Influences on International Business in Latin America*, AIB Latin America, https://doi.org/10.1007/978-3-319-98340-0_2

business expression (Dunning and Lundan 2008), standing out as a relevant strategy, and to some extent inevitable, since it allows companies to explore new markets, access new technologies, gain skills, learn, and achieve economies of scale (Cyrino and Penido 2007); the same way that the effects provided by the exposure to international competition eventually induce and foster innovation (European Commission 2014).

However, despite being a typically entrepreneurial phenomenon, internationalization is also an emerging subject of the contemporary government agenda. It is of interest to national governments that enterprises in their territories acquire the international competitiveness required to contend for foreign markets and to be able to engage and advance in global value chains. Because, as argued by Porter (1993), companies are the real drivers of domestic economies, since they are responsible for jobs, income, and taxes, as well as productivity and technological externalities.

As a result of this scenario, a new global debate about national development strategies has been initiated based on the role that governments begin to take on their economies, in order to promote an environment that induces competitive advantages capable of raising domestic companies to privileged positions in comparison to international competitors. Contemporary experiences of growth, such as in China, seem to nurture this analysis, given that a large part of the determinants of the rise of Chinese companies is based on a national strategy called going global, which was promoted by horizontally and vertically articulated government policies to promote the industrial competitiveness of the country (Masiero and Coelho 2014). Apparently, a new form of government action has been organized, going beyond the scope of traditional macroeconomic policies, such as monetary and exchange policies, and involves the internal variables of enterprises and a national competitive environment.

Similar to the reality of major emerging countries, these aspects are also present in Brazil, and the interaction between the internationalization of companies and government involvement is opening new fronts. With regard to the Brazilian private sector, it is possible to observe that domestic companies have been seeking international insertion as a strategy for competitiveness. Several studies conducted in that country have observed this trend (Cyrino et al. 2010; Borini et al. 2010; Valor 2011), based on which it is already possible to say that the internationalization of Brazilian companies and their growth has ceased to be an incipient phenomenon to become an ongoing and relatively sharp trend. With regard to the government, Brazil follows the international agenda, and a broad public debate (headed largely by the government) has been placed on the national level with regard to the existence, format, and implementation of government policies to support international business.

Several signals from the Brazilian government in recent years have indicated the increasing international insertion of domestic companies' support (Sennes and Mendes 2009). Through the Ministry of Foreign Affairs (MFA), Ministry of Development, Industry and Foreign Trade (MDIC), Ministry of Finance (MF), National Bank for Economic and Social Development (BNDES), and the Brazilian Trade and Investment Promotion Agency (Apex- Brazil), various measures to support internationalization have been recently announced (Sennes and Mendes 2009), most of them arising and derived from trade policies to support exports and industrial and technological policies currently underway in that country. The greatest recent institutional frameworks for these measures were the *Termo de Referência: Internacionalização de Empresas Brasileiras* (Internationalization of Brazilian Companies), sponsored and released by the Executive Secretariat of the Chamber of Foreign Trade (Camex), in 2009, and *Plano Brasil Maior 2011/2014*, established in 2011 by the Presidency of the Republic (PR).

Therefore, this chapter proposes the investigation of instrumental forms that the Brazilian government (policymaker) has chosen to use to support the internationalization of Brazilian companies, aiming to discuss their relevance from the perspective of policytakers; that is, the executives of the target companies. Therefore, among the public instruments available, we have chosen the specification of one of the most institutionally vaunted actions by that country, whose operationalization takes place in partnership with the private sector: the Sector Projects on the Promotion of Exports (Apex-Brazil) of the Brazilian Trade and Investment Promotion Agency (Apex-Brazil).

Based on that, we sought to investigate the following research problem: could the participation in a Sector Project of Apex-Brazil be an action that facilitates the internationalization of Brazilian companies? Thus, we intended to investigate whether Brazilian internationalized companies that integrate this type of project consider that the actions and instruments provided by the project, whether those directly accessed or indirectly facilitated, were relevant or not for their current stage of international involvement.

In order to achieve these research goals, we decided to study the Sector Project concerning Brazil Machinery Solutions (BMS), which, intended for the mechanical capital goods sector and managed by the Brazilian Association of Machinery and Equipment Manufacturers (Abimaq), has been in a new phase since 2010, being one of the oldest Apex-Brazil cases currently involving the participation of over 100 companies. To address the research problem, we started with the theoretical framework of the Nordic School of International Business, particularly the studies of Johanson and Vahlne (2006, 2009), who argue in their latest line of reflection that the expansion of companies to foreign markets is not an isolated strategic action, but a broad trend triggered and facilitated by the insertion in chains of national and international relationships.

From this perspective, it is considered that the relationship and the position of a company in a network tends to facilitate its process of international integration, because it is capable of reducing the perceived psychic distance and other types of information asymmetry. Therefore, we consider the expectation that the Brazil Machinery Solutions (BMS) Sector Project can be considered as a network promoted in partnership with the federal government capable not only of promoting experiences among participants, but especially enabling the facilitated access to government instruments of support. It thus confirms that this kind of national project should be regarded as an important action for the internationalization of domestic companies, notably those with fewer resources; that is, small and medium enterprises (SMEs) within the scope of government policies to support international business.

This chapter is organized as follows: first, we develop the theoretical framework of the study, which is based on the Nordic School of International Business and the public policy dimensions, in particular, the instruments usually provided by governments. Then, we describe the methodology used, guided by the application of a survey conducted with companies in the sector, using the t-test as a technique of analysis. The results of the survey appear to be relevant to both the Brazilian government instruments to support internationalization and the descriptive analysis of the companies contemplated in this study. Finally, we discuss the main findings.

## Literature Review

### The Internationalization of Companies and the Role of Networks

Despite a fairly diversified set of approaches regarding the phenomenon of internationalization, one can be highlighted: the behavioral. Its basic characteristics lie in the use of fundamentals that, not exclusive to Economics, are supported in both the behavioral dimensions of decision makers and in issues strongly related to strategy, innovation, and processes of companies in markets and networks.

The behavioral approach was established through theoretical and empirical studies in Norway, Finland, Denmark and Sweden by several researchers, who ended up suggesting a new framework for the phenomenon of internationalization, subsequently identified and integrated into what was known as the Nordic School of International Business. Its origin dates back to the agenda started in the 1960s, with the launch of the international business research program from the University of Uppsala, Sweden, by Professor Sune Carlson. According to Johanson and Vahlne (2003), the major questions proposed by Carlson and founding members of the program were addressed in the reflection regarding "if", "how" and "to what extent" the operations internationally conducted by the companies differ from those performed in a single country, nationally.

In the wake of these questions, several studies with a strong empirical trend were placed in the field, with results that revealed a perceptible tension between the theories hitherto available and the reality observed by the researchers. The main hiatus occurred when references about markets and companies failed to provide support for the answers of executives registered in interviews, which therefore led researchers to conclude that "the theories were totally irrelevant to the current scenario of the business activities of executives and the decisions they made" (Johanson and Vahlne 2003, p. 4). Purposely, two new problems became clearly present, drawing attention and establishing a new direction for the research agenda: the choice of target countries and how to operate in these markets (Johanson and Vahlne 2003).

The studies started to interpret the phenomenon of internationalization aiming to explain their processes and determining characteristics, rather than, as predominantly in the economic frameworks, the reasons that lead companies to invest abroad (Weisfelder 2001). It was through this perspective that Johanson and Wiedersheim-Paul (1975) and Johanson and Vahlne (1977), in seminal texts, initiated the creation of a model for the internationalization of companies that became internationally known later as the Uppsala Model (U-Model).

The basic assumptions of the Uppsala Model lie on the emphasis that the process of internationalization of the company is a strategy of an incremental and sequential nature, both in exports and in direct investments. Ours are based on the understanding that the operations and business in markets across borders are inherently risky, given the differences in terms of politics, culture marketing systems to which companies must adapt (Pan and Tse 2000). In this framework, the option to enter a market takes place after acquiring prior experience in another market, and large part of its explanatory factors is related to the contrast between the internal environment of organizations, particularly the attitudes, behavior, and competence of the executives responsible for making decisions, and the external environment. Consequently, the organizational learning and the acquisition of knowledge and experience about foreign markets are key dynamics that not only determine the speed of business expansion abroad, but also the direction for the regions in which this process will occur and the means by which the operating modes will be performed (Petersen et al. 2003).

Internationalization is understood as a cautious strategic decision, deepened and perfected in time, given that the foreign environment is strongly marked by considerable uncertainty and imperfections, where information asymmetry stands out. Thus, for decision makers, the control of risks tends to direct them to the most appropriate processes, and somewhat more interactive, through accumulated experience, skills, and expertise. Therefore, the more inexperienced the executives are in international affairs and activities, as well as the lower the expertise and practice in the target markets, the higher the probability of a company starting its involvement through strategies of lower risk, for example, trade, through indirect exports.

Not coincidentally, one of the main concepts of this approach is the psychic distance (Johanson and Weidersheim-Paul 1975, p. 308), defined as "the sum of the factors that hinder or impede the flow of information between the company and the markets" such as differences in language, cultural, institutional, political, business differences, and development levels, among others, which would be, largely, an important predictor of destinations and forms of international insertion. Since, through the psychic distance perceived by decision makers, companies would seek, in theory, to initially expand their activities to markets that are more similar to their country of origin and their expertise and experience, as well as assume initial strategies of insertion with lower commitment of resources.

Based on the assumptions of the Uppsala Model, it is possible to note that the strategy of internationalization, despite being a process of allocation of resources to and abroad, is determined not only by efficiency and optimization, but also by incremental and perceptual adjustments of the conditions in constant change regarding companies and environments (Neumann and Hemais 2005; Aharoni 1966). According to Pan and Tse (2000), the dynamics regarding the choice of destination and entry occurs hierarchically based on expertise about the market, with the prediction given in large part by the psychic distance. The expertise about the market is thoroughly presented in their approaches as the indispensable condition of internationalization, being the most relevant type "the one acquired through the experience obtained in doing business in the markets" (Blomstermo et al. 2001, p. 127), in clear predilection to experiential knowledge.

On the other hand, as observed by Blomstermo et al. (2001), it was not clear in the first works that constituted the Uppsala Model what types of market experiences would be most useful for internationalization—a relevant question, so much so that in subsequent text, Johanson and Vahlne (1990), by contrasting their Model with the Eclectic Paradigm of

(Dunning 2002), started from the limitations observed in Uppsala, a review of its processes, giving opportunity for the incorporation of ideas of relationships and bonds of trust between market and industry players.

Johanson and Vahlne (1990, p. 18) noted that empirical research conducted in the 1980s began to "show that companies in industrial markets establish, develop and maintain long lasting business relationships with other players", and that the interactions occurring in its core end up strengthening the bonds of trust, commitment, and understanding among the parties involved. After that, based on the Uppsala Model, it led to a strong incorporation of industrial networks to the understanding of the phenomenon of internationalization, since these relationships are connected by networks that are developed as a result of the interaction between companies from different segments and positions in the industrial value chains: producers, consumers, competitors, suppliers (final and intermediate), distributors, agents, consultants, and regulatory bodies and government agencies (Johanson and Vahlne 1990). This procedure turns networks into compositions routinely built, dynamic, and a complex of important means of knowledge and experience, especially among markets.

Inevitably, for their characteristics, the networks become relevant determinants of the process of internationalization in the approaches of the Nordic School. In this framework, we assume the understanding of business expansion to foreign markets not as an isolated strategic action, but as a broad movement triggered and facilitated by the insertion in chains of national and international business relationships. From this perspective, it is considered that the relationship and the position of a company in a network tends to facilitate its process of international integration, because it is capable of reducing the perceived psychic distance.

As emphasized by Johanson and Vahlne (2006), the networks allow developing opportunities in foreign markets and thereby also contribute to reduce uncertainties, thus facilitating and inducing processes of international integration—factors that had been corroborated in previous studies, as stated by Blomstermo et al. (2001)—since it was demonstrated that companies primarily act through their business relationships, and then, when they decide to expand abroad, they often associate this process with their networks.

Purposely, Chen and Chen (1998) showed evidence that the experience of insertion in various types of networks is extremely useful in the entry and expansion in foreign markets, in such a way that becomes a significant determinant not only for the beginning of internationalization, but also the choice of modes and forms of operation. In this perspective, Johanson and Vahlne (2009) added to their model the concept of liability of outsidership, which starts being understood as the disadvantage provided to a company by the fact of not being integrated into a relevant network, which will be, more than psychic distance, the determining source of uncertainty.

It is possible to note, therefore, the evolution of the Uppsala Model to an approach that incorporates networks; that the market experiences capable of developing essential expertise and skills for the international involvement of a company, including the destination to be chosen, have their process enhanced, or facilitated, by the active interaction with other companies and agents.

## Government Policies to Support Internationalization: Scope and Dimensions

Until the mid-twentieth century, governments were restricted to the development of commercial and industrial policies of horizontal rather than sectoral action. The government interventions that occurred through these policies aimed at encouraging the commercial standards considered to be the most interesting to the welfare of their populations, determined by the allotment of factors and the structure of production and productivity of their economies. Thus, the traditional policies of competitiveness of domestic companies were commercial with a protectionist bias and, based on the incentive of the insertion in international contexts, their instruments were targeted by the incentives and subsidies to export; which led to a model that can be considered neomercantilist.

However, when internationalization was considered a public problem, it triggered the beginning of cycles of public policies that heralded a new frontier of specific government actions, since, given the complexity of the phenomenon, its stages of creation, guidelines, mechanisms and instruments of action ultimately required new dimensions of interventions, as well as new proposals and strategies, both isolated as articulated, which inaugurated new institutional milestones. Therefore, government policies to support internationalization, in countries where they have been an option, are not drawn exclusively based on the deterministic pattern of comparative advantages based on productivity and relative allotment of factors. Currently, government policies also incorporate aspects of microeconomic and strategic determinants of companies, from their motivations and characteristics to their advantages of ownership, and other factors of a behavioral nature.

Everything indicates that these policies are being formulated and implemented through mechanisms and instruments that are strategically aligned with the determining factors of the strategic behavior of internationalization and geoeconomically contextualized, in addition to being articulated with other complementary policies. The cycles of government policies to support internationalization tend to be highly contextualized with respect to their interests, guidelines, industries, and enterprises supported, including with respect to national characteristics and those of the countries of destination and/or origin, without the possibility, as noted by Unctad (2006), of a policy considered as "one-size-fits-all".

Consequently, there are two challenges for studies on this subject: one empirical, related to the cycle of public policy; and one analytical, focused on the ways of analyzing and mainly comparing this particular profile of governmental policy between countries.

With regard to the fact that governmental policies to support internationalization are developed, formulated, and implemented in context, it can be seen that governments are compelled to develop their approaches and instruments necessarily based on the specific conditions prevailing in their countries and that reflect their stage of development, "comparative advantages, geopolitical position, business structure and sectoral expertise, and of course, the national development strategy of their government" (Unctad 2006, p. 201). Thus, given the significant variation between the countries, the analysis of governmental policies to support internationalization has been usually addressed in the literature through some typical dimensions, which, by demarcating the scope of operation, not only allows us to characterize them as a specific policy, but to analyze them through and from their specificities and proposed instruments.

In this context, the most appropriate pattern of classification of this type of government policy was the one developed by IPEA (2012), whose primary references were the dimensions and instruments defined in the report published by UNCTAD (2006)—which, in addition, take up the dimensions and common organizational structure previously used for policies exclusively intended to promote exports. According to IPEA (2012), the specific government policies to support internationalization can be typically comprised of six dimensions: (i) informational support, technical assistance and other guidance, (ii) creation of comfort zone, (iii) tax and fiscal instruments, (iv) risk mitigation instruments, (v) financing instruments, and (vi) international agreements.

In this classification, the first dimension encompasses all government mechanisms and instruments intended to provide informational and sometimes experiential support to companies under the process of internationalization, whose primary goals are directed to the reduction of information asymmetries and transaction costs. In the second, understood as "creation of comfort zone", are the actions intended to create, in the destination countries, one-stop-point institutions, where it is possible to create and develop services and contact networks capable of providing for the demanding company a facilitated and supported arrival to its destination, which, as suggested, is usually referred to in the literature as a "soft landing". In turn, the "tax and fiscal instruments" are characterized by all fiscal and tax incentives promoted by government entities, including exemptions, suspensions, reductions, or refunds. The fourth dimension, regarding "risk mitigation instruments", includes all guarantees of coverage and insurance aimed at mitigating the risks associated with currency transfer restrictions, expropriation, war, and other situations of economic and political instability. In the dimension "financing instruments" are credit incentives provided by governments to their companies, notably the credit facilities specific to internationalization, preferential loans, equity, and credits. And, finally, are the "international agreements", which include all international negotiations that constituted institutional arrangements for the legal protection of investments and the elimination of double taxation, in particular.

It is possible to note, therefore, a classification that is structured around the critical variables of the strategic process of expansion of any contemporary company. Namely, information, support, the tax burden, risks, financing, and legal certainty, with the merit of contextualizing them in the involvement with foreign markets. It is worth noting that it specifies these instruments and mechanisms as a targeted policy.

## Methods

For the development of the survey for this study, we used an intersectional drawing with its data prospected in only one moment of time, through a collection instrument consisting of a questionnaire of predominantly closed questions, primarily using the five-point Likert scale (Babbie 1999). The population considered for the study included manufacturers of mechanical capital goods associated with the Brazilian Association of Machinery and Equipment Manufacturers (Abimaq) in 2013 Brazil: approximately 1496 companies nationwide.

The completion of the survey occurred with the application of a self-administered online web-based questionnaire. Aiming to minimize the occurrence of errors of interpretation throughout the application of the questionnaire, we conducted a pretest with two industry executives and two companies. After that, we evaluated the performance of the online platform as positive, considering it as appropriate. With regard to the content and information of the questionnaire, a few adjustments to the text, concepts, and information were made, seeking—through the suggestions made by Abimaq and companies in the pretest—to adapt the text and questions to the reality of the sector.

The variables used to conduct the survey were developed based on the theoretical framework proposed, with special mention of the behavioral determinants of internationalization. In addition, the questionnaire was structured to be clear, objective, and straightforward, aiming to meet the criteria of self-administration, predominantly consisting of basic and closed questions, with preference given to the use of the five-point Likert scale. We chose to use the Likert scale, which is widely used in Business Administration, because it is a metric guided by the perception of the respondents, which, in view of a situation, expresses their impressions and assessments, thus being the most appropriate method to capture the opinion of the executive decision makers of the process of internationalization of companies.

The questionnaire was divided into eight blocks, as follows: (A) Qualification of the Company; (B) International Involvement; (C) Motivators; (D) Justifications; (E) Destinations; (F) Government Policies; (G) Evaluation of the role of government; (H) Final. In the section "Qualification of the Company" we included questions that allowed respondents to characterize the company by segment, size, revenue, and origin of capital. In the following section, "International Involvement", we sought to identify whether the company is internationalized or not; and, if not, the reasons why (internal and external barriers), and, if so, what the profile and direction of insertion is: trade; contracts; investments. In this sense, the sections "Motivators", "Justifications", and "Destinations" sought, in an associated manner, to characterize aspects of the strategic behavior of internationalization of companies considered internationalized, and in the section "Government Policies" and "Evaluation of the Role of Government" the measurement of the perceptions of executives from these companies regarding the performance of the Brazilian government in the processes of international involvement.

The motivators of the internationalization of companies, which make up the construct motivators, relate to the drivers that motivate companies to engage internationally. Basically, according to the theoretical framework elaborated, the motivators/drivers are very well associated with the reasons that explain the process of international insertion considered by the executives. In the limit, it is the justifications and reasons of internationalization undertaken by decision makers that usually materialize into expected benefits that are associated, to a greater or lesser degree, with the end goal of the companies—all being indiscriminately rooted in economic, market, transactional, behavioral, and/or governmental issues, with the ultimate horizon being the increase of profitability and market value.

Developed in the survey questionnaire based on UNCTAD (2006, p. 155), these drivers can be understood as "the factors that trigger the process of internationalization of the companies or intensify it", usually addressed, or classified, based on their local characteristics; that is, their country of origin, the push factors, and/or those of the destination, the so-called pull factors, where the studies of Uppsala, together with the

**Table 2.1** Construct of the motivators of internationalization

| | Dimensions | Variables | Scale | Cronbach's alpha | References |
|---|---|---|---|---|---|
| Motivators | Market | var31<br>var32<br>var33<br>var34<br>var35<br>var36 | 5-point Likert<br>1 (Strongly disagree);<br>5 (Strongly agree) | 0.767 | Cyrino and Penido (2007), UNCTAD (2006), Dunning (2002), Dunning and Lundan (2008) |
| | Efficiency | var37<br>var38<br>var39<br>var40<br>var41<br>var42 | 5-point Likert<br>1 (Strongly disagree);<br>5 (Strongly agree) | 0.731 | |
| | Transaction | var43<br>var44<br>var45<br>var46<br>var47<br>var48 | 5-point Likert<br>1 (Strongly disagree);<br>5 (Strongly agree) | 0.783 | |
| | Behavioral | var49<br>var50<br>var51<br>var52<br>var53 | 5-point Likert<br>1 (Strongly disagree);<br>5 (Strongly agree) | 0.700 | |
| | Governmental | var54<br>var55<br>var56<br>var57<br>var58 | 5-point Likert<br>1 (Strongly disagree);<br>5 (Strongly agree) | 0.850 | |

**Table 2.2** Assertions of the construct motivators

| | |
|---|---|
| var31 | Access new customers, given the size and growth potential of foreign markets |
| var32 | Approach foreign customers, increasing responsiveness (feedback), especially in the after-sales |
| var33 | Approach foreign competitors, aiming to strengthen the company's competitive position |
| var34 | Access frontier technology |
| var35 | Promote the geographical diversification of markets, diluting the risk |
| var36 | Improve the company's image/products in the domestic market |
| var37 | Reduce production costs through the access to resources at lower prices |
| var38 | Promote economies of scale and scope in production and processes |
| var39 | Existence of more efficient infrastructure abroad for the exploration of resources and production |
| var40 | Existence of more efficient infrastructure abroad for outflow and logistics |
| var41 | Obtain gains through differences in rates, such as exchange, interest, and tax rates (arbitrage gains) |
| var42 | Existence of wide availability of natural resources and production factors (capital and labor) in foreign markets |
| var43 | Lower trade barriers and entry barriers in foreign markets |
| var44 | Existence of few market distortions abroad |
| var45 | Existence of more efficient institutions abroad, especially those related to the legal protection of property rights |
| var46 | Reduce the information asymmetry existing between the Brazilian and foreign market |
| var47 | Reduce the costs of trading with foreign customers and suppliers |
| var48 | Participate in clusters and/or export processing zones (EPZs) |
| var49 | Develop and leverage market experiences |
| var50 | Acquire and develop managerial and marketing skills |
| var51 | Improve know-how about the competitive dynamics in foreign markets |
| var52 | Develop negotiation skills and practices based on international expansion |
| var53 | Undertake strategic alliances for interaction and joint exploitation of know-how and technologies |
| var54 | Existence of government policies of attraction in foreign markets formulated by the government of the destination |
| var55 | Existence of tax incentives from the Brazilian government for international expansion |
| var56 | Existence of support and informational and training assistance from the Brazilian government for international expansion |
| var57 | Existence of tax incentives from the Brazilian government for international expansion |
| var58 | Support and assistance from ABIMAQ for international expansion |

variables specified in the Eclectic Paradigm of Dunning (2002), become fundamental approaches and frameworks for such dimensions. Table 2.1 shows the indicators used to structure this construct, and Table 2.2 describes their assertions.

The common thread of the analysis of potential government involvement in the internationalization of Brazilian mechanical capital goods companies occurred through the process of government policies formulated and deliberately intended for these purposes, which are currently in force in Brazil. The conformation of public and government policies to support internationalization was addressed based on six dimensions, according to the theoretical framework: (i) informational support, technical assistance, and other guidance, (ii) creation of comfort zone, (iii) tax and fiscal instruments, (iv) risk mitigation instruments, (v) financing instruments, and (vi) international agreements, which listed all instruments provided by the Brazilian government, by dimension. Thus, all Brazilian government instruments currently in force were listed and grouped based on such dimensions, according to Tables 2.3 and 2.4.

To analyze the consistency of the constructs theoretically proposed for the motivators and government policies, hence their measurement reliability and empirical consistency, a Cronbach's alpha test was conducted. The coefficients found for all constructs had their results above 0.60, which is considered acceptable in the literature (Pestana and Gageiro 2005), particularly in exploratory studies, as advocated by Hair et al. (2005).

The sample consisted of 104 valid questionnaires, which represented 6.95 percent of the population of considered companies associated with Abimaq. For the purposes of comparison, and the calculation of conjunctural indicators of the entity, monthly disclosed and used as parameters for studies and national sectoral disputes, we used an average sample of approximately 110 associate companies, with profiles approximate to that obtained. Thus, it is possible to say that although we had only 6.95 percent of total valid questionnaires given the total number of associated companies, this figure can be considered adequate for the purposes of this study, as it is next to the regular figure and officially used by the organization representing the industry.

**Table 2.3** Construct of government policies to support internationalization

| | Dimension | Variables | Scale | Cronbach's alpha | References |
|---|---|---|---|---|---|
| Government policies to support internationalization | Informational support, technical assistance, and other guidance | var78<br>var79<br>var80<br>var81<br>var82<br>var83<br>var84<br>var85<br>var86 | 5-point Likert<br>1 (Strongly disagree);<br>5 (Strongly agree) | 0.858 | UNCTAD (2006), IPEA (2012) |
| | Comfort zone | var87<br>var88 | 5-point Likert<br>1 (Strongly disagree);<br>5 (Strongly agree) | 0.807 | |
| | Tax and fiscal instruments | var89<br>var90<br>var91<br>var92 | 5-point Likert<br>1 (Strongly disagree);<br>5 (Strongly agree) | 0.744 | |
| | Risk mitigation instruments | var93<br>var94 | 5-point Likert<br>1 (Strongly disagree);<br>5 (Strongly agree) | 0.738 | |
| | Financing instruments | var95<br>var96<br>var97<br>var98<br>var102<br>var103<br>var104 | 5-point Likert<br>1 (Strongly disagree);<br>5 (Strongly agree) | 0.912 | |
| | International agreements | var99<br>var100<br>var101 | 5-point Likert<br>1 (Strongly disagree);<br>5 (Strongly agree) | 0.664 | |

**Table 2.4** Assertions of the construct government policies to support internationalization

| | |
|---|---|
| var78 | Participation in the PEIEX program of APEX-BRAZIL |
| var79 | Participation in seminars/events on the subject promoted by the federal government |
| var80 | Participation in business roundtables organized by APEX-BRAZIL (PS Brazil Machinery Solutions) |
| var81 | Participation in trainings/courses/seminars organized by APEX-BRAZIL (PS Brazil Machinery Solutions) |
| var82 | Access to market intelligence reports prepared by APEX-BRAZIL (PS Brazil Machinery Solutions) |
| var83 | Legal assistance for international expansion sponsored by APEX-BRAZIL in Brazil |
| var84 | Participation in trade shows abroad with the support from APEX-BRAZIL (PS Brazil Machinery Solutions) |
| var85 | Use of services from SECOMs in the Brazilian embassies/consulates abroad |
| var86 | Access to market intelligence material and databases sponsored/conducted by the Brazilian government |
| var87 | Using the APEX-BRAZIL business centers abroad for local settlement |
| var88 | Use of legal assistance and information services of APEX-BRAZIL business centers abroad |
| var89 | Use of special drawback customs regime |
| var90 | Use of Ex-tariff |
| var91 | Use of SISPROM |
| var92 | Use of tax and fiscal incentives (exemption/suspension/reduction) for international expansion |
| var93 | Use of Reciprocal Credit Agreement (RCA) |
| var94 | Use of guarantees and credit insurance (BNDES; SBCE; FGE; SCE) |
| var95 | Use of credit facility BNDES-Exim |
| var96 | Use of credit facility BNDES-Finem |
| var97 | Use of credit facility PROEX-Equalização [equalization] |
| var98 | Use of credit facility PROEX-Financiamento [financing] |
| var102 | Use of credit facility BNDES PSI—Exportação Pré-embarque [export preshipment] |
| var103 | Use of credit facility BNDES—Revitaliza Exportação [revalize exports] |
| var104 | Use of credit facility PROGER Exportação [exports] |
| var99 | Use of trade agreements signed by Brazil |
| var100 | Use of agreements to eliminate double taxation (ABT) |
| var101 | Use of agreements for the legal protection of investments (APPI) |

# Results

## A Network

Developed by Abimaq, based on the new Sector Project (PS) model of the Brazilian Trade and Investment Promotion Agency (Apex-Brazil), Brazil Machinery Solutions, launched in 2010, is the result of a partnership between these entities. Its purpose is to promote Brazilian exports of machinery and equipment, as well as strengthen the image of Brazil as a manufacturer of mechanical capital goods (BMS 2014). This is, therefore, a conceptual and strategic reformulation of the former Integrated Sector Project that Abimaq had been undertaking with Apex-Brazil since the early 2000s, becoming a network of agents to build a sector brand of international scope.

The logic of Brazil Machinery Solutions operates through actions aimed at approximating the Brazilian enterprises to markets considered strategic, aiming to present to potential foreign buyers the quality and advantages of Brazilian machinery and equipment. Among its main actions are those related to trade promotion, with special mention of the participation in international trade shows, both in Brazil and abroad. In the computation of activities involving participation in trade shows, the project promotes Warm Ups, which are characterized by the networking meetings between Brazilian entrepreneurs and interested parties, which occur before the beginning of the events, and are aimed to match potential clients to associated manufacturers. In addition to the Warm Up there are also traditional actions in sectoral projects sponsored by Apex-Brazil, such as: (i) the Buyer Project, which promotes meetings between manufacturers and foreign buyers in Brazil; (ii) the Vendor Project, which follows the same logic as the Buyer Project, though it is held abroad; (iii) the Image Project, whose actions are focused on seeking foreign opinion makers, such as journalists and experts companies, and inviting them to come to the country, with their expenses paid—, with the aim of promoting the image of domestic products; and finally (iv) the business missions abroad, motivated to carry out exchanges between countries, as well as seeking clients. In addition, and where relevant, courses and training are also offered in areas considered essential for the start-up and advancement of companies participating in exports.

Currently, the Brazil Machinery Solutions program includes 176 affiliated companies and members of various segments of the mechanical capital goods industry, specifically those manufacturing machines for the following sectors: agricultural, plastics and containers, cement, mining, and wood. In any event, even though this involves a project with actions that are more engaged in trade promotion and training, by being associated with Apex-Brazil and the works of Abimaq, this also becomes a channel that facilitates access to and information about other government instruments to support internationalization, such as credit facilities, international agreements, and risk mitigation instruments, with a view to facilitate agents to participate in its network. Thus, it can be said that the project, via Abimaq, is an important means of dialogue between companies and relevant government agencies on the subject of international business.

## International Involvement of Companies

According to data from the sample of the 104 companies surveyed, 88.5 percent own international businesses that are considered internationalized. The majority, 55.4 percent, consists of exporting companies. Out of these companies, 62 are said to integrate Brazil Machinery Solutions, which means, in relative terms, 67.4 percent of the internationalized companies studied.

The data analysis of the survey regarding government instruments in the process of international involvement revealed that support and assistance from the government was not deemed relevant by the decision makers, on average, in none of the six dimensions. That is, values lower than three were assigned on average to the six dimensions of government policies, which suggests the instruments provided by the government were viewed as irrelevant from the perspective of executives responsible for the internationalization of their companies.

However, although considered irrelevant, the government instruments that on average were better evaluated were those associated with informational

**Table 2.5** Results of constructs of government instruments to support internationalization

| | N | Minimum | Maximum | Average | Standard-deviation |
|---|---|---|---|---|---|
| Informational and technical assistance | 92 | 1.00 | 4.67 | 2.2297 | 0.96286 |
| Comfort zone | 92 | 1.00 | 4.50 | 1.7033 | 1.05346 |
| Tax incentives | 92 | 1.00 | 4.75 | 2.1916 | 1.10571 |
| Risk mitigation instruments | 92 | 1.00 | 5.00 | 1.9489 | 1.23154 |
| Financing | 92 | 1.00 | 5.00 | 1.8009 | 1.07273 |
| Trade agreements | 92 | 1.00 | 4.67 | 1.8901 | 0.95062 |
| Valid | 92 | | | | |

support and technical assistance, with an average of 2.23, followed by tax incentives, with 2.19. Table 2.5 shows the results.

In any event, it should be noted that the standard deviations for government instruments reached significant levels, larger than one, which suggests changes regarding these factors in relation to the strategic behavior adopted by the companies. Thus, it was possible to question, from the perspective of the theoretical framework of the Nordic School, whether the evaluation of government instruments differs between the internationalized companies integrating the Brazil Machinery Solutions project versus those that are not part of it. To evaluate this possible difference in perception, we chose to test the means assigned by the executive through a t-test, which statistically assesses whether there are differences between the means of these groups.

The outputs of the t-test show that, at the 0.05 ($p < 0.05$) level of significance, except for the comfort zone instruments, since they indicated a p-value of 0.08 ($p > 0.05$), the means are statistically different. Thus, it can be stated that the perception of the executives from internationalized companies integrating the Brazil Machinery Solutions project is different from that expressed by executives of companies that are not part of the project. It is noted, however, that although the two groups have classified the role of government as less than three—that is, of little relevance—there are differences of appraisal between the groups. Figure 2.1 illustrates the average differences.

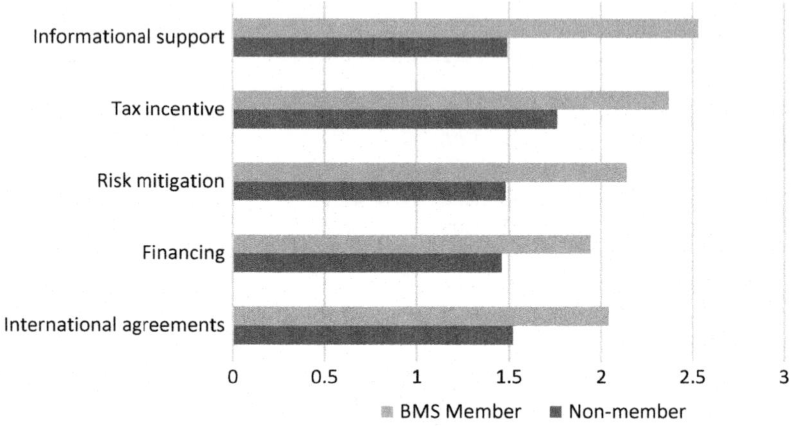


**Fig. 2.1** Differences in perception regarding the role of government instruments in the process of internationalization among executives

Based on the data, it can be seen that the group of executives from companies integrating Brazil Machinery Solutions has averages with higher levels of appraisal of government instruments than those who are not in the project. The largest difference occurs on the relevance of informational support instruments, wherein companies integrating the project reached an average of 2.53, while non-members reached 1.49. The resulting analysis is that, apparently, being part of the project between Abimaq and Apex-Brazil to promote the internationalization of companies in the industry positively impacts the perception of executives involved regarding the relevance of public instruments in the process of international integration of their companies.

Furthermore, it is worth noting that the instruments more often provided by Brazil Machinery Solutions, precisely those of informational support, training, and trade promotion, to its members differ from the non-members. One possible explanation for this result is that participating in the Brazil Machinery Solutions project exposes executives to the possibility of using government instruments in the internationalization of their companies in comparison to non-members. However, as can be seen, the two groups line up in one analysis: the instruments are considered of little relevance for the internationalization of both groups of companies.

Thus, although the participation exposes executives to the use and appraisal of government instruments, it is not sufficient to substantially change the perceived impact of the relevance of government on the reality of international involvement.

Therefore, what could motivate a company to integrate the Brazil Machinery Solutions project? That is, is there any motivation in the internationalization process that drives executives to seek participation in this project? To investigate this question, we performed a t-test on the groups of internationalized company members and non-members of the Abimaq/Apex-Brazil project regarding the motivators of internationalization.

According to the results of the t-test, at the 5 percent significance level, only the averages of motivators by drivers guided by governmental factors can be considered statistically different, since this p-value was 0.015. The result is relevant because it refers precisely to the set of motivators in which the variable government is central. As analyzed in the sections on the theoretical framework and methodology, the construct of motivators by government factors comprises variables of perception on a five-point Likert scale, where one is "strongly disagree" and five "strongly agree", regarding assertions such as: whether the existence of government policies, either in the origin or destination, is a factor that motivated the company to engage internationally. It can be noted, therefore, that internationalized companies integrating Brazil Machinery Solutions consider the existence of government policies as a significant motivation for internationalization, since the average was above three. While companies that are not members reached an average below three; that is, government policies were not considered by their executives as a motivator for internationalization.

It can be concluded, therefore, that being aware of the existence of a sector program that encourages internationalization can motivate entrepreneurs to appreciate it as supporting international involvement and, when they start being part of it, they tend to evaluate government instruments, on average, better than the executives who are not part of a program, who find no motivation for internationalization in the government. However, even if the entrepreneur integrates the Brazil Machinery Solutions project and sees in the government a motivator for internationalization, the government instruments currently available are not yet considered very relevant, on average, for the international involvement of companies.

To analyze which entrepreneurs consider government instruments relevant in the international involvement of their companies, we verified the proportion of internationalized companies (members and non-members of Brazil Machinery Solutions project) who expressed this relevance, using as a criterion the average results in the Likert scale above three points. Figure 2.2 shows the proportion of the total number of companies integrating the Brazil Machinery Solutions project that considered government instruments relevant in their internationalization, just as for the total number of non-member companies.

As expected, the highest proportion of relevance is among the participants of the project. Informational support stands out, with the highest relevance among the companies adopting Brazil Machinery Solutions, with over 25 percent of companies considering that the use of these instruments was relevant to their international involvement. Among the non-members, no government instrument reached a relevant appraisal exceeding 15 percent of the total. The instruments that were better appreciated in this group of companies were the fiscal and tax incentive instruments, with approximately 15 percent of the total.

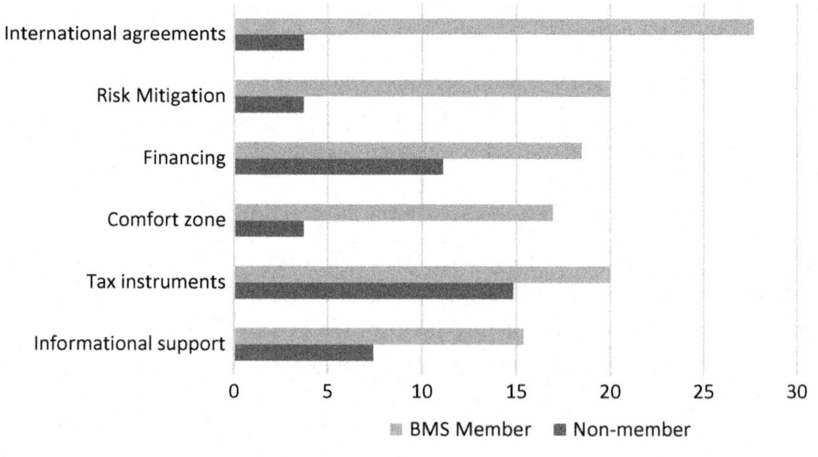


**Fig. 2.2** Proportion of relevant appraisal of government instruments from the total number of companies

After analyzing the distribution of appraisal of government instruments by size of company, following the criteria of the Ministry of Industry, Development and Foreign Trade (MDIC), it was found that out of the total number of internationalized microenterprises, none of them attributed relevance to the government in their international involvement. The data is interesting because it reveals that large companies presented a relevant appraisal of the instruments. For example, 28 percent of large internationalized enterprises considered financing instruments relevant, compared to only 18.8 percent of small enterprises and 10.9 percent of medium enterprises. In addition, 20 percent or more of large enterprises also considered as relevant risk mitigation, informational support, and tax instruments. As for small enterprises, the most prominent were tax instruments, with 31.3 percent considering them relevant. As for medium enterprises, the largest proportion was found in informational support, with 19.6 percent. Therefore, from the internationalized companies that used government instruments, when considering their size, it is possible to say that the concentration of large enterprises that appreciated their impact as relevant was proportionally higher than in other segments (Fig. 2.3).

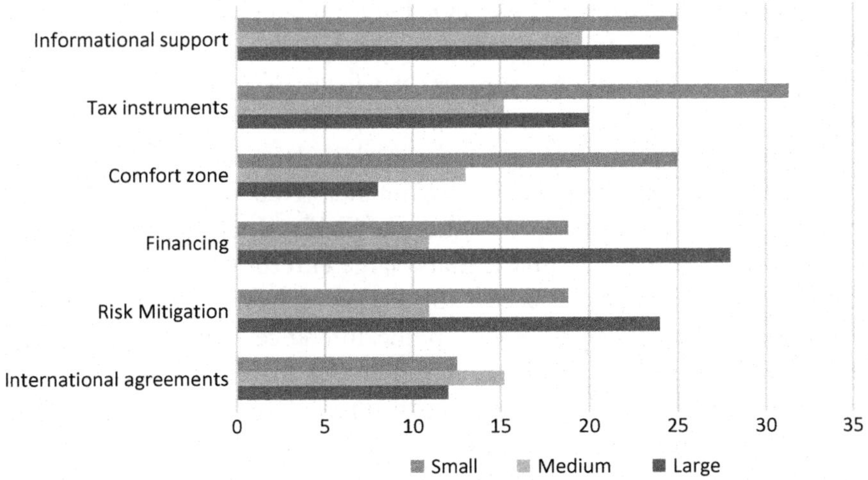


**Fig. 2.3** Proportion of relevant appraisal of governmental instruments of all companies

## Discussion

The study of the Brazil Machinery Solutions project has shown that there is evidence that executives from companies participating in this project tend to better evaluate, on average, the government instruments when compared to executives from companies that are not integrating the project. However, both groups did not consider, on average, that the government instruments were relevant. In addition, it was also found that a large proportion of the companies that viewed the government instruments as relevant integrated the Brazil Machinery Solutions project, and when analyzing this appraisal by company size, proportionally, a larger share of executives from large companies assumed that the government policies were relevant, which is what happened in almost all instruments provided by the government. On the other hand, a significant portion of small enterprises, a predominant part of the sample is in the project, assessed three dimensions of instruments as relevant, and in two with significant portions, compared to large enterprises: these being tax and comfort zone instruments, the latter being offered via Sector Project.

Therefore, some final considerations can be raised. The resulting situation has shown that, if only those companies whose executives considered government instruments as relevant are analyzed, the highest proportion is found in companies integrating the Brazil Machinery Solutions project—basically the instruments of informational support, the focus of action of the project studied.

Another fact that stands out is the analysis by size, which indicated better appraisals of government instruments given by executives from large enterprises in comparison to those of SMEs. There are two possible explanations for this. The first is that a large enterprise, better informed and prepared, manages to access the various government instruments more easily. The second is based on the inference that SMEs, despite being members of the project—that is, being aware of the instruments—are either unable to use them owing to internal factors (organizational and/or staff training) or the Brazil Machinery Solutions project is failing to communicate the whole range of government instruments available, which is plausible, since the highest proportions of relevance regarding

SMEs were for instruments of informational support (25 percent) and comfort zone (25 percent), both basically offered by Apex-Brazil, the providing agency of the project, along with Abimaq, in addition to tax instruments, which are the most disseminated nationally.

Thus, it can be noted, as an overall result, that although many executives consider the government as a motivator for internationalization, especially executives who sought to integrate their companies with the Brazil Machinery Solutions project, the government instruments are not considered, on average, by the respondents, as relevant factors in the international involvement of their companies. Even if the project promotes some kind of positive impact on the subject, the executives of companies integrating the Brazil Machinery Solutions project tend, on average, to appreciate government instruments better than those belonging to non-member companies. This result is pertinent because it reveals the possibility of implying that the Brazil Machinery Solutions network may reduce the information asymmetry of entrepreneurs regarding government instruments: however, its use is not effective in the perception of policytakers. What can be a consequence of internal problems of enterprises, as well as the instruments, particularly their suitability to the business dynamics required in the process of internationalization, is their bureaucratic complexity and operational delays.

Therefore, we conclude that it is necessary to expand the Brazilian public debate on government policies to support internationalization, which should occur through a closer relationship between companies and governments. For governments, the need is to find out why executives from companies that have gone global do not consider the available instruments to be relevant. And, for the executives, it is important that they express and argue about the reasons why their appraisals tend to the low impact of instruments in the international insertion of their companies. In addition, as indicated by the study, a possible and interesting way for this debate to develop could be via Apex-Brazil sector projects, since the results for the Brazil Machinery Solutions project showed that the executives from companies integrating the project tend to find in the government a motivation for international insertion, although without significant impact, and that their exposure to use and positive appraisal of their instruments may be greater.

## References

Aharoni, Y. 1966. *The foreign investment decision process*. Boston: Division of Research, Graduate School of Business Administration.

Babbie, E. 1999. *Métodos de pesquisas de survey*. Belo Horizonte: Ed. da UFMG.

Blomstermo, A., K. Eriksson, L. Johanson, and D.D. Sharma. 2001. The usefulness of network relationship experience in the internationalization of the firm. In *Business network learning*, ed. H. Håkansson and J. Johanson. Oxford: Elsevier Science.

Borini, F.M., M.T.L. Fleury, A.C.C. Fleury, and M.M. Oliveira Jr. 2010. Performance e internacionalização das empresas brasileiras. In *Multinacionais brasileiras: internacionalização, inovação e estratégia global*, vol. 1, 111–126. Porto Alegre: Bookman.

Brazil Machinery Solutions – BMS. 2014. O Programa, January. Retrieved from www.brazilmachinery.com

Chen, H., and T.J. Chen. 1998. Network linkages and location choice in foreign direct investment. *Journal of International Business Studies* 29 (3): 445–467.

Cyrino, A., and E. Penido. 2007. Benefícios, riscos e resultados do processo de internacionalização das empresas brasileiras. In *Internacionalização de empresas brasileiras: perspectivas e riscos*, 79–116. Rio de Janeiro: Elsevier.

Cyrino, A.B., M.M. Oliveira Junior, and E.P. Barcellos. 2010. Evidências sobre a internacionalização de empresas brasileiras. In *Multinacionais brasileiras: internacionalização, inovação e estratégia global*, ed. M.M. Oliveira Junior. Porto Alegre: Bookman.

Dunning, J.H. 2002. The eclectic paradigm as an envelope for economic and business theories of MNE activity. In *Theories and paradigms of international business activity: The selected essays of John H. Dunning, Vol. I*, ed. J.H. Dunning. Cheltenham: Edward Elgar.

Dunning, J.H., and S.M. Lundan. 2008. *Multinational enterprises and the global economy*. Cheltenham: Edward Elgar Publishing.

European Commission. 2014. *Supporting the internationalisation of SMEs*, Guidebook series: How to support SME policy from structural funds. Luxembourg: European Union. PDF: https://tinyurl.com/y75lqnxp

Graves, C., and J. Thomas. 2006. Internationalization of Australian family businesses: A managerial capabilities perspective. *Family Business Review* 19 (3): 207–224.

Hair, J.F., et al. 2005. *Análise multivariada de dados*. Porto Alegre: Bookman.

Instituto De Pesquisas Econômicas Aplicadas – IPEA. 2012. *Internacionalização de empresas: experiências internacionais selecionadas,* Comunicados do Ipea, n. 150. Brasília: IPEA. PDF: https://tinyurl.com/y79s9oyt

Johanson, J., and J.E. Vahlne. 1977. The internationalization process of the firm – A model of knowledge development and increasing foreign market commitments. *Journal of International Business Studies* 8 (1): 23–32.

———. 1990. The Mechanism of Internationalisation. *International Marketing Review* 7 (4): 11–24.

———. 2003. Building a model of firm internationalisation. In *Learning in the internationalisation process of firms,* ed. A. Blomstermo and D.D. Sharma. Cheltenham: Edward Elgar Publishing Limited.

———. 2006. Commitment and opportunity development in the internationalization process: A note on the Uppsala internationalization process model. *Management International Review* 46 (2): 165–178.

———. 2009. The Uppsala internationalization process model revisited: From liability of foreignness to liability of outsidership. *Journal of International Business Studies* 40 (9): 1411–1431.

Johanson, J., and F. Weidersheim-Paul. 1975. The internationalization of the firm: Four Swedish cases. *Journal of Management Studies* 12 (3): 305–322.

Masiero, G., and D. Coelho. 2014. A política industrial chinesa como determinante de sua estratégia going global. *Revista de Economia Política 34* (1): 139–157.

Neumann, R.W., and C.A. Hemais. 2005. Produção internacional e comportamento organizacional no processo de internacionalização: podem as teorias explicar o comércio internacional. In *O desafio dos mercados externos: teoria e prática na internacionalização da firma,* ed. C.A. Hemais. Rio de Janeiro: Mauad.

Pan, Y., and D. Tse. 2000. The hierarchical model of market entry modes. *Journal of International Business Studies* 31 (4): 535–554. Retrieved from http://www.jstor.org/stable/155660

Pestana, M.H., and J.N. Gageiro. 2005. *Análise de dados para ciências sociais: complementaridade do SPSS.* 4th ed. Lisboa: Edições Sílabo.

Petersen, B., T. Pedersen, and D.D. Sharma. 2003. The role of knowledge in firms' internationalisation process: Wherefrom and whereto. In *Learning in the internationalisation process of firms,* 36–55. Cheltenham/Northampton: Edward Elgar.

Porter, M.E. 1986. *Competition in global industries.* Boston: Harvard Business Press.

———. 1993. A vantagem competitiva das nações.

Ricupero, R., and F.M. Barreto. 2007. A importância do investimento direto estrangeiro do Brasil no exterior para o desenvolvimento socioeconômico do país. In *Internacionalização de Empresas Brasileiras*. Rio de Janeiro: Elsevier.

Sennes, R., and R. Mendes. 2009. Políticas públicas e as multinacionais brasileiras. In *A ascensão das multinacionais brasileiras: o grande salto de pesos-pesados regionais a verdadeiras multinacionais*, ed. J. Ramsey. Rio de Janeiro: Elsevier.

United Nations Conference on Trade and Development – UNCTAD. 2006. *FDI from developing transition economies: Implications for development*. World investment report 2006. Geneva: ONU.

Vahlne, J.E., and J. Johanson. 2003. Building a model of firm internationalization. In *Learning in the internationalization process of the firm*.

Valor. 2011. Presença global: empresas avançam no exterior. Revista Multinacionais Brasileiras, ano 4, n. 4.

Weisfelder, C.J. 2001. Internationalization and the multinational enterprise: Development of a research tradition. In *Reassessing the internationalization of the firm*, ed. C. Axinn and P. Matthyssens. Amsterdam: JAI.

# 3

# Regime Structure, Institutional Stability and Pro-market Reforms

Luis Alfonso Dau, Elizabeth M. Moore, and Catherine Bradley

## Introduction

Pro-market reforms are recognized as a major catalyst for firm performance in the developing world (Lin 1992; Griffith et al. 2007; McMillan and Naughton 1992). By granting this axiom, a link is formed between political economy and international business scholars and practitioners. In order for both politicians and executives to perform optimally, there must be an open dialogue between the two streams of literature. This research will attempt to strengthen this dialogue.

In the political economy literature, development scholars are often faced with difficult questions: What is the best path to development? What government structure is most conducive to economic prosperity, particularly in the developing world? How do pro-market reforms and other regulatory changes instigated by states affect their markets?

L. A. Dau (✉) • E. M. Moore • C. Bradley
Northeastern University, Boston, MA, USA
e-mail: L.Dau@northeastern.edu; e.moore@northeastern.edu; Bradley.c@husky.neu.edu



W. Newburry et al. (eds.), *Contemporary Influences on International Business in Latin America*, AIB Latin America, https://doi.org/10.1007/978-3-319-98340-0_3

Relatedly, the international business literature has paid increased attention to the effects of pro-market reforms and other institutional adjustments on companies (Banalieva and Eddleston 2015; Klapper and Love 2004; Lopez et al. 2009; Selowsky and Martin 1997) in an attempt to ask similarly difficult questions. For example: How close is the correlation between firm performance and pro-market reforms? What policies are most conducive to firm success and prosperity? These examinations span across different levels of analysis (country and firm) as they attempt to provide business executives with an insight on how to best manage their companies.

By combining the two literatures, scholars on both sides can benefit. Economic policies, after all, are developed in part to influence business, and businesses must work within the confines of the rules set by the policies. Furthermore, the type of government regime can have an impact on regulatory policies, and these policies can in turn affect firm performance, leading to a natural curiosity to better understand the link between regime type, regulatory changes, and firm performance.

The purpose of this chapter is to assess how political regime and institutional stability affect the relationship between regulatory reforms and company performance. The chapter first argues that institutional stability enhances the potential benefits of reforms for firm performance. Then, it proposes that authoritarian regimes may be more beneficial for firm performance initially but a transition to democracy is necessary to retain and expand those benefits over time. Using a comparative case study methodology, the chapter studies the diverse institutional paths pursued by Chile and Argentina to examine these propositions. A case methodology provides the advantage of allowing researchers to look closer into the countries, firms, and relationships in question. This project is conducted with the hope of bettering strategic decisions made at the firm level and public policy decisions made at the country level while connecting two closely related disciplines.

The remainder of this chapter is organized as follows. The following sections provide a survey of the literature and develop the arguments of the study. This in turn is followed by a description of the methodology. The chapter closes with a discussion and conclusion, including a description of potential areas for future research.

## Theoretical Development

The theoretical logic behind this examination stems from two streams of literature: pro-market reforms and firm performance from international business and the debate within political economy between authoritarianism and democracy. Before analyzing the literature and logic, it is important to outline two theoretical assumptions on which this manuscript rests.

First, it is assumed that pro-market reforms can have a meaningful impact on the performance of companies (Banalieva 2014; Del Sol and Kogan 2007; Klapper and Love 2004). Both in political economy and international business, there is often a debate as to whether or not economic liberalization and the opening of a country's borders are beneficial for both the country as a whole and for local firms (Henisz et al. 2005). This chapter does not study the direct effect of reforms on firm performance as this has been analyzed in prior work, but instead develops the mechanisms whereby political structure and institutional stability can have a critical impact on whether reforms are effective and beneficial for firms.

Second, a transition to democracy is assumed. The research here focuses on countries that have transitioned or are transitioning to democracy as opposed to the possibility of a permanent dictatorship. Permanent dictatorships fall outside the scope of this particular research endeavor, despite the interesting impacts that they may have on international businesses. For this reason, a transition from authoritarian rule to a freer, more open society is assumed.

## Pro-market Reforms and Firm Performance

For the purpose of this research, pro-market reforms are broadly defined as any policy that aims to liberalize the economy and open a particular market to the global economy (Boas and Gans-Morse 2009; Borras 2003). Moreover, within the nature of pro-market reforms, there is a wide variety of individual policies. For example, tariff barriers can be eliminated or reduced, intellectual property rights may be strengthened, subsidization may take place for certain industries, income taxes may be elevated or diminished, foreign direct investment may be sought or reduced, and so on (Baldwin et al. 2012; Dau 2011, 2012, 2013; Dau and Wesley 2016). Each of these reforms not only has an effect on business-level decisions, but they also may mutually impact one another. Pro-market reforms are a form of institutional change and institutions are, put one way, the "rules of the game" (North 1990: 3). Institutions provide the boundaries and guidelines for businesses and other economic actors on how to behave in a particular context (Henisz et al. 2005; Hill 2014). In order to create an optimal business environment, it is important to understand what types of institutions are most beneficial to executives and owners of firms (Chacar et al. 2010) seeking to expand in the developing world, where institutions are not always as clear-cut as they may be in the developed world.

There are three critical factors for pro-market reforms to be effective: clarity, consistency, and stability. First, the rules must be clear in order for economic actors—such as executives and those in charge of making business decisions—to understand the rules of the game (Behrman and Grosse 1990; Boddewyn and Brewer 1994; Peng et al. 2008). While this may appear basic, such rules are not always clearly stated and made readily available for all the participants involved in the developing world (Krugman 2009). When pro-market reforms are implemented and institutions become formalized within a country, the rules must be accessible and clear for businesses to be effective actors (Child and David 2001; Dunning 2012; Newburry and Yakova 2006).

A second characteristic of effective pro-market reforms is stability. Oftentimes, if a policy does not work immediately, the first action that government officials and business owners may expect is for a change in that policy (Leigh and Blakely 2016). Based on this rationale, governments often change the institutional structure based on short-term logic (Barnett and Finnemore 2004; Henisz and Swaminathan 2008). Policies designed for the long-term can be altered to fit the immediate business or political climate and hence the policy is not afforded the opportunity to become effective (Barnett 2006; Muller 2007).

As such, stability, or a long-term vision of a policy, is a critical factor of an effective pro-market reform. If a policy is constructed to enhance the economic climate of the country, government officials would be wise to let the policy run its course (Muller 2007). Moreover, the perception that institutions will remain stable is critical for investors. The logic behind stability, then, is quite clear: if policies are constantly changing, businesses will never adequately adapt to them, potentially resulting in uncertainty, confusion, and potential mismanagement (Baldwin et al. 2012). If a pro-market reform is initiated in an unstable environment, the risk for executives increases as the future of their decisions also becomes unstable (Ghoshal and Bartlett 1999; Leung et al. 2005).

A third critical factor of an effective pro-market reform is consistency. As governments change hands, new policies and reforms are added and old ineffective measures are oftentimes subtracted—politics, after all, is rarely a stagnant game (Goldstein and Pevehouse 2012; Kingdon 2010). However, within these normal changes, governments should be cognizant of the continuation of consistent pro-market reforms. Oftentimes, government officials making policy are not aware of the effects these policies have on businesses (Muller 2007; Schumpeter 1950). For example, one administration may recommend increasing foreign direct investment and a slight increase in a tariff barrier, while the next administration may decrease government subsidies and decrease income taxes. While all of the policies may remain intact and stable, the policies are not consistent with one another and may clash, canceling out the effectiveness of any given policy (Buckley and Casson 1994; Djelic and Quack 2003; Nayyar 2002; Taoka and Beeman 1991). If businesses are to operate at an optimal level of performance, policies must remain relatively consistent from administration to administration and there should be a general consensus on how to achieve economic liberalization in a systemic fashion (Mahoney and Chi 2001; Cantwell et al. 2010; Miller 1992).

The preceding literature and arguments lead to the following proposition:

**Proposition 1** *The benefits of pro-market reforms for firm performance are greater in markets characterized by clear, stable, and consistent institutions.*

## Regime Type and Institutions

Following this discussion of the optimal characteristics of institutions and pro-market reforms, we must now determine how these characteristics are implemented. In its most basic form, governments set up institutions and the individual pro-market reforms by which businesses must abide (Muller 2007; Goldstein and Pevehouse 2012; Schumpeter 1950). Within the field of international relations, there is an active debate between two different regime types and their effectiveness for country-level development: democracy and authoritarianism (Dahl 1971; Ogden 2002; Przeworski et al. 1995). Many scholars suggest that democracy is the only path to development (Lipset 1959; Williamson 1993; Valenzuela and Valenzuela 1978). Other scholars suggest, however, that authoritarian regimes are best suited for bringing about macro-level economic development (Bellin 2004; Diamond 2010; Femia 1972; Romer 1992). The purpose of this examination is not to choose one side or the other, but rather to shift the debate to examine the impact of regime type on institutional clarity, stability, and consistency. Rather than asking which regime type is better for development, this chapter examines which regime type is better suited to construct institutions that are conducive to business-friendly pro-market reforms. What follows will be a discussion of the impacts of both democracy and authoritarianism on institutions.

## Democracy and Institutions

Democracy is often thought of as the champion of the free flow of ideas (Aristotle 2009; Teegen et al. 2004). Proponents of a democratic system suggest that it is the best regime type for developing countries as it allows the majority to be heard, rather than just the voices of big government and those with power (Dahl 1971; Hirschman 1970).

Democracy allows for policy recommendations from many different interest groups (Hill and Hupe 2002; Parekh 1992). One tool of democracy is that it can reach out to many different sectors of a given society and process the information to make policy-level decisions that represent many different interests (Goggin et al. 1990; Heineman et al. 1991; Hood and Margetts 2007). While some may argue that businesses have a privileged position and that groups with more money have more power, an often-cited benefit of democracy is that it allows for many different voices to be heard, leaving maximum potential for the most informed decisions to be made (Downs 1957; Kingdon 2010; Olson 1971; Rose 1993). With more opinions and more information, the likelihood of positive pro-market reforms increases.

A second benefit of democracy is flexibility. Within a democracy, policies are not set in stone (Osborne and Plastrik 1997; Rochefort and Cobb 1994) and interest groups can impact government at a variety of levels (Fischer 1995; Howlett et al. 1995; Schneider and Ingram 1997). Furthermore, it is not solely the decision of those in power to weigh whether or not a policy is helpful. In a democracy, individual actors, such as businesses, can voice their opinions regarding the effectiveness of a particular policy and instigate actual change (Schneider and Ingram 1997; Stimson et al. 1995; Stone 2002). Power, therefore, does not just lie in the hands of one, a fact that becomes critical when change is necessary.

However, while democracies positively influence institutions in some ways, there are ways in which democracies can have detrimental impacts on institutions. Democracies are usually defined by an electoral system whereby politicians make promises to influence society via reforms and policies (Dahl 1954). In both the developing and developed world, one negative impact on institutional stability and consistency is legislative turnover (Kingdon and Thurber 1984; Samuels 2000). Democracy is highly susceptible to institutional instability as new political leadership comes into power (Brady 1991; Iannaccone and Lutz 1970; Stimson et al. 1995).

In stable democracies, this turnover may not be so drastic. In the developing world, however, where countries may be prone to several elections in a short time span, this presents serious problems in terms of institutional stability and consistency (Diamond 2003; Mahoney 2001). Politicians seeking office may change policies and implement new reforms not for the benefit of the country, businesses, or even the population, but rather because they made a promise to a certain interest group or voting bloc (Keeler 1993; Kingdon 2010). Pro-market reforms created under emerging democracies are highly vulnerable to drastic changes.

Another drawback of democracies is gridlock (Diamond et al. 1989; Skocpol 1979). As previously noted, democracies champion the voice of the people and many different interest groups. While this is usually beneficial, since it allows policies to be more representative of the entire population, it is also a drawback as it can sometimes result in a long-drawn-out process that may not see the creation of a policy for several years (Baumgartner and Jones 1993; Gandhi and Lust-Okar 2009; Kingdon 2010). A particular idea may take years to become concrete policy.

Thus, democracies may not always be the most conducive to creating policies at the right time. Democracies allow many different interests to be heard, such as businesses, but if these interests do not translate into actual policies or if policies are changed too often, the regime does a disservice to the potential effectiveness of pro-market reforms.

## Authoritarianism and Institutions

Authoritarian regimes are those in which power is highly centralized and decisions are made by either one central political figure or a small cohort of top officials (Arendt 1968; Bursey 2013; Friedrich and Brzezinski 1965). Authoritarian regimes at the macro level are often thought of as unstable because they are vulnerable to revolutions and coups, but this study aims to understand the merits and flaws of authoritarianism in terms of institutional clarity, stability, and consistency rather than stability of the regime itself (Duckitt 1989; Levitsky and Way 2002). Since this research is contingent upon a transition to democracy, it is outside the scope of this chapter to determine if an authoritarian regime itself has enough internal consistency to remain in power indefinitely and resist upheaval.

One benefit of a regime led by a dictator is that policies and reforms can be made immediately and are rarely contested (Bunce and Wolchik 2010; Purcell 1975). The ruler therefore can bypass legislative roadblocks that are inherent in a democracy, and make a timely decision without having to worry about the policy being rejected (Alesina and Rodrik 1994; Arendt 1993). Policies under a dictator can run their course without being altered by the public or parties (Brunetti and Weder 2003; Dahl et al. 2003).

In terms of pro-market reforms, this potential benefit can be critical. In a skeptical world where the position of business is often being challenged and questioned, an authoritarian regime may be better equipped to protect stable pro-market reforms at the onset (Cardoso 1979; Purcell 1973; Stoner-Weiss 2006). With many different interest groups, business regulations are often under scrutiny, and with this threat removed, there is a higher likelihood that these reforms can grow and transform society rather than be rejected because their long-term benefits cannot be seen in the short term (Ball 2012; Bangura 1991).

A second benefit of an authoritarian regime is the potential for policy consistency and a long-term vision. In a democratic society, elections and leadership turnover are inevitable. In an authoritarian style regime, however, the dictator is typically in power for the foreseeable future (Bellin 2004; Goodwin 2001; Remmer and Merkx 1982). As such, an authoritarian leader can make policies with a long-term vision, since they are not implementing policies to stay in office or please a particular interest group (Lieberthal 1992; Remmer and Merkx 1982). In other words, different interest groups and the fear of demotion do not cloud a dictator's vision. Policies stemming from an authoritarian regime have the potential to be made with the very distant future in mind.

Like democracy, however, authoritarianism also has its limitations. One such limitation is the dictators themselves. If a dictator does not have the best interest of the country in mind, the policies may be stable, consistent and clear, but they may also be detrimental in nature (Arendt 1968; Manion 2006; Mertha 2009; Ross 1999). Democracies have the luxury of changing political leadership with relative ease if the leadership is not having a positive impact (Sen 1999). Authoritarian regimes, however, are designed in a way that turnover and leadership change only come because the dictator steps down willingly or is forcibly removed by a revolt or upheaval—there is no mechanism in place for regular turnover (Ayoob 1995; Evans 1996; Hadenius and Teorell 2005). The potential drawback for pro-market reforms is evident: if an authoritarian leader does not believe in pro-market reforms, or is generally uninformed, the probability that effective pro-market reforms will be implemented is low.

Another drawback of authoritarian rule is a lack of dissent and differing opinions. A dictator is allowed to select their own advisors, like a president or other head of state in a democratic system, but unlike a stable democracy where a leader usually has checks on their power, a dictator does not have such constraints (Gerring et al. 2005; Geyer and Fitzpatrick 2009). Consistency implies that a reform is constantly evolving in the same direction, but an authoritarian regime is unlikely to allow policy and reform evolution because fewer opinions and interests are acknowledged (Goodwin 2001; Kimber 1989; Mill 1859; Prebisch 1950; Remmer and Merkx 1982).

Once again, this authoritarian characteristic has a high potential for negative impacts on pro-market reforms. As global economic conditions are constantly in flux and markets rise and fall, pro-market reforms must evolve. Authoritarian regimes, unless they are highly invested in business interests, are less likely to carry out proper pro-market reform evolution for long periods of time.

Based on this reasoning, we propose that the benefits of reforms for firms are greater initially under authoritarian regimes, but a transition to a more democratic style of rule is necessary to maintain their success and evolution once reforms have been adequately established. The logic behind this argument stems from the benefits and drawbacks of both authoritarian regimes and democracies and attempts to reconcile the two forms of regimes by taking advantage of the benefits of each while simultaneously minimizing the deficiencies. Based on past exploration and literature (Dahl 1954; Manion 2006; Schmitter and Karl 1991; Sen 1999; Williamson 1993), democracies seem to flourish once positive ideas are firmly in place and only need to evolve slightly over time to enhance growth. At the same time, the characteristics inherent in a democratic system of rule pose problems for the creation of stable and lasting policies at the onset. Authoritarianism, on the other hand, has the strong-handed ability to enforce policies immediately whether or not they are widely accepted. Authoritarianism, however, risks a dictator overusing his or her power and being unwilling to change and evolve when necessary. The transition from authoritarianism to democracy, then, may be most beneficial for optimal pro-market reforms, eventually leading to the greatest improvement in the average performance of firms.

Based on the preceding logic and literature, the following argument is formulated:

**Proposition 2** *The benefits of pro-market reforms for firm performance are greater initially under authoritarian regimes, but a transition to democracy is necessary to maintain the success and evolution of these reforms once they have been adequately established.*

## Methods

For the purpose of this examination a comparative case study method will be used to assess the impact of the type and stability of political institutions on the effectiveness of pro-market reforms as positive moderators for firm performance. Within this examination, Chile will serve as a model for pro-market reforms born under temporary authoritarianism and Argentina will serve as a representative model of pro-market reforms stemming out of democracy. It is important to note that Chile and Argentina were selected as representatives of the two different models toward effective pro-market reforms being assessed within this manuscript since each country was one of the forerunners for their respective models and other countries have since followed similar paths, but are in different stages of the pro-market reform process. Both Chile and Argentina have implemented pro-market reforms for a substantial period of time and as such, make for richer examinations.

This study aims to understand what type of political regime fosters the characteristics of institutions that most positively influence effective pro-market reforms. As such, Douglass North's definition of institutions as, "the rules of the game" will be utilized (North 1990: 3). Within this particular research endeavor, two types of political regimes will be assessed: authoritarian regimes and democratic regimes. This is not to suggest that many intermediary regimes do not exist between these two types on the political spectrum, but for the purpose of this chapter these two categorizations are used. A democratic regime is defined as one that considers many different interest groups and that has free and fair elections (Dahl 1954). An authoritarian regime, on the other hand, is defined as a government that "promotes a centralized source of power at the hands of one dictator" marked by a decrease in citizen interaction (Friedrich and Brzezinski 1965). Pro-market reforms are defined as the government policies aimed at reducing government interactions in economic affairs and enhancing government oversight mechanisms over market activities (Baldwin et al. 2012; Dau 2016a, b).

Within the context of this examination and based on prior work, "effective" pro-market reforms are those reforms that are clear, stable, and consistent (DiMaggio 1988). Their effectiveness will be examined through a historical analysis of the pro-market reforms in each country, a series of exclusive interviews with managers performed by the first author at various firms throughout Chile and Argentina,[1] as well as the World Bank Index for "ease of doing business." A critical assumption that relates to the methodology of this chapter is that pro-market reforms that are effective are those that facilitate doing business for firms within a given country (Cuervo-Cazurra and Dau 2009). This index was included to provide an external examination of the effectiveness of the pro-market reforms to supplement the historical account and interviews, which could represent individual level preference rather than a realistic depiction of the pro-market reforms.

In order to best understand the path to pro-market reforms as well as the impacts that the political institutions have had transitively on firm performance, this case-study examination will rely heavily on both historical analyses of each country's path to pro-market reforms as well as exclusive interviews of managers conducted by the first author, as mentioned above. The historical analysis and in-depth interviews will be supplemented with various measures provided by the World Bank in order to provide the most holistic view on the effectiveness of pro-market reforms. The historical context for each country will be provided

[1] The interviews were conducted primarily in Spanish and then translated into English. The identity of the companies is concealed when discussing the interviews below for the sake of anonymity.

first, followed by a synthesis of the interviews and World Bank measurements.

# Data

## Brief History of Pro-market Reforms: Chile

Throughout the early part of the 1970s, Chile was in economic turmoil, facing hyperinflation of 140% and the third lowest gross domestic product (GDP) per capita in Latin America (Klein 2007). Socialist President Salvador Allende was well-known for implementing protectionist barriers, which lead to a constantly declining GDP, a severe lack of foreign exchange reserves, and non-existent foreign investment (Labán and Larraín 1995). Moreover, the Chilean economy was faltering with revenues only reaching 23.3% of total GDP (Labán and Larraín 1995). With many sectors of the economy nationalized, the private sector growth rate dipped to −1.7% and employment growth was sluggish (World Bank 2014). In the year prior to the coup led by Augusto Pinochet, inflation in Chile had reached an all-time high of 150% (IMF 2014a). In response to the economic struggles, the Minister of Finance Hernán Buchi declared that "price controls, protectionism and expropriations" were to blame. It is significant to note that prior to the beginning of military rule, there was a general sentiment in Chile that pro-market reforms were the suggested remedy to the ailing economy (Armijo and Faucher 2002; Teichman 2001).

In 1973, Augusto Pinochet led a military coup to overthrow the Allende government. Shortly after the coup, Pinochet began to implement "El Ladrillo" (the brick), an economic plan prepared by a group of economists now known as the "Chicago Boys" (Klein 2007). In complete opposition to the Allende government's economic policy, "El Ladrillo" suggested a set of economic reforms that included deregulation, privatization, a reduction in tariffs, a reduction in taxes, and overall increased economic liberalization (Ricardo 2010; Martínez and Díaz 1996). Under the influence of the "Chicago Boys," Pinochet aimed to "make Chile not a nation of proletariats, but a nation of entrepreneurs" (BBC News 2001).

In an attempt to liberalize the economy, reforms were implemented in Chile in three rounds: 1974–1983, 1985, and 1990. During the first round of reforms, all protectionist trade barriers were eliminated and foreign direct investment was incentivized, forcing Chilean businesses to compete with foreign manufactured products or close their doors (Valdés 1995). During this period, the only company of significance that remained nationalized was Codelco, the main copper company (Bulmer-Thomas 2003; Collier and Sater 2004). In the spirit of liberalization and reform, however, private companies were allowed to develop new mines (Edwards and Cox-Edwards 1991; Klein 2007). Pinochet simultaneously pursued free-trade agreements and cut tariffs by 10% (Coatsworth 2005; Sokoloff and Engerman 2000). Before this change, the Cato and Fraser Institutes' annual reports had ranked Chile 71 out of 72 on a scale of "most protectionist economies" in the world.

Shortly after these reforms, Chile slightly departed from the path of economic liberalization and implemented a pegged exchange rate of 39 pesos per dollar in 1979 (IMF 2014b). The result was a severe recession that lasted from 1982 to 1984. GDP fell by 13%, industrial production plummeted, and unemployment hit 20% (Valdés 1995).

In response to the ensuing recession, Chile entered into the second set of reforms in 1985 with the goal of reinvigorating pro-market oriented economic policies. Tariff barriers were reduced an additional 10% and Codelco was deconstructed and privatized (Ricardo 2010). It soon became apparent that the country as a whole and businesses alike benefitted enormously from liberalization policies.

Before the second round of reforms was implemented, however, a significant change in the political regime type of the Chilean government had taken place. In 1980, legal dispositions were signed declaring that all citizens of Chile would ratify a candidate (proposed by the Chief of Staff and the General Director of the Carabineros) who would become the President of Chile for an eight-year term (Martínez and Díaz 1996). Seven years later, political parties became legalized and the national registers of voting were officially open (Klein 2007; Valdés 1995).

It is significant to note the transition from an authoritarian-military regime to a free-democratic regime in Chile. The first set of pro-market reforms (and their subsequent success) came under a military regime with complete control and limited citizen involvement. The Pinochet government made decisions alone and dissent was illegal. The government was under no restraints or pressure from public opinion to alter its policies. Pinochet's pro-market reforms were enormously successful. As a result, once Chile began to transition to a democratic system in the early 1980s, the pro-market reforms had already been shown to positively influence both the overall economy and business conditions for entrepreneurs.

The result was a third set of reforms in 1990, shortly after Pinochet legally stepped down from office. Chile signed a variety of free-trade agreements with Canada, México, and Nicaragua, as well as preferential trade agreements with Venezuela, Colombia, and Ecuador (International Monetary Fund 2014a; World Bank 2012). The culmination of the 1990 reforms came in 1996 when Chile joined MERCOSUR, solidifying its transition to an open and free market system (Martínez and Díaz 1996).

By the time Chile had a democratic system of rule, pro-market reforms had become arguably the most positive policy implementation. Although the people and the successive governments had the legal right to remove the pro-market policies or reimplement protectionist policies, economic liberalization had already been cemented as a priority (Bethell 1993; Fischer 1995). While Chilean democracy brought about social change and freedom, economic freedom had already come and a vision for a stable, consistent and clear plan had already become a goal of the country.

## Brief History of Pro-market Reforms: Argentina

The story of the Argentine economy is cyclically marked with a series of sharp spikes followed by devastating depressions. In September 1984, shortly after Raúl Alfonsín was elected as the first democratic president of Argentina's post-military dictatorship, the country reached out to the International Monetary Fund (IMF) for financial help. The IMF officially agreed in July 1987 to implement the Austral Plan, aimed at renegotiating debt with Argentina's creditors (Teichman 2001). The short-lived program, however, failed a year later due to government budget spending issues and loose monetary policy coupled with a lack of adequate market reforms (International Monetary Fund 2014a).

After a series of failed economic plans, Peronist Carlos Menem was elected president in May 1989. In an attempt to salvage the struggling economy, he announced a "shock program" that was closely correlated to the Washington Consensus plan outlined by economic experts from the United States (Levy 2004). Privatization became the primary objective of the Menem government and nearly all state-owned enterprises were quickly turned over to private hands, with the exception of several banks. Initially, privatization led to great success for the people of Argentina. Services like transportation were expedited dramatically. In 1991, Finance Minister Domingo Cavallo introduced a series of free-market reforms such as open trade, monetary reform, pegging the peso to the dollar, devaluation, and a complete reduction of tariff barriers. In the years following, GDP increased and unemployment fell under 10% for the first time in a decade. Success slowed in the second half of the 1990s and citizen protests followed as unemployment rose again to 14.2% in 1998 (Levy 2004; Nouzeilles and Montaldo 2002). In 1999, in the face of a growing economic crisis, Fernando de la Rúa won the presidency. In an attempt to quell social unrest, the administration continued with pro-market reforms but overhauled many of the reforms that the Menem government had initiated. In an attempt to make the market enticing for business exports, relevant policies were incentivized and the government embarked on subsidization programs to spur entrepreneurship (International Monetary Fund 2014a). At the same time, the government strongly favored a pension reform program intended to increase jobs and GDP, but at a cost of 3% of overall GDP (The Economist 2002). As the pro-market reform policies changed shape, deflation, falling wages and rapidly growing unemployment ensued. The public was quick to blame the neoliberal agenda, as promoted within the IMF arrangements (Bulmer-Thomas 2003; Collier and Sater 2004).

As a result of this economic turmoil, Argentina experienced a period of extreme political instability that led to the election of five different presidents within a period of two weeks in 2001. Eduardo Duhalde finally brought stability to the office in January 2002 (Levy 2004). In response to the failing economy, he and Finance Minister Roberto Lavagna stabilized both commodity prices and the exchange rate, while maintaining the neoliberal policies from the de la Rúa administration (Teichman 2001).

In the decade that followed (and continuing into the present day), Argentine presidents have continued implementing policies that mirror the neoliberal agenda, but have slightly altered them with each term. Néstor Kirchner, for example, raised export and import taxes (which had been lowered to increase foreign direct investment), but pushed hard to liberalize domestic business policies and nationalize banks and comestible products (Richardson 2008). President Kirchner also favored reinvesting into the international debt market and liberalized the economy to allow a total debt sale of $500 million dollars at a yield of 8.36% (Richardson 2008).

In 2007, however, when Cristina Fernández de Kirchner took over the presidency, the pro-reform policies were once again changed. The import and export taxes that had just been raised in 2005 were now nearly eliminated, while pension funds that were previously privatized were nationalized (Richardson 2008). Higher-income households were receiving subsidies in the hopes of spurring innovation and investment.

While the economic agenda could broadly have been defined as pro-market liberalization, the specific policies and tools being used toward this liberalization were heavily in flux from one administration to the next. While there seemed to be consistency of macro-level ideas, the micro-level implementation of these ideas was anything but consistent. As a result, the Argentine government defaulted on its debt once again in July 2014 (The Economist 2014). In Argentina, democratic institutions have allowed for political stability and gradual social growth, but have made for less stable pro-market reform implementation.

## Effectiveness of Institutional Stability on Pro-market Reforms and Firm Performance

The purpose of this examination is to bridge the gap between government type; institutional clarity, stability, and consistency; and pro-market reforms. Once this link has been solidified, it can be concluded transitively that institutional stability and government types that increase the effectiveness of pro-market reforms thus enhance the potential benefits on firm performance. For both the Chilean and Argentine cases, data from exclusive interviews and the World Bank will be provided to highlight the impact that institutional stability and government type has had on the effectiveness of pro-market reforms. Note that we do not study the direct effect of reforms on firm performance as this has been analyzed in prior work (e.g., Cuervo-Cazurra and Dau 2009), but instead develop the mechanisms whereby the political structure and institutional stability can have a critical impact on whether the reforms are effective and beneficial for firms.

## Chile

Throughout the series of managerial interviews, where open-ended questions regarding the nature and history of pro-market reforms in Chile were asked, several commonalities became apparent. First, almost all of the participants interviewed quickly cited 1973 as the critical year in which tariffs were reduced significantly and the beginning of pro-market reforms were initiated.

In an interview with a managing partner from the real estate industry, the strengths of the Chilean model were discussed. "From 1973 to 1978 the model was changed to reduce the tariff barriers. If you bring that tariff down by about 50%, [this] would cause a reconversion of everything in the Chilean industrial system…," he noted. The interview highlighted the importance of economic liberalization in the early to late 1970s and its subsequent impact on the Chilean industrial system.

The same time frame of Chilean reforms was corroborated in an interview with a board member from the production development industry who pointed out that, "the great revolution of the Chicago boys that was largely started from 1973 to 1974 right after the government changed hands." This interview complemented the real estate industry interview in pinpointing when the Chilean reforms started taking form:

It becomes important to highlight the time frame when the reforms started because when correlated to the political context of Chile, it is evident that the reforms began when Pinochet took control of Chile.
From the interviews, a second commonality was stressed: because the government was authoritarian, the policies could not be changed and institutional stability and consistency were strong.

A CEO from the pharmaceutical industry noted how important reform was in producing stability within the country and within the business environment itself: "The key to reform was in reform itself and in stability. That was the program that the Chicago boys set up."

In an interview with an expert from the field of education in Chile, the importance of consistency and a long-term vision for reforms was brought up. "Here in Chile we are moving towards the same direction," he said.

What many Chilean CEOs and practicing managers point out when they talk about Pinochet's reforms is that they remained for a long period of time and each reform complemented one another as they all worked toward the same goal. Because the policies were implemented under an authoritarian regime, liberalization was non-negotiable. This created institutional stability in the form of lasting pro-market reforms. These policies were in effect for a long period of time and brought economic success in the long term. Thus, when Pinochet willingly stepped down and legalized democracy, leaving the policies vulnerable, they had become so normalized and effective that the new leaders opted to keep them. The population was generally convinced of the efficacy of such reforms and did not demand change through the voting booths.

Furthermore, it is helpful to look at other indicators for signs of effectiveness stemming from these policies. According to the World Bank's Ease of Doing Business indicator, Chile's average score from 2000 to

2013 was a 34 out of 150 (with 150 being the least amount of ease and 0 being the most amount of ease), which is ranked among the top 10 of the countries within the developing world. Moreover, other entrepreneurs and business owners—in a series of other interviews from Colombia, Brazil, and Peru—also indicated that Chile is the easiest country within the region to operate in because of its pro-market reforms and the stability of its institutional framework. Because the rules are transparent and constant, the business environment in Chile is highly conducive to success and growth.

## Argentina

A similar series of interviews with the same type of participants (e.g., managers, CEOs, and entrepreneurs) was conducted in Argentina. From the interviews, several patterns also became apparent.

In an interview with the manager of an electronics store in Argentina, she explained how the reform process and institutional conditions have affected doing business in the country. This interview is based on notes, so the ideas are paraphrased. The manager mentioned that because taxes are so high, it makes it very difficult for businesses to be successful. She discussed how reforms have been unstable in the country—as one government implements them and then the next government takes them away—and how that has made it very difficult to operate a successful business over time. She added that governments develop many rules without any knowledge of how the market works or the rules of the industry. They are looking to make an impact on the next election or to link the government's image to the launch of a new project. As elections change, so do policies. She proposed that what Argentina needs is stability. She closed by stating that Argentina abused the electoral process and the freedom to change policies and leaders, and as a result the country fell into debt as the policies around liberalization changed over time.

What is significant about these ideas is that they highlight, at the company level, the impact that institutional stability has on firm strategy and performance. Many of the interview participants were quick to point out that while democracy has brought a spirit of economic freedom, it has also allowed for the policies to change as quickly as the leaders do. Consistent with the historical context, individuals mentioned that as policies change, it is difficult to do business because companies and executives are uncertain how long the new "rules of the game" will be in effect. This is because there is no consistency and stability, making long-term decisions extremely difficult.

A second commonality from the series of interviews in Argentina was a comparison with the Chilean pro-market reform history, emphasizing the stability of the pro-market reforms that came out of the authoritarian regime.

When conducting an interview with a CEO from the production and development industry in Argentina it became apparent that even within Argentina, the stability of the Chilean model was highly recognized: "… even when going back to democracy, carrying on the policies and the consistency of the policies is amazing. Every presidency since '89 has been a left wing coalition government but their policies have been a continuation of these winning policies that were established during the 17-year Pinochet regime and that is consistency."

A managing partner, also from the production and development industry, echoed similar sentiments in a subsequent interview. "Even in countries like Chile that had just changed the style of government but has had something consistent. They had a completely free market where no one can dispute that the long-term goal was in investments and private investments. This has not changed."

A board member from the real estate industry in Argentina also spoke of the Chilean model. "What were the critical factors in Chile? What were the critical factors in the…country after Franquism? Well, having a leadership with a strategic vision of systemic competitiveness is a key factor. When you have a stable and consistent state policy—that is a key factor. Having institutions that work is a key factor. Having a business leadership is essential."

A board member who commented on the benefits of the Chilean model also discussed the difficulty within the Argentine market. He pointed out that sometimes doing business is rarely easy. "Argentina is a 'difficult market.' It is highly liberalized with many resources but the politics sometimes create barriers to doing business and because of this, decisions must be made whether to remain here or go elsewhere, like Chile, where doing business is easier."

It is interesting to note how often Chile was discussed, unprompted, within the series of interviews from Argentina. From the comments and frequency, two things deserve emphasis. First, that the Chilean pro-market reform model has merit in the minds of a number of Latin American businessmen and entrepreneurs. Even within the context of interviews from other countries, the Chilean model was constantly cited as the vision of success within Latin America. Second, that the key to the Chilean success is institutional stability. One commonality throughout the interviews was the importance of consistency, which in Chile was attributed to Pinochet's authoritarian style of government.

Furthermore, it is helpful to highlight other indicators regarding the effectiveness of the pro-market reforms in Argentina. According to the World Bank's Ease of Doing Business research project, Argentina's average score 2000–2013 was 123.5 out of 150, again with 150 being the least amount of ease and 0 being the most amount of ease. Although this is only one indicator, when analyzed in conjunction with the interviews, it becomes apparent that the business environment in Argentina is a relatively difficult market to sustain successful and profitable operations. Despite the fact that the market is liberalized and has sought to follow the Washington Consensus prescriptions closely, the lack of policy consistency is not necessarily "business friendly."

## Discussion and Conclusions

There are several theoretical implications and several considerations for managers and policy-makers that can be deduced from the preceding discussion. The theoretical implications will be discussed, followed by a practical discussion for firm-level strategy. The chapter will conclude with recommendations for future research and suggested methods to expanding the scope of this particular project. Before these sections, the limitations of this research will be noted.

## Limitations of the Research

As is true for all case-based research, this project is limited by examining only a small sample selection (Yin 2008). Only two countries were assessed in the context of this project, and, as such, more countries (perhaps from other regions around the globe) may be analyzed in future work in order to examine the generalizability of the aforementioned claims.

While the interviews referenced were from a pool of countries around Latin America and were protected and honest, interview-level research always comes with a risk of reliability (Yin 2008). The questions posed were open-ended, rather than leading, and, as such, the answers and quotations come with merit and reliability. Nevertheless, challenges with interviews must always be brought to the attention of the reader in order to promote honest and valued research.

Furthermore, this chapter focuses on the relationship between regime type, institutional stability, and pro-market reforms and how they each interact with one another to affect firm performance. However, it does not study how these factors affect other important aspects of a country. Future work may focus on how these factors may impact other aspects, such as equality, employment, or security.

Despite the limitations of the project, the results yield influential and significant theoretical implications as well as many implications for strategy decisions at the firm level. The theoretical implications will be highlighted first.

## Theoretical Implications

In political economy, there is an on-going debate surrounding the type of government that is most conducive to economic development, namely an authoritarian government or a democratic government (Remmer and Merkx 1982; Sen 1999; Valenzuela 2004). This chapter, however, does not look to settle that debate but rather argues that while democracy is often assumed as the desired outcome, there may be merit in authoritarian regimes serving as precursors to democratic ones, provided they are "enlightened" and business-friendly. From this chapter, the idea of an "enlightened dictator" or one with a positive vision for his/her people surfaces. This research recognizes a major potential drawback of authoritarian regimes, as laid out by the political science literature, to be the dictator him- or herself. If the dictator is shortsighted, selfish, narcissistic, and uninformed about best policy practices, it is inevitable that the country will face serious difficulty. What is illuminated by this research, however, are the benefits of having a dictator with foresight and one who sees the benefits of making informed policy decisions, as was the case in Chile. An "enlightened dictator" (the type described in the preceding sentence) is critical to firm profitability because if an authoritarian regime is in place and the dictator is not enlightened, it is unlikely that effective, stable, and consistent policies will be developed and implemented. If, on the other hand, such a leader does exist, at least as far as policies are concerned, this type of government may have serious benefits. This research by no means ignores the social restrictions and risks that authoritarian governments may present, but rather turns the attention of the reader to the potential benefits of cementing stable policies and institutions for businesses on the path toward democracy.

A second theoretical implication that stems from the results of this research lies within the field of international business. Much attention in the literature has been given to the connection between governance and firm performance (Bhagat and Bolton 2008; Fan et al. 2007). Less of a connection, however, has been drawn between government type, institutional stability, and firm performance. If the assumption is granted that pro-market reforms lead to increased firm performance, a critical theoretical implication from this chapter is that regime type is a precursor to policy stability, and policy stability directly impacts the effectiveness of pro-market reforms.

What can be concluded, then, is that government type has an impact on firm-performance, which is a significant finding within the scope of literature for international business. Rather than perpetuating the discussion at the macro-economic level, this chapter attempts to bring government type and institutional stability down to the firm level in order to analyze the correlation that exists within that realm. From this, it can be concluded that while democracies may be most conducive and supporting of liberal economic policies, and that these democracies may provide the best social outcomes for individuals, pro-market reforms that are implemented and enforced within an authoritarian regime first, have a better chance at long-term stabilization and maintenance. That is not to say that a democratic society is incapable of promoting and protecting pro-market reforms, but rather that authoritarian governments have a higher probability of doing so effectively. In a democratic system where elections occur frequently, policies are at risk of fluctuation. In an authoritarian system, on the other hand, where the dictator decides alone, policies are not subject to the same kind of democratic process and therefore are less likely to be rejected or overturned.

Finally, this chapter has implications for literature surrounding economic development. Development is a central issue in both the fields of political economy and international business (Romer 1992; Ross 1999; Williamson 1993). While this chapter does not attempt to answer how nations develop, it does add to the literature by highlighting some of the overlooked merits of authoritarian regimes serving as a precursor to democratic regimes on firm performance. From this conclusion, it can be deduced that one way to positively impact development is to support local firm performance, as such firms can provide the motor that drives their economies, and this support may be received from authoritarian regimes that precede democratic ones. Many studies have been introduced that emphasize the drawbacks of authoritarian regimes on social development (Dahl 1954; Lipset 1959). Again, this chapter does not contest the potential drawbacks and risk potential that exists with authoritarianism, but wishes to add to the debate by looking at the potential policy benefits of authoritarianism preceding a transition to a democratic regime.

## Practical Implications

International business attempts to provide strategy analysis and recommendations for managers and firms seeking to internationalize or move into new markets. However, many managers and firms do not know where to take their businesses or what markets are most conducive to growth in their particular sector. Prior work suggests that economically liberalized markets that support pro-market reforms may offer the best business conditions (Klapper and Love 2004). The results of this research, however, point to another indicator that executives could look to: the history of the political and institutional structures that led to the pro-market reforms in any given society.

Based on this particular project, there may be a benefit for companies to look at the path that a country took when implementing pro-market reforms, prior to entering that country to do business. If a country implemented the policies under an authoritarian structure and the policies have remained after a transition to democracy, these policies may provide a more stable institutional and business context. On the other hand, if the country in question implemented the policies under a democratic regime, executives may want to consider the possibility that these policies are more fragile and susceptible to a fluctuating political environment. Scenarios such as elections, policy turnovers, changes in leadership, and mass support or disdain for a particular policy all have the potential to shift any particular policy, regardless of its impact on the business environment. From this, executives should first consider the political context and progression of pro-market reforms as this could shed insight on the stability and effectiveness of reforms.

Furthermore, this research has practical implications for politicians and officials within developing countries. As a country faces the questions of development, including what type of government structure is best at both the macro- and micro-levels, policy-makers and government personnel are forced to make critical decisions involving government structure (Dau et al. 2015, 2016c; Suchman 1995). This chapter implies that a long-term vision for authoritarianism preceding a transition to democracy may be best for countries aiming to promote business development. This chapter does not contest that one type of government is better than another, but rather nuances that each type of government may have different strengths and the timing of each government structure may be critical for bringing about the most effective pro-market reform policies. Regardless of the political system in place, politicians are urged to develop a long-term rather than short-term approach when making structural and institutional decisions. Decisions made for the next election may not create the best business environment.

A final practical implication this research presents is for entrepreneurs and business executives. As Douglass North points out, institutions are the "rules of the game" (North 1990: 3). Understanding the rules is critical for business executives to operate effectively, but understanding the larger political system in which these rules are embedded becomes especially critical when trying to influence and change these rules if they are not working (Dau et al. 2016a; North 1990). When dealing with developing and emerging markets, business executives may be wise to become involved from the ground level of pro-market reform policy-making. Businesses, like any other interest group, have the ability to influence government and vice versa (Dau et al. 2016b; Fox 2000; Zurn 2002). Executives with proper resources and time could better serve not only their private business interests, but also business interests of a given market as a whole if they actively participate in influencing government.

## Future Research and Conclusion

This research project represents the strengthening of a dialogue between academics within political economy and international business. The project attempts to encompass the correlation between country-level policy decisions and firm-level performance. While there have been studies that have aimed to capture the influence that policy has on business and vice versa, this study attempts to dig deeper to understand the influence that this connection has on the strategy level.

While this research project propels the conversation in the right direction and frames the discussion by presenting a broad picture, future research on this topic is necessary. One such project that might be of interest on the large-n scale relates to election timing and policy change and the subsequent impact that the two have on firm performance. From the case studies presented within this research, it seemed apparent that one of the inhibitors to firm performance was the fluctuation of policies due to political turnover, specifically elections. Future scholars could find a fruitful analysis in attempting to discover a potential correlation between the timing of policy adjustments and changes in leadership, to better assess policy and institutional stability within democracies. This information could be invaluable for understanding how to create lasting and effective pro-market reforms, that could in turn have countless effects on development, economic success, and firm performance.

Future research could also include additional case studies not only within Latin America but also throughout other areas of the developing world. By exploring case studies from other countries and regions, one would add credibility, depth, and richness to the logic within this manuscript. Furthermore, an analysis could be performed on countries within Latin America that appear (at the onset) to be following one of the two model paths to pro-market reforms described here. Peru and Colombia, for example, are said to be following a similar path to that of Chile and could be observed for a better understanding if the circumstances in Chile are unique to the country or generalizable to a larger population of countries and firms. Furthermore, future work could examine the dissimilar paths that India and China have pursued, with the former implementing reforms under a democracy and the later under an authoritarian regime, which may or may not transition to a democracy in the future. South Korea is another example of a country that developed relatively quickly from a rural society to one that is highly industrialized with an authoritarian regime and then transitioned to a democracy once the institutional framework had demonstrated its benefits to the population. Authoritarian regimes also often fail to provide benefits for their populations or business environments, so it is also critical to study the effects of different types of authoritarian regimes.

Finally, future research could include rhetorical analyses of the actual pro-market reforms in question. Is there a correlation between the strength of language and the effectiveness and duration of the reforms themselves? If the rhetoric behind the reforms is analyzed, executives and politicians alike can have an even fuller understanding of how to influence pro-market reforms at the ground level to ensure the most durable and effective policies are developed and nurtured.

The findings of this chapter have a place not only within the academic world—including several different streams of literature across political economy and international business—but also within the practical world. While they may be preliminary, they serve as a vehicle to facilitate future research and conversation.

## References


Alesina, A., and D. Rodrik. 1994. *Distributive politics and economic growth* (No. w3668). National Bureau of Economic Research.

Arendt, H. 1968. *Imperialism: Part two of the origins of totalitarianism.* New York: Houghton Mifflin Harcourt.

———. 1993. *Between past and future: Eight exercises in political thought.* New York: Penguin.

Argentina Interview Series. Interviews by first author.

Aristotle. 2009. *Politics – Aristotle.* [S.l.]: Nuvision Publications.

Armijo, L.E., and P. Faucher. 2002. "We have a consensus": Explaining political support for market reforms in Latin America. *Latin American Politics and Society 44* (2): 1–40.

Ayoob, M. 1995. *The third world security predicament: State making, regional conflict, and the international system.* London: Rienner Publishers.

Baldwin, R., M. Cave, and M. Lodge. 2012. *Understanding regulation: Theory, strategy, and practice.* Oxford: Oxford University Press.

Ball, S.J. 2012. *Politics and policy making in education: Explorations in sociology.* London: Routledge International Press.

Banalieva, E.R. 2014. Embracing the second best? Synchronization of reform speeds, excess high-discretion slack, and performance of transition economy firms. *Global Strategy Journal* 4 (2): 104–126.

Banalieva, E.R., and K.A. Eddleston. 2015. When do family firms have an advantage in transitioning economies? Toward a dynamic institution-based view. *Strategic Management Journal* 36 (9): 1358–1377.

Bangura, Y. 1991. *Authoritarian rule and democracy in Africa: A theoretical discourse.* Geneva: United Nations Research Institute for Social Development.

Barnett, M. 2006. Building a republican peace: Stabilizing states after war. *International Security* 30 (4): 87–112.

Barnett, M., and M. Finnemore. 2004. *Rules for the world: International organizations in global politics*. New York: Cornell University Press.
Baumgartner, F., and B.D. Jones. 1993. *Agendas and instability in American politics*. Chicago: University of Chicago Press.
BBC News. 2001. Pinochet's rule: Repression and economic success.
Behrman, J.N., and R.E. Grosse. 1990. *International business and governments: Issues and institutions*. Columbia: University of South Carolina Press.
Bellin, E. 2004. The robustness of authoritarianism in the Middle East: Exceptionalism in comparative perspective. *Comparative Politics* 1 (2): 139–157.
Bethell, L. 1993. *Chile since independence*. Cambridge: Cambridge University Press.
Bhagat, S., and B. Bolton. 2008. Corporate governance and firm performance. *Journal of Corporate Finance* 14 (3): 257–273.
Boas, T.C., and J. Gans-Morse. 2009. Neoliberalism: From new liberal philosophy to anti-liberal slogan. *Studies in Comparative International Development* 44 (2): 137–161.
Boddewyn, J.J., and T.L. Brewer. 1994. International-business political behavior: New theoretical directions. *Academy of Management Review* 19 (1): 119–143.
Borras, S. 2003. Questioning the pro-market critique of state-led agrarian reforms. *The European Journal of Development Research* 15 (2): 109–132.
Brady, D.W. 1991. *Critical elections and congressional policymaking*. Stanford: Stanford University Press.
Brunetti, A., and B. Weder. 2003. A free press is bad news for corruption. *Journal of Public Economics* 87 (7): 1801–1824.
Buckley, P.J., and M. Casson. 1994. A theory of cooperation in international business. *Cooperative Forms of Transnational Corporation Activity* 13 (1): 91.
Bulmer-Thomas, V. 2003. *The economic history of Latin America since independence*. Cambridge: Cambridge University Press.
Bunce, V.J., and S.L. Wolchik. 2010. Defeating dictators: Electoral change and stability in competitive authoritarian regimes. *World Politics* 62 (01): 43–86.
Bursey, G. 2013. Structure of dictatorship. Totalitarianism and oppressive forms of government. 306 Meserve Hall, Northeastern University, 25 October 2013. Lecture.
Cantwell, J., J.H. Dunning, and S.M. Lundan. 2010. An evolutionary approach to understanding international business activity: The co-evolution of MNEs and the institutional environment. *Journal of International Business Studies* 41 (4): 567–586.

Cardoso, F.H. 1979. *The new authoritarianism in Latin America*. Princeton: Princeton University Press.
Chacar, A., W. Newburry, and B. Vissa. 2010. Bringing institutions into performance persistence research: Exploring the impact of the product, financial and labor market institutions. *Journal of International Business Studies* 41 (7): 1119–1140.
Child, J., and K.T. David. 2001. China's transition and its implications for international business. *Journal of International Business Studies* 32 (1): 5–21.
Chile Interview Series. Interviews by first author.
Coatsworth, J.H. 2005. Structures, endowments, and institutions in the economic history of Latin America. *Latin American Research Review* 40 (3): 126–144.
Collier, S., and W.F. Sater. 2004. *A history of Chile, 1808–2002*. Cambridge: Cambridge University Press.
Cuervo-Cazurra, A., and L.A. Dau. 2009. Pro-market reforms and firm profitability in developing countries. *Academy of Management Journal* 52 (6): 1348–1368.
Dahl, R.A. 1954. *A preface to democratic theory*. Chicago: University of Chicago Press.
———. 1971. *Polyarchy*. New Haven: Yale University Press.
Dahl, R.A., I. Shapiro, and J.A. Cheibub, eds. 2003. *The democracy sourcebook*. Boston: MIT Press.
Dau, L.A. 2011. Reforms, multinationalization, and profitability. In L. Toombs (Ed.), *Academy of management best paper proceedings*. Academy of Management. Briarcliff Manor, NY.
———. 2012. Pro-market reforms and developing country multinationals. *Global Strategy Journal* 2 (3): 262–276.
———. 2013. Learning across geographic space: Pro-market reforms, multinationalization strategy, and profitability. *Journal of International Business Studies* 44 (3): 235–262.
———. 2016a. Knowledge will set you free: Enhancing the firm's responsiveness to institutional change. *International Journal of Emerging Markets* 11 (2): 121–147.
———. 2016b. Contextualizing international learning: The moderating effects of mode of entry & subsidiary networks on the relationship between reforms & profitability. *Journal of World Business*. https://doi.org/10.1016/j.jwb.2016.10.005, in press.
Dau, L.A., and Wesley, D. 2016. Overcoming the home field disadvantage: How BRICS firms adapt to market reforms. In *Progress in international busi-*

*ness research, volume 11: The challenge of BRIC multinationals*, edited by Rob van Tulder, Alain Verbeke, Jorge Carneiro, and Maria Alejandra Gonzalez-Perez. Emerald Group Publishing Limited, in press.

Dau, L.A., E.M. Moore, and C. Bradley. 2015. Institutions and international entrepreneurship. *International Business: Research, Teaching and Practice* 9 (1): 1–20.

Dau, L.A., E.M. Moore, and M. Soto. 2016a. Informal transnational political actors and emerging markets: Understanding entrepreneurship in a changing normative atmosphere. In *Entrepreneurship and firm performance*, ed. Antoinette Walsh, 19–41. New York: NOVA Publishers.

———. 2016b. The great recession and emerging market firms: Unpacking the divide between global and national level sustainability expectations. In *Advances in sustainability and environmental justice: Lessons from the Great Recession*, ed. Liam Leonard, Maria Alejandra Gonzalez-Perez, and Constantin Gurdgiev, 165–189. Bingley: Emerald Group Publishing Limited.

———. 2016c. How globalization sparked entrepreneurship in the developing world: The impact of formal economic & political linkages. In *Corporate espionage, geopolitics, and diplomacy issues in international business*, ed. Bryan Christiansen, 72–91. Hershey: E-Editorial Discovery. IGI Global.

Del Sol, P., and J. Kogan. 2007. Regional competitive advantage based on pioneering economic reforms: The case of Chilean FDI. *Journal of International Business Studies* 38 (6): 901–927.

Diamond, L. 2003. *Can the whole world become democratic? Democracy, development, and international policies*. Washington, DC: Center for the Study of Democracy.

———. 2010. Why are there no Arab democracies? *Journal of Democracy* 21 (1): 93–112.

Diamond, L.J., J.J. Linz, and S.M. Lipset, eds. 1989. *Democracy in developing countries*. Vol. 4. Boulder: Lynne Rienner.

Dimaggio, P.J. 1988. Interest and agency in institutional theory. *Institutional Patterns and Organizations: Culture and Environment* 1 (1): 3–22.

Djelic, M.L., and S. Quack. 2003. *Globalization and institutions. Redefining the rules of the economic game*. New York: Edward Elgar Publications.

Downs, A. 1957. *An economic theory of democracy*. New York: Harper.

Duckitt, J. 1989. Authoritarianism and group identification: A new view of an old construct. *Political Psychology* 10: 63–84.

Dunning, J.H. 2012. *International production and the multinational Enterprise (RLE international business)*. London, UK: Routledge International Publishing.

Edwards, S., and A.C. Edwards. 1991. *Monetarism and liberalization: The Chilean experiment*. Chicago: University of Chicago Press.

Evans, P. 1996. Government action, social capital and development: Reviewing the evidence on synergy. *World Development* 24 (6): 1119–1132.

Fan, J.P., T.J. Wong, and T. Zhang. 2007. Politically connected CEOs, corporate governance, and post-IPO performance of China's newly partially privatized firms. *Journal of Financial Economics* 84 (2): 330–357.

Femia, J.V. 1972. Barrington Moore and the preconditions for democracy. *British Journal of Political Science* 2 (1): 21–46.

Fischer, F. 1995. *Evaluating public policy*. London: Wadsworth Publishing Company.

Fox, S. 2000. Communities of practice, Foucault and actor-network theory. *Journal of Management Studies* 37 (6): 853–867.

Friedrich, C.J., and Z.K. Brzezinski. 1965. *Totalitarian dictatorship*. Cambridge, MA: Harvard University Press.

Gandhi, J., and E. Lust-Okar. 2009. Elections under authoritarianism. *Annual Review of Political Science* 12 (1): 403–422.

Gerring, J., P. Bond, W.T. Barndt, and C. Moreno. 2005. Democracy and economic growth: A historical perspective. *World Politics* 57 (3): 323–364.

Geyer, M., and S. Fitzpatrick. 2009. *Beyond totalitarianism: Stalinism and Nazism compared*. Cambridge: Cambridge University Press.

Ghoshal, S., and C.A. Bartlett. 1999. *The individualized corporation: A fundamentally new approach to management*. New York City: Harper Collins.

Goggin, M.L., A.M. Bowman, J.P. Lester, and L.J. O'Toole. 1990. *Implementation theory and practice: Toward a third generation*. Glenview: Scott Foresman/ Little Brown.

Goldstein, J.S., and J.C. Pevehouse. 2012. *International relations*. Boston: Pearson Print.

Goodwin, J. 2001. *No other way out: States and revolutionary movements, 1945–1991*. Cambridge: Cambridge University Press.

Griffith, R., R. Harrison, and G. Macartney. 2007. Product market reforms, labour market institutions and unemployment. *The Economic Journal* 117 (519): C142–C166.

Hadenius, A., and J. Teorell. 2005. Cultural and economic prerequisites of democracy: Reassessing recent evidence. *Studies in Comparative International Development* 39 (4): 87–106.

Heineman, R., W.T. Bluhm, S.A. Peter, and E.N. Kearny, eds. 1991. *The world of the policy analyst*. Chatham: Chatham House.

Henisz, W., and A. Swaminathan. 2008. Institutions and international business. *Journal of International Business Studies* 39 (4): 537–539.

Henisz, W.J., B.A. Zelner, and M.F. Guillén. 2005. The worldwide diffusion of market-oriented infrastructure reform, 1977–1999. *American Sociological Review* 70 (6): 871–897.

Hill, C. 2014. *International business: Competing in the global market place*. 10th ed. New York City: McGraw Hill Educational Press.

Hill, M.J., and P.L. Hupe. 2002. *Implementing public policy: Governance in theory and practice* (No. 04; H97, H5.). London: SAGE International Press.

Hill, C.W., and A.K. Jain. 2000. *International business 10/e: Competing in the global marketplace*. New York: McGraw-Hill Education.

Hirschman, A.O. 1970. The search for paradigms as a hindrance to understanding. *World Politics* 22 (3): 329–343.

Hood, C.C., and H.Z. Margetts. 2007. *The tools of government in the digital age*. New York: Palgrave Macmillan.

Howlett, M., M. Ramesh, and A. Perl. 1995. *Studying public policy: Policy cycles and policy subsystems*. Vol. 3. Toronto: Oxford University Press.

Iannaccone, L., and F.W. Lutz. 1970. *Politics, power and policy: The governing of local school districts*. Columbus: CE Merrill Publishers.

IMF. 2014a. Country profiles: Argentina. www.imf.org/en/Countries/ARG. Accessed 1 Feb 2014.

———. 2014b. Country profiles: Chile. www.imf.org/en/Countries/CHL. Accessed 1 Feb 2014.

Keeler, J.T. 1993. Opening the window for reform mandates, crises, and extraordinary policy-making. *Comparative Political Studies* 25 (4): 433–486.

Kimber, R. 1989. On democracy. *Scandinavian Political Studies* 12 (3): 199–219.

Kingdon, J. 2010. *Agendas, alternatives, and public policies*. Update ed. New York: Harper Collins Press.

Kingdon, J., and Thurber. 1984. *Agendas, alternatives, and public policies*. Boston: Little, Brown, Print.

Klapper, L.F., and I. Love. 2004. Corporate governance, investor protection, and performance in emerging markets. *Journal of Corporate Finance* 10 (5): 703–728.

Klein, N. 2007. *The shock doctrine: The rise of disaster capitalism*. London: Macmillan.

Krugman, P. 2009. *The conscience of a liberal*. New York: WW Norton & Company.

Labán, R., and F. Larraín. 1995. Continuity, change, and the political economy of transition in Chile. In *Reform, recovery, and growth: Latin America and the Middle East*, 115–148. Chicago: University of Chicago Press.

Leigh, N.G., and E.J. Blakely. 2016. *Planning local economic development: Theory and practice*. New York: SAGE Publications.

Leung, K., R.S. Bhagat, N.R. Buchan, M. Erez, and C.B. Gibson. 2005. Culture and international business: Recent advances and their implications for future research. *Journal of International Business Studies* 36 (4): 357–378.

Levitsky, S., and L. Way. 2002. The rise of competitive authoritarianism. *Journal of Democracy* 13 (2): 51–65.

Levy, M.L. 2004. *We are millions: Neo-liberalism and new forms of political action in Argentina*. New York: SAGE Publishers.

Lieberthal, K.G. 1992. Introduction: The 'fragmented authoritarianism' model and its limitations. In *Bureaucracy, politics, and decision making in post-Mao China*, 1–30. London: Routledge Press.

Lin, J.Y. 1992. Rural reforms and agricultural growth in China. *The American Economic Review* 82: 34–51.

Lipset, S.M. 1959. Some social requisites of democracy: Economic development and political legitimacy. *American Political Science Review* 53 (1): 69–105.

Lopez, L.E., S.K. Kundu, and L. Ciravegna. 2009. Born global or born regional: Evidence from an exploratory study in the Costa Rican software industry. *Journal of International Business Studies* 40 (7): 1228–1238.

Mahoney, J. 2001. Path-dependent explanations of regime change: Central America in comparative perspective. *Studies in Comparative International Development* 36 (1): 111–141.

Mahoney, J.T., and T. Chi. 2001. Business strategies in transition economies. *Academy of Management Review* 26 (2): 311–313.

Manion, M. 2006. Democracy, community, trust- the impact of elections in rural China. *Comparative Political Studies* 39 (3): 301–324.

Martínez, J., and A. Díaz. 1996. *Chile: The great transformation*. Washington, DC: Brookings Institution.

McMillan, J., and B. Naughton. 1992. How to reform a planned economy: Lessons from China. *Oxford Review of Economic Policy* 8 (1): 130–143.

Mertha, A. 2009. "Fragmented authoritarianism 2.0": Political pluralization in the Chinese policy process. *The China Quarterly* 200: 995–1012.

Mill, J.S. (1859[1975]). *On Liberty*. New York: Routledge International Publishing Company.

Miller, K.D. 1992. A framework for integrated risk management in international business. *Journal of International Business Studies* 23 (2): 311–331.

Muller, J.Z. 2007. *The mind and the market: Capitalism in Western thought*. New York: Anchor Press.

Nayyar, D. 2002. *Governing globalization: Issues and institutions*. Oxford: Oxford University Press.
Newburry, W., and N. Yakova. 2006. Standardization preferences: A function of national culture, work interdependence and local embeddedness. *Journal of International Business Studies* 37 (1): 44–60.
North, D.C. 1990. *Institutions, institutional change and economic performance*. Cambridge: Cambridge University Press.
Nouzeilles, G., and G. Montaldo. 2002. *The Argentina reader: History, culture*. Politics: Duke University Press.
Ogden, S. 2002. *Inklings of democracy in China*. Vol. 210. Boston: Harvard University Asia Center.
Olson, M. 1971. The logic of collective action. Vol. 124. *Harvard Economic Studies Series*. Boston: Harvard University Press.
Osborne, D., and P. Plastrik. 1997. *Banishing bureaucracy: The five strategies for reinventing government*. Boston: Addison-Wesley Publishing Company, Inc..
Parekh, B. 1992. The cultural peculiarity of liberal democracy. *Political Studies* 40 (1): 160–175.
Peng, M.W., D.Y. Wang, and Y. Jiang. 2008. An institution-based view of international business strategy: A focus on emerging economies. *Journal of International Business Studies* 39 (5): 920–936.
Prebisch, R. 1950. *The economic development of Latin America and its principal problems*. New York: United Nations Press.
Przeworski, A., F. Limongi, and S. Giner. 1995. Political regimes and economic growth. In *Democracy and development*, 3–27. London: Palgrave Macmillan.
Purcell, S.K. 1973. Decision-making in an authoritarian regime: Theoretical implications from a Mexican case study. *World Politics* 26 (01): 28–54.
———. 1975. *The Mexican profit-sharing decision: Politics in an authoritarian regime*. Berkeley: University of California Press.
Remmer, K.L., and G.W. Merkx. 1982. Bureaucratic-authoritarianism revisited. *Latin American Research Review* 17 (2): 3–40.
Ricardo, F.D. 2010. *Economic reforms in Chile: From dictatorship to democracy*. London: Palgrave Macmillan Press.
Richardson, N.P. 2008. Export-oriented populism: Commodities and coalitions in Argentina. *Studies in Comparative International Development* 44 (3): 228.
Rochefort, D.A., and R.W. Cobb. 1994. *The politics of problem definition: Shaping the policy agenda*. Lawrence: University of Kansas Press.
Romer, P.M. 1992. Two strategies for economic development: Using ideas and producing ideas. *The World Bank Economic Review* 6 (1): 63–91.

Rose, R. 1993. *Lesson-drawing in public policy: A guide to learning across time and space*. Vol. 91. Chatham: Chatham House Publishers.

Ross, M.L. 1999. The political economy of the resource curse. *World Politics* 51 (2): 297–322.

Samuels, D. 2000. Ambition and competition: Explaining legislative turnover in Brazil. *Legislative Studies Quarterly* 1 (1): 481–497.

Schmitter, P.C., and T.L. Karl. 1991. What democracy is… and is not. *Journal of Democracy* 2 (3): 75–88.

Schneider, A.L., and H.M. Ingram. 1997. *Policy design for democracy*. Lawrence: University Press of Kansas.

Schumpeter, J. 1950. *Capitalism, socialism and democracy*. New York: Harper.

Selowsky, M., and R. Martin. 1997. Policy performance and output growth in the transition economies. *The American Economic Review* 87 (2): 349–353.

Sen, A.K. 1999. Democracy as a universal value. *Journal of Democracy 10* (3): 3–17.

Skocpol, T. 1979. *States and social revolutions: A comparative analysis of France, Russia, and China*. Cambridge: Cambridge University Press.

Sokoloff, K.L., and S.L. Engerman. 2000. History lessons: Institutions, factors endowments, and paths of development in the new world. *The Journal of Economic Perspectives* 14 (3): 217–232.

Stimson, J.A., M.B. MacKuen, and R.S. Erikson. 1995. Dynamic representation. *American Political Science Review* 89 (03): 543–565.

Stone, D. 2002. *Policy paradox: The art of political decision making*. revised ed. London/New York: WW Norton and Company.

Stoner-Weiss, K. 2006. Russia: Authoritarianism without authority. *Journal of Democracy* 17 (1): 104–118.

Suchman, M.C. 1995. Managing legitimacy: Strategic and institutional approaches. *Academy of Management Review* 20 (3): 571–610.

Taoka, G.M., and D.R. Beeman. 1991. *International business: Environments, institutions, and operations*. New York: Harpercollins College Division.

Teegen, H., J.P. Doh, and S. Vachani. 2004. The importance of nongovernmental organizations (NGOs) in global governance and value creation: An international business research agenda. *Journal of International Business Studies* 35 (6): 463–483.

Teichman, J.A. 2001. *The politics of freeing markets in Latin America: Chile, Argentina, and Mexico*. Chapel Hill: University of North Carolina Press.

The Economist. 2002. Argentina's bottomless pit. 8 August. Print.

———. 2014. The tragedy of Argentina: A century of decline. 17 Feb. Print.

Valdés, J.G. 1995. *Pinochet's economists: The Chicago school of economics in Chile*. Cambridge: Cambridge University Press.

Valenzuela, A. 2004. Latin American presidencies interrupted. *Journal of Democracy* 15 (4): 5–19.

Valenzuela, J.S., and A. Valenzuela. 1978. Modernization and dependency: Alternative perspectives in the study of Latin American underdevelopment. *Comparative Politics* 10 (4): 535–557.

Williamson, J. 1993. Democracy and the "Washington consensus". *World Development* 21 (8): 1329–1336.

World Bank. 2012. Country development indicators database. http://www.worldbank.com/data/developmentindicators. Accessed 11 Nov 2013.

———. 2014. Ease of doing business database. http://www.worldbank.com/data/DoingBusiness. Accessed 11 Nov 2013.

Yin. 2008. *Case study research: Design and methods*. New York: SAGE Publications.

Zurn, M. 2002. From interdependence to globalization. In *Handbook of international relations*, 235–254. Cambridge: Routledge Press.

# 4

# Country Development Stage and the Level of Corporate Social Disclosure

Simone R. Barakat, Greici Sarturi, and Keysa Manuela Cunha de Mascena

## Introduction

Given the increasingly evident impacts of business activities, society now requires companies to adopt more ethical, transparent, and socially responsible behavior (Carroll 2008). In this context, companies' concerns about the responsibility for their activities has also increased, leading them to implement actions to incorporate corporate social responsibility (CSR) in policies and practices (Cheng et al. 2014), as well as to document such actions in their annual reports (Frías-Aceituno et al. 2013).

S. R. Barakat (✉) • G. Sarturi
Business Administration Department, University of São Paulo, São Paulo, Brazil
e-mail: simonebarakat@usp.br; greici@usp.br

K. M. C. de Mascena
University of Fortaleza, Fortaleza, Brazil
e-mail: keysamascena@unifor.br



W. Newburry et al. (eds.), *Contemporary Influences on International Business in Latin America*, AIB Latin America, https://doi.org/10.1007/978-3-319-98340-0_4

CSR can be conceptualized as voluntary company activities that consider social and environmental concerns in business operations and in interactions with stakeholders (Van Marrewijk 2003). In this setting, CSR exists only if adopted voluntarily by the company and extends to groups such as customers, employees, suppliers, government, and local communities (Jones 1980). However, despite the notable increase in the attention given to CSR, there are different levels of CSR activities and practices among companies.

Many internal factors may explain the variations in the extent of firms' CSR and, consequently, in their voluntary corporate social disclosure (CSD). Some examples of these factors are firm's size (Xiao et al. 2005; Naser et al. 2006) and managers' values (Haniffa and Cooke 2005). Since large companies are more visible to the public and receive more pressure than small firms, they tend to voluntarily disclose more social responsibility information (Naser et al. 2006). Also, when managers have intrinsic motivations and care about a broader set of stakeholders, they tend to act to increase the responsibilities of firms and to promote more CSD (Schaltegger and Burritt 2010).

However, external factors, such as institutional pressures, market efficiency, financial market development, governance, transparency, and accountability, also affect the degree of CSD, especially voluntary disclosure. Since the country where firms operate largely determines these external factors, it is important to examine the country's influence on CSD. Several studies have investigated the factors that explain variations in the extent of voluntary information disclosed by firms, but a limited number of studies have focused on countries' characteristics that may influence the level of CSD. Therefore, this research seeks to contribute to the CSD literature by analyzing the phenomenon through the country level and not the firm level, as most studies do.

More specifically, this chapter investigates the association between countries' development stages and the level of CSD of firms operating in these countries. It was done by adopting the five stages of countries' development presented in the Global Competitiveness Report (GCR), and the number of GRI reported by 144 countries in 2014.

# Literature Review

## Corporate Social Responsibility

CSR has become a prominent topic for different actors (Lockett et al. 2006). For governments, CSR is a means of encouraging better corporate governance and ethical practices. For firms, CSR may represent a source of competitive advantage, once it can differentiate companies with better CSR practices from their competitors (Nalband and Al-Amri 2013). As the involvement of governments and firms increases, scholars also have an important opportunity to engage in CSR research (Aguinis and Glavas 2012).

Despite the growing evidence of the theme, it is neither possible to verify a consensus on the meaning of CSR (McWilliams et al. 2006) nor an operationalization of the core general concepts of CSR (De Bakker et al. 2005). Here, it is considered that CSR is voluntary company activities that consider social and environmental concerns in business operations and in interactions with stakeholders (Van Marrewijk 2003). CSR accounts for a company's direct impacts as well as indirect impacts considering the entire value chain and the entire life cycle of its products. So, CSR includes a wide range of issues such as relationships between customers and suppliers, contributions to community development, environmental protection, employee participation in the results and the company's decisions, diversity, safety, and professional development (Michalos 1997).

In order to describe CSR in a conceptual approach, Carroll (1979, 1991) proposed a pyramid-shaped model that covers four categories for CRS: economic, legal, ethical, and philanthropic. The economic dimension is the basis for all the others and reflects the company's need to maintain its financial health, ensuring its survival and growth. The second level refers to the adequacy of the company's actions to comply with current legislation. The third level corresponds to a behavior based on the existing expectations among society. Finally, the fourth level refers to the company's voluntary initiatives concerning solutions to social problems (Carroll 1979, 1991).

Reconciling these levels can become a challenge for managers, since it is normally assumed that complying with legal and ethical requirements sacrifices economic results (Husted and Salazar 2006). However, such an interface seems to have competitive potential for organizations.

Companies that consistently operate at all levels of responsibility can economically benefit from their responsible actions (Porter and Kramer 2006; McWilliams and Siegel 2001).

Following the same logic, the triple bottom line (TBL) has emerged as an interpretation of CSR commonly adopted by companies, once it indicates the dimensions that CSR should cover. The model was created by Elkington (1997), who argued that organizations can pursue sustainable development by assessing the economic, social, and environmental aspects of their activities. In this model, each of the three dimensions has an equivalent weight.

The TBL is based on the concept of sustainable development, which gained notoriety after publication of the Brundtland Report, conducted by the World Commission on Environment and Development (WCED), of the United Nations (UN) in 1987. The report highlights that companies must meet the needs of the present generation without compromising the ability of future generations to meet their own needs, in order to achieve sustainable development.

The basic idea is that the success and health of the company should not be evaluated only by traditional financial measures, but also for its social responsibility and environmental performance (Norman and MacDonald 2004). Although each of these TBL dimensions represents a great challenge for managers, organizations are increasingly allocating a considerable amount of time and resources to CSR strategies (Cheng et al. 2014).

## Corporate Social Disclosure

CSD is used to address the exposure firms face regarding social and environment issues, and should be related more closely with public-pressure variables than profitability measures (Patten 1991, 2002). CSD covers a broad and diverse set of issues, such as product information, environmental impact of corporate operations, labor practices and relations with suppliers and customers (Van der Laan Smith et al. 2005).

In the past two decades, there was a dramatic increase in firms' reporting on CSR activities around the world (Dhaliwal et al. 2012). This increase is twofold: there has been an increase in the number of companies adopting social disclosure as well as an increase in the amount of information provided (García-Sánchez et al. 2013).

According to KPMG (2011), 95% of the G250 companies issue reports on their corporate responsibility activities. However, there is not a single globally accepted report or a commonly accepted format that reporting should follow (Dilling 2010). Currently, the Global Reporting Initiative (GRI) is the most widely used standard for CSR reporting and it covers the economic, environmental, and social impacts caused by a company in its everyday activities. According to the GRI, its framework is "a reporting system that provides metrics and methods for measuring and reporting sustainability-related impacts and performance" (GRI 2015).

In the academic perspective, corporate social reporting has been discussed for more than two decades under multiple theories. For instance, social contracting theory understands that firms and society have a social contract where they should perform certain tasks within the principles of justice. Legitimacy theory is also used in the understanding of firms' social disclosure. It extends social contracting theory and explains that companies respond to the demands of divergent interest groups by legitimizing their actions. Accountability theory also extends social contracting theory by considering companies' compliance with the law. Finally, decision usefulness theory understands CSD as incorporating users other than investors (Tilt 1994; Haniffa and Cooke 2005).

Based on such theories, empirical research looked for evidence that could explain social disclosure patterns. Some of the key research questions addressed include: (1) what companies are reporting; (2) the relationship between social and environmental disclosure practices and economic performance; and (3) companies' motivations to make social and environmental disclosures (Haniffa and Cooke 2005).

One prominent author of the field was Ullmann (1985) who reviewed studies that analyzed the correlation between CSD and corporate social performance (CSP) as well as CSD and corporate finance performance (CFP). Regarding the relationship between CSD and CSP, the social performance could be under-reported due to the accountability traditionally made only to shareholders. On the other hand, the firm could over-report social performance in order to create a good impression to other stakeholders. He also found that social disclosure was more linked with other variables such as company size, visibility, and external pressure than social performance. Regarding the CSD and CFP relationship, Ullmann (1985) found that in a positive correlation, high CSD could attend to ethical investors reducing the risk associated with reputation, while in a negative correlation, high CSD could indicate high investments not necessary under an economic perspective. Based on this research, Ullmann (1985) proposed a model wherein the power of the stakeholder, the strategic posture, and the economic performance influence the level of social disclosure and performance.

However, more recent studies have shown that firms with superior CSP are more likely to disclose their responsible activities and practices by issuing public CSR reports (Al-Tuwaijri et al. 2004; Dhaliwal et al. 2012). CSR reporting: (1) increases transparency related to the social and environmental impact of companies and their governance structure; and (2) leads to changes in internal control systems that may improve the compliance with regulations and the reliability of reporting (Cheng et al. 2014). Also, the best CSR performers will provide a higher quality of CSD in order to signal their commitment to CSR (Mallin and Michelon 2011).

Aerts, Cormier, and Magnan (2008) point out some factors found in the literature that contribute to social disclosure. These factors include: firm size, industry, and ownership; legal exposure regarding environment issues; probability of social or environmental accidents; and concerns of environmental lobby groups. Schaltegger and Burritt (2010) also presented some factors that contribute to social disclosure. Focusing on managerial decisions about social disclosure, the authors argue that besides managers' intrinsic motivation there are six reasons that can encourage managers to establish an accounting system with information on sustainability issues that show firm actions. These reasons include: (1) greenwashing; (2) mimicry and industry pressure; (3) legislative pressure, stakeholder pressure, and ensuring the license to operate, (4) self-regulation, (5) corporate responsibility and ethical reasons, and (6) managing the business case for sustainability.

## The Influence of Country on CSR and CSD

Research in the CSR area has been dedicated to explaining variations in CSR practices and disclosure; however, few have focused on a country's influence on the level of firms' CSR and CSD. Since the country in which firms operate largely determines external factors, such as institutional pressures, market efficiency, financial market development, governance, transparency, and accountability, it is expected that it will also affect the level of CSR and CSD.

Institutional theory and culture differences may be used to explain variations in CSR and CSD practices. For instance, Fifka and Pobizhan (2014) considered institutional theory to investigate the degree that national, political, and socio-economic institutions determine CSR practices. They analyzed 50 Russian companies and investigated the CSR areas in which such companies are active, the relevant stakeholders, the form and financial extent of their activities, the application of international standards, and how the reporting was conducted. Results suggested a strong relationship between national, political and socio-economic environments and companies' CSR practices, wherein most attention is paid to employees and the immediate community. Specific issues, such as support for veterans, orphans, and ethnic minorities are also considered in the CSR practices of those companies.

Frías-Aceituno et al. (2013) also studied CSR under an institutional perspective by analyzing the impact of the legal system on the elaboration and publication of an integrated report that includes a set of information such as financial information, management commentary, governance, remuneration disclosure, and sustainability reporting. The authors identified external pressures that affect firms in their decisions to disclose integrated reports. The results indicated that general norms and enforcement mechanisms to regulate stakeholders' rights have a significant impact on business disclosure practices. Opposite to what was expected, non-Anglo-Saxon firms produce integrated financial and non-financial information more rapidly than Anglo-Saxon firms. This result was counterintuitive since the Anglo-Saxon firms have traditionally been considered more transparent with regard to financial issues.

Dilling (2010) also found some factors that influence CSR and sustainability reporting. According to the study's results, legislation, location, sector, and the profitability and growth situation of the firm are significant characteristics related to CSR. With regards to legislation, the author argues that, when the legislation does not require sustainability reports, firms might voluntarily adhere to standardized sustainability reports in order to show their CSR commitment to internal and external stakeholders. In the opposite, firms in countries with CSR legislation already in place might find no reason to prepare an additional sustainability report due to the additional cost associated with doing so.

In order to analyze the differences on CSR across three types of economies, Robertson (2009) selected Singapore, Turkey, and Ethiopia to represent a range of economic development levels from high to low. The results illustrate variation across the countries, indicating that institutional factors such as firm ownership structure, corporate governance, openness of the economy to international investment, and the role of civil society contribute to explain variations of CSR. Singapore presented a CSR similar to the United States and the UK, in other words countries that present more public companies, effective corporate governance structures, a relatively open economy to international investment, and a tradition of citizen voice and action. Similarly, Ethiopia showed a weak orientation to CSR, characterized by firms' association with non-governmental organizations (NGOs) in order to deliver aid and education (Robertson 2009).

A recent study that sought to investigate the effect of a country's characteristics on the level of CSD found that firms are more predisposed to disclose CSR information in countries with better investor protection, higher levels of democracy, more effective government services, higher-quality regulations, and more press freedom (De Villiers and Marques 2016). Following this logic, developed countries tend to have greater concern about social and environmental issues and, consequently, companies in these countries face greater public and institutional pressures for more CSD than those from less-developed countries (Xiao et al. 2005; Jamali 2007).

Another stream of research has focused on cultural aspects that influence the level of CSR and CSD of firms. For instance, Orij (2010) applied the model of national culture dimensions proposed by Hofstede (1984) to analyze differences in the level of CSD. Orij (2010) argues that there are differences between the stakeholder orientations of countries that can explain the variation of CSD levels. He tested the hypotheses that secrecy and masculinity are negatively related to CSD levels as cultures characterized by secrecy present a non-stakeholder orientation, and greater masculinity is related to a weaker social orientation. The author also tested the influence of long-term orientation on CSD. As result, Orij (2010) found evidence of a negative relationship between secrecy and masculinity orientation and level of CSD. However, long-term orientation did not present a significant relationship with level of CSD.

García-Sánchez et al. (2013) used Hofstede's model as representative of the values of local stakeholders in order to analyze the influence of national culture on disclosure of integrated reporting, which includes financial, management, governance, remuneration, and sustainability reports information. According to the study's results, companies located in countries with strong values of collectivism and feminism presented a greater interest in developing integrated reporting. On the other hand, and similar to Orij's (2010) findings, long-term orientation and tolerance of uncertainty were not determinant factors to explain differences on disclose of integrated reporting.

Thus, previous studies have shown differences on CSR and CSD based on institutional theory and cultural orientation. However, the stage of the countries' development is less explored. In the studies about CSR, some exceptions can be found in Robertson's (2009) work, where the economic development stage was considered an influence on CSR. Here, the development stage of countries was considered as a variable associated with variations of CSD. Therefore, the stages of development of the country influence the level of CSD because the institutions' and stakeholders' pressures are different in each stage of development. These differences can be understood by analyzing the characteristics of the stages.

## Stages of Countries' Development

Based on economic development, countries can be classified into five stages of development. There are three main stages: (1) factor-driven, (2) efficiency-driven, and (3) innovation-driven, and two transitions stages between them (Porter 1990; Porter et al. 2002). Figure 4.1 shows the key pillars for each of the stages. Stage 1 consists of factor-driven economies, where countries compete primarily based on unskilled labor and natural resources. This stage is characterized by the pillars 1, 2, 3, and 4. Stage 2 refers to economies driven by efficiency, where countries develop more

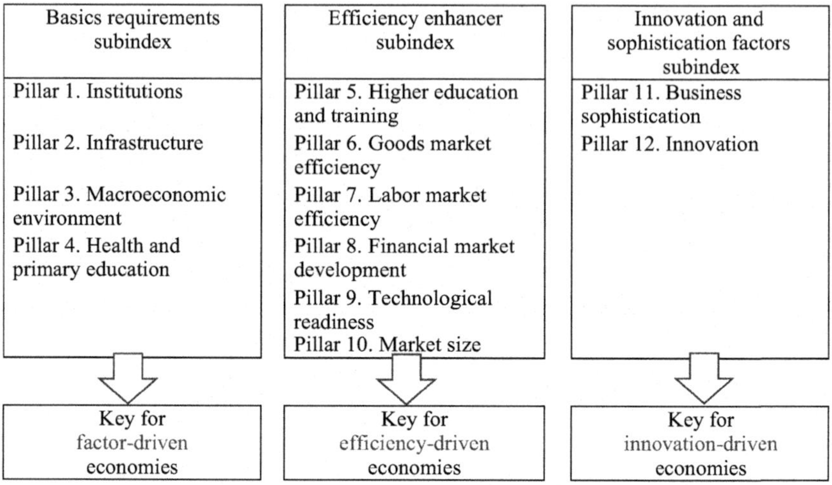


**Fig. 4.1** Stages of development: key pillars. Source: WEF (2015, p. 9)

efficient production processes and increase product quality. In this stage, the main pillars are 5, 6, 7, 8, 9, and 10. Finally, stage 3 includes countries that are innovation-driven, where they employ sophisticated production processes for the production of new and different goods. This stage is characterized by pillars 11 and 12. The two transition stages relate to the transition from stage 1 to stage 2 and the transition from stage 2 to stage 3.

The factor-driven stage is characterized by countries wherein production is based on low-cost efficiencies or low value-added. The knowledge is not used for exporting or to improve innovation. Normally, countries in this stage included a large amount of small manufacturing and service firms as well as high rates of non-agricultural self-employment (Acs et al. 2008). Countries in this stage compete primarily based on unskilled labor and natural resources, and companies compete through price bases and selling basic products or commodities. The low productivity of this type of economy is reflected in low wages (WEF 2015).

To move from the first to the second stage, countries must increase their production efficiency and workforce education. Countries in the efficiency-driven stage compete through efficient productive practices in large markets, where companies increase product quality and can use economies of scale (Acs et al. 2008; WEF 2015). This stage presents decreasing rates of self-employment and entrepreneurial activity since increases in the capital stock (i.e., through private enterprise, direct foreign investment or government ownership) will increase returns relative to the earlier activities (Acs et al. 2008).

Finally, countries in the innovation-driven stage employ sophisticated production processes for the production of new and different goods. This stage included higher levels of export-oriented entrepreneurship, improvements in information technologies, reduction of geographic distances provided by mail services, internet and mobile phones, and so on (Acs et al. 2008). At the innovation-driven stage, the wages are high and companies are able to compete with new and unique products (WEF 2015).

## Hypotheses Development

The growing numbers of corporations publishing sustainability reports represent a growing concern for firms regarding all of their stakeholders, the environment, and society (Dilling 2010). However, it is possible to observe different levels of disclosure among firms due to internal and external factors. One of the external factors is related to country characteristics, such as institutional and cultural environments (Dilling 2010; Orij 2010; Ernstberger and Grüning 2013; García-Sánchez et al. 2013).

The extent to which a society strengthens its civilian base, using practices related to CSR—composed of a set of rules, customs, and laws—can result in legal obligations. In this way, the civil foundation of a society and, consequently, the demand for CSR tends to grow with the increasing economic development of the country (Martin 2002; Abreu et al. 2015). Since CSD is closely related with public-pressure variables (Patten 2002), companies operating in countries whose society and stakeholders impose diverse pressure for CSR will present different levels of CSD. Companies are most likely to behave responsibly when operating in institutional contexts where there is more pressure through a more-developed legal system that protects stakeholders (Campbell 2006). Therefore, we propose the following hypothesis:

**Hypothesis 1** *The country's stage of development is associated with the level of CSD.*

Developed countries have greater awareness of social and environment issues and their institutions generally have a greater concern for such issues. Firms embedded in this context tend to adopt a higher level of CSR practices if compared with those in a context where there is lower concern for social and environment issues (Xiao et al. 2005; Abreu et al. 2015). Such firms must deal with a broader and more complex range of stakeholders' expectations. In addition, societies concerned with social issues might present stakeholder groups with more power, greater legitimacy, and claims viewed with greater urgency (Van der Laan Smith et al. 2005). Since superior CSR performers are more likely to disclose their responsible activities and practices (Al-Tuwaijri et al. 2004; Dhaliwal et al. 2012) and better CSR performers will provide a higher quality of CSD in order to signal commitment to CSR (Mallin and Michelon 2011), it is expected that companies operating in countries in the innovation-driven stage will present higher levels of disclosure. Therefore, we propose the following hypothesis:

**Hypothesis 1a** *Countries in more advanced stages of development have a higher level of CSD.*

Following the same logic, companies based in countries in the middle stages of development (i.e., in the efficiency-driven economies and in transition economies) receive less pressure from stakeholders than companies operating in countries in more advanced stages of development. Therefore, we propose the following hypothesis:

**Hypothesis 1b** *Countries in the middle stages of development present a medium level of CSD.*

Finally, companies operating in countries in the less-advanced stages of development (i.e., in factor-driven economies) face a weaker institutional environment and receive less stakeholder pressures. Since weaker corporate governance arrangements lead to lower levels of voluntary CSD

(Ernstberger and Grüning 2013), companies operating in such environments tend to disclose less. Therefore, we propose the following hypothesis:

**Hypothesis 1c** *Countries in less-advanced stage of development have a lower level of CSD.*

# Methods

## Data Collection

We collected data from the Global Competitiveness Report 2014–2015 in order to measure the stage of the development of countries. The report is released by the World Economic Forum (WEF) and gathers information about the microeconomic and macroeconomic foundations of national competitiveness of 144 countries.

In order to classify countries in the development stages, we used the Global Competitiveness Report (GCR) categorization. The GCR categorizes countries into five stages of development according to two indicators: (1) the level of GDP per capita at market exchange rates and (2) share of exports of mineral goods in total exports (goods and services). The first indicator is used as a proxy for wages and the second indicator is based on income and is used to adjust for countries that would have moved beyond stage 1, but their economy is based mainly on the extraction of resources (WEF 2015) (Fig. 4.2).

We considered the disclosure of Global Reporting Initiative (GRI) in 2014. The GRI is the most widely spread model of social, environmental, and economic reporting and was created in 1997 by the NGO of the same name. The GRI was founded by the Coalition for Environmentally Responsible Economies (CERES) and the United Nations Environment Programme (UNEP) in Boston, USA.

We measured the CSD by the number of GRI reports per country. However, since the number of firms in the country impacts the number of reports, it was necessary to minimize such influence. Therefore, we weighted the number of reports by the country market size.

| | STAGE OF DEVELOPMENT | | | | |
|---|---|---|---|---|---|
| | Stage 1: Factor-driven | Transition from stage 1 to stage 2 | Stage 2: Efficiency-driven | Transition from stage 2 to stage 3 | Stage 3: Innovation-driven |
| GDP per capita (US$) thresholds* | <2,000 | 2,000–2,999 | 3,000–8,999 | 9,000–17,000 | >17,000 |
| Number of countries | 37 | 16 | 30 | 24 | 37 |
| | Bangladesh | Algeria | Albania | Argentina | Australia |
| | Burkina Faso | Angola | Armenia | Bahrain | Austria |
| | Burundi | Azerbaijan | Bulgaria | Barbados | Belgium |
| | Cambodia | Bhutan | Cape Verde | Brazil | Canada |
| | Cameroon | Bolivia | China | Chile | Cyprus |
| | Chad | Botswana | Colombia | Costa_Rica | Czech_Repub |
| | Côte d'Ivoire | Gabon | Dominican_Rep | Croatia | Denmark |
| | Ethiopia | Honduras | Egypt | Hungary | Estonia |
| | Gambia, The | Iran | El_Salvador | Kazakhstan | Finland |
| | Ghana | Kuwait | Georgia | Latvia | France |
| | Guinea | Libya | Guatemala | Lebanon | Germany |
| | Haiti | Moldova | Guyana | Lithuania | Greece |
| | India | Mongolia | Indonesia | Malaysia | Hong_Kong_SAR |
| | Kenya | Philippines | Jamaica | Mauritius | Iceland |
| | Kyrgyz Rep | Saudi_Arabia | Jordan | Mexico | Ireland |
| | Lao PDR | Venezuela | Macedonia,_FYR | Oman | Israel |
| | Lesotho | | Montenegro | Panama | Italy |
| | Madagascar | | Morocco | Poland | Japan |
| | Malawi | | Namibia | Russian_Feder | Korea, Rep. |
| | Mali | | Paraguay | Seychelles | Luxembourg |
| | Mauritania | | Peru | Suriname | Malta |
| | Mozambique | | Romania | Turkey | Netherlands |
| | Myanmar | | Serbia | United_Arab_Emirates | New_Zealand |
| | Nepal | | South_Africa | Uruguay | Norway |
| | Nicaragua | | Sri_Lanka | | Portugal |
| | Nigeria | | Swaziland | | Puerto_Rico |
| | Pakistan | | Thailand | | Qatar |
| | Rwanda | | Timor-Leste | | Singapore |
| | Senegal | | Tunisia | | Slovak_Republic |
| | Sierra Leone | | Ukraine | | Slovenia |
| | Tajikistan | | | | Spain |
| | Tanzania | | | | Sweden |
| | Uganda | | | | Switzerland |
| | Vietnam | | | | Taiwan,_China |
| | Yemen | | | | Trinidad and Tobago |
| | Zambia | | | | United_Kingdom |
| | Zimbabwe | | | | United_States |

**Fig. 4.2** Countries classified in the development stages. Source: WEF (2015, pp. 10, 11)

In 2014, 91 countries reported GRI and, among these countries, seven were not in the Global Competitiveness Report 2014–2015. Therefore, these seven countries were excluded from the sample. The countries excluded were Afghanistan, Andorra, Bermuda, Ecuador, Greenland, Macao Special Administrative Region (China), and Papua New Guinea.

## Data Analyses

For data analysis, we employed the correspondence analysis, which is the cross-tabulation of two categorical variables (Hair et al. 2006). In this study, the CSD level was cross-tabulated on countries' development stages by indicating the number of countries that fall into each category of the development stages.

The number of GRI reports per country, weighted by the country market size, generates the GRI score. The CSD level was defined by the criterion of quartiles of the GRI score, with the first group of countries having a score of zero (60 countries); the second group of countries having a score greater than zero and less than or equal to 0.68 (12 countries); the third group having scores higher than 0.68 and less than or equal to 6.9 (36 countries); and the fourth group having scores greater than 6.9 and less than or equal to 78.1 (36 countries).

With regards to stages of development, we adopted the stages proposed by the Global Competitiveness Report: Stage 1—Factor-driven (S1); Transition from stage 1 to stage 2 (T1-2); Stage 2—Efficiency-driven (S2); Transition from stage 2 to stage 3 (T2-3); Stage 3—Innovation-driven (S3).

## Results

As previously mentioned, the number of GRI reports published in 2014 by each country was weighted by the market size, generating a metric variable (i.e., the GRI score). Descriptive statistics of the variables are presented in Tables 4.1 and 4.2.

The highest average CSD is for the countries that are at the highest level of development, while the lowest average CSD is for less-developed countries. The graphical representation of the average is shown in Fig. 4.3.

Also in a descriptive analysis, Table 4.3 shows the 20 countries with the highest number of GRI reports published in 2014 and their respective stages of development.

Most of the top 20 reporting countries are at higher stages of development. However, the highlighted points are the five countries in developing

**Table 4.1** Descriptive statistics

| | N | Minimum | Maximum | Mean | Std. deviation | Variance |
|---|---|---|---|---|---|---|
| GRI | 144 | 0.00 | 542.00 | 34.9931 | 74.55326 | 5558.189 |
| Market size | 144 | 1.30 | 6.94 | 3.7850 | 1.15825 | 1.342 |
| GRI score | 144 | 0.00 | 78.10 | 6.6622 | 12.92111 | 166.955 |

**Table 4.2** Descriptive statistics by stages of development

| | Stage | N | Mean | Std. deviation | Minimum | Maximum |
|---|---|---|---|---|---|---|
| GRI score | S1 | 37 | 0.4784 | 2.00925 | 0.00 | 12.14 |
| | T1-2 | 16 | 0.6712 | 1.04798 | 0.00 | 3.85 |
| | S2 | 30 | 5.9303 | 14.60817 | 0.00 | 66.60 |
| | T2-3 | 24 | 5.8617 | 9.15575 | 0.00 | 42.76 |
| | S3 | 37 | 16.5492 | 16.63225 | 0.00 | 78.10 |
| | Total | 144 | 6.6622 | 12.92111 | 0.00 | 78.10 |

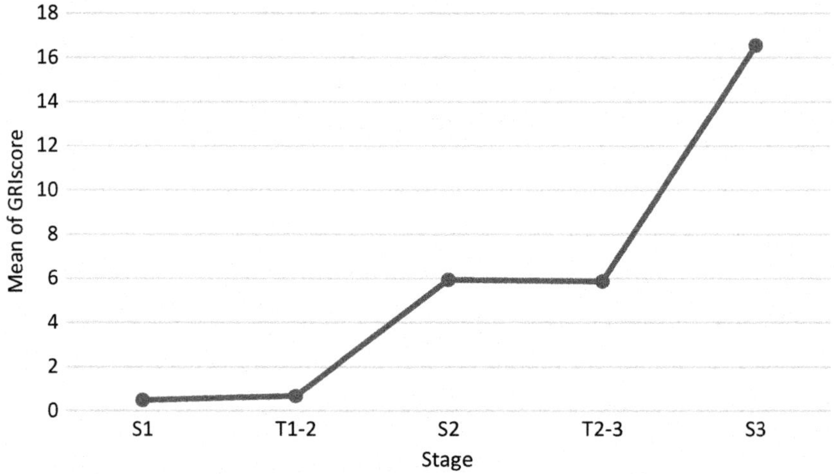


**Fig. 4.3** Mean plot

economies, specifically, South Africa, Brazil, China, Colombia, and Argentina, all of which also appear in the list. Among the five countries with the highest number of GRI reports that are not in developed economies, three are Latin American countries, which may indicate a tendency in the

**Table 4.3** Countries with more GRI reports

| Country | GRI | Stage | Country | GRI | Stage |
|---|---|---|---|---|---|
| United States | 542 | S3 | Australia | 167 | S3 |
| South Africa | 327 | S2 | Switzerland | 137 | S3 |
| Japan | 275 | S3 | France | 135 | S3 |
| Brazil | 242 | T 2-3 | Netherlands | 132 | S3 |
| China | 222 | S2 | Sweden | 130 | S3 |
| Taiwan, China | 212 | S3 | Finland | 121 | S3 |
| Colombia | 184 | S2 | Canada | 119 | S3 |
| United Kingdom | 179 | S3 | Korea, Rep. | 118 | S3 |
| Spain | 175 | S3 | Italy | 96 | S3 |
| Germany | 170 | S3 | Argentina | 82 | T2-3 |

**Table 4.4** Cross-tabulation

| | Stage of development | | | | | |
|---|---|---|---|---|---|---|
| CSD level | S1 | T1-2 | S2 | T2-3 | S3 | Total |
| 1 | 29 | 8 | 14 | 5 | 4 | 60 |
| 2 | 2 | 4 | 3 | 2 | 1 | 12 |
| 3 | 5 | 4 | 7 | 10 | 10 | 36 |
| 4 | 1 | 0 | 6 | 7 | 22 | 36 |
| Total | 37 | 16 | 30 | 24 | 37 | 144 |

region for a higher level of CSD. Such evidence is in accordance with Cuevas-Mejía, Escobar-Váquiro, and Maldonado-García (2013), who analyzed the disclosure of CSR in Latin American countries and demonstrated that the disclosure in these countries occurs in response to institutionalizing mechanisms, such as isomorphism.

## Correspondence Analysis

The GRI score was categorized into four groups, used as targeting criteria quartiles, generating the CSD level variable. Table 4.4 displays the cross-tabulated data. The data shows that the number of GRI disclosures vary substantially across CSD levels and stages of development.

Table 4.4 shows that most countries with CSD Level 1 are in the first stage of development and most countries with CSD Level 4 are at the third stage of development.

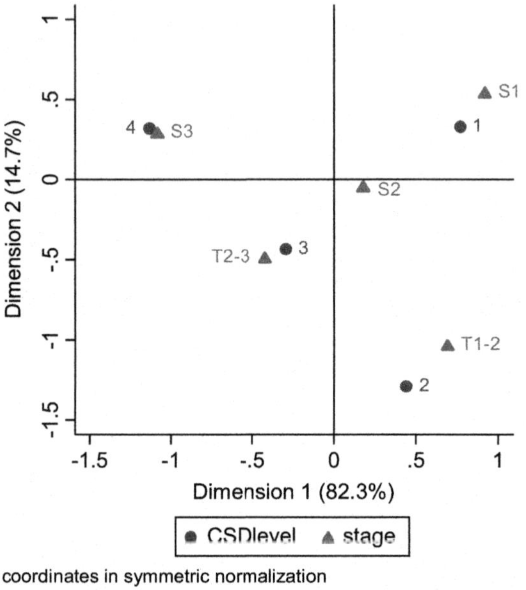


**Fig. 4.4** Correspondence analysis biplot

Through the correspondence analysis, we found an association between the stage of development and the CSD level with a chi-squared of 65.7, significant at 0.000. The total inertia of 0.4493 indicates that the row-column correlation is significant.

The association between variables is shown in a two-dimensional map and presented in Fig. 4.4.

The map shows an association between the Stage of Development 5 and the CSD Level 4; between the Stage Transition 2 to 3 and the CSD Level 3; between the Stage Transition 1 to 2 and the CSD Level 2; and between the Stage of Development 1 and the CSD Level 1.

# Discussion and Conclusions

## Discussion

The findings support the hypotheses proposed, in an exploratory way, showing an association between the country's development stage and the

CSD level. The first hypothesis was that *the country's stage of development is associated with the level of CSD*. We confirmed this hypothesis by the chi-squared test that indicated a significant association between the variables' stage of development and CSD level. The results show that the country's development stage may be a potential determinant of the level of disclosure of companies.

Our findings contribute to the literature investigating this association in a larger sample of countries, since previous similar studies (Robertson 2009) investigated an association between the stage of development and CSR practices restricted to three countries. Robertson's (2009) study found that factors such as firm ownership structure, corporate governance, openness of the economy to international investment, and the role of civil society contribute to explain variations in CSR. These factors could also influence the CSD, since the literature advocates a relationship between the CSR level and the CSD level (Al-Tuwaijri et al. 2004; Dhaliwal et al. 2012).

Our second hypothesis was that *countries in more advanced stages of development have a higher level of CSD*. We supported the hypothesis by finding an association between the higher stage of development and the higher CSD level. The association can be understood by assuming Xiao et al.'s (2005) argument that developed countries have higher levels of awareness of social and environment issues. The high concern about these issues can explain the high level of CSD. Also, developed economies offer an organized institutional environment and stronger financial markets, which can lead to more disclosure requirements and greater propensity to voluntary disclosure, such as GRI reporting. Companies operating in countries in the innovation-driven stage may have to deal with higher expectations of stakeholders, as well as global organizations influencing companies embedded in these economies to have high levels of CSR and CSD.

Our third hypothesis proposed that *countries in the middle stages of development present medium levels of CSD*. We supported this hypothesis by finding an association between the Stage Transition from stage 2 to stage 3 and the CSD Level 3 and between the Stage Transition from stage 1 to stage 2 and the CSD Level 2. Companies operating in countries with middle stages of development (i.e., in the efficiency-driven economies and in transition economies) receive less pressure from stakeholders than companies operating in countries in more advanced stages of development. Similarly, they receive more pressure than companies in a factor-driven stage.

Our fourth hypothesis was that *countries in less advanced stages of development have a lower level of CSD.* We support the hypothesis finding an association between the lower stage of development and the lower CSD level, as displayed on the map. In the sample, among the 60 countries that do not have reports on the GRI database, 30 are from countries in factor-driven economies. These results may reveal that, in these economies, awareness of disclosure needs and stakeholder power to demand high levels of CSD are still weak. Companies in less-developed countries may also have fewer international investors who require greater accountability of companies; therefore, companies in these economies have lower disclosure levels.

## Conclusion

Our chapter contributes to the CSD literature by analyzing the association between the development stage of countries and the social disclosure of firms operating in these countries. Such analysis is important for understanding the factors that influence differences in disclosure among firms and countries. Since most studies focus on characteristics at the firm level such as size, industry, and managers' motivations, this study contributes by presenting evidence of characteristics at the macro level.

The findings confirm the hypotheses that there is an association between countries' stage of development and the disclosure level of these countries. The results showed that countries in the first stages of development present lower levels of CSD, countries in the middle stages are associated with medium levels of CSD, and countries in the advanced stage present higher levels of CSD. This association was explained considering institutional issues and stakeholder pressures. The extent to which a society strengthens its institutions, enables practices related to CSR and CSD to become more evident.

This chapter has some limitations. First, CSD was measured by the number of GRI reporting for each country. However, firms can also disclose their CSR actions through other types of reporting, such as sustainability reports and other integrated reports. These other types of disclosures could also be considered. Second, we weighted the number of reports using the country market size; however, the disclosure level could be weighted directly by the number of firms in each country.

Future research could explore the relation between more specific country characteristics (e.g., innovation, level of education and stock market) in order to understand which characteristics are more closely associated with disclosure and which are less so.

## References


Abreu, M.C.S.D., L.T.D. Cunha, and C.Y. Barlow. 2015. Institutional dynamics and organizations affecting the adoption of sustainable development in the United Kingdom and Brazil. *Business Ethics: A European Review* 24 (1): 73–90.

Acs, Z.J., S. Desai, and J. Hessels. 2008. Entrepreneurship, economic development and institutions. *Small Business Economics* 31 (3): 219–234.

Aerts, W., D. Cormier, and M. Magnan. 2008. Corporate environmental disclosure, financial markets and the media: An international perspective. *Ecological Economics* 64 (3): 643–659.

Aguinis, H., and A. Glavas. 2012. What we know and don't know about corporate social responsibility a review and research agenda. *Journal of Management* 38 (4): 932–968.

Al-Tuwaijri, S.A., T.E. Christensen, and K.E. Hughes. 2004. The relations among environmental disclosure, environmental performance, and economic performance: A simultaneous equations approach. *Accounting, Organizations and Society* 29 (5): 447–471.

Campbell, J.L. 2006. Institutional analysis and the paradox of corporate social responsibility. *The American Behavioral Scientist* 49 (7): 925–938.

Carroll, A.B. 1979. A three-dimensional conceptual model of corporate performance. *Academy of Management Review* 4 (4): 497–505.

———. 1991. The pyramid of corporate social responsibility: Toward the moral management of organizational stakeholders. *Business Horizons 34* (4): 39–48.

———. 2008. A history of corporate social responsibility. In *The Oxford handbook of corporate social responsibility*, ed. A. Crane, A. McWilliams, D. Matten, J. Moon, and D.S. Siegel. Oxford: Oxford University Press.

Cheng, B., I. Ioannou, and G. Serafeim. 2014. Corporate social responsibility and access to finance. *Strategic Management Journal* 35 (1): 1–23.

Cuevas-Mejía, J.J., S. Maldonado-García, and N. Escobar-Váquiro. 2013. Aproximación a los factores que influyen en la divulgación de información sobre RSC en empresas de América Latina. *Cuadernos de contabilidad 14* (34): 91–131.

De Bakker, F.G., P. Groenewegen, and F. Den Hond. 2005. A bibliometric analysis of 30 years of research and theory on corporate social responsibility and corporate social performance. *Business & Society 44* (3): 283–317.

De Villiers, C., and A. Marques. 2016. Corporate social responsibility, country-level predispositions, and the consequences of choosing a level of disclosure. *Accounting and Business Research* 46 (2): 167–195.

Dhaliwal, D.S., S. Radhakrishnan, A. Tsang, and Y.G. Yang. 2012. Nonfinancial disclosure and analyst forecast accuracy: International evidence on corporate social responsibility disclosure. *The Accounting Review* 87 (3): 723–759.

Dilling, P.F. 2010. Sustainability reporting in a global context: What are the characteristics of corporations that provide high quality sustainability reports-an empirical analysis. *The International Business & Economics Research Journal* 9 (1): 19–30.

Elkington, J. 1997. *Cannibals with forks: The triple bottom line of 21st century.* Oxford: Capstone Publishing.

Ernstberger, J., and M. Grüning. 2013. How do firm-and country-level governance mechanisms affect firms' disclosure? *Journal of Accounting and Public Policy* 32 (3): 50–67.

Fifka, M.S., and M. Pobizhan. 2014. An institutional approach to corporate social responsibility in Russia. *Journal of Cleaner Production* 82: 192–201.

Frías-Aceituno, J.V., L. Rodríguez-Ariza, and I.M. García-Sánchez. 2013. Is integrated reporting determined by a country's legal system? An exploratory study. *Journal of Cleaner Production* 44: 45–55.

García-Sánchez, I.M., L. Rodríguez-Ariza, and J.V. Frías-Aceituno. 2013. The cultural system and integrated reporting. *International Business Review 22* (5): 828–838.

GRI. 2015. *Global reporting initiative.* Retrieved from https://www.globalreporting.org/Pages/default.aspx

Hair, J.F., W.C. Black, B.J. Babin, R.E. Anderson, and R.L. Tatham. 2006. *Multivariate data analysis* (Vol. 6). Upper Saddle River, NJ: Pearson Prentice Hall.

Haniffa, R.M., and T.E. Cooke. 2005. The impact of culture and governance on corporate social reporting. *Journal of Accounting and Public Policy* 24 (5): 391–430.

Hofstede, G. 1984. National cultures revisited. *Asia Pacific Journal of Management* 2 (1): 22–28.
Husted, B.W., and J. de Jesus Salazar. 2006. Taking Friedman seriously: Maximizing profits and social performance. *Journal of Management Studies 43* (1): 75–91.
Jamali, D. 2007. The case for strategic corporate social responsibility in developing countries. *Business & Society Review* 112 (1): 1–27.
Jones, T.M. 1980. Corporate social responsibility revisited, redefined. *California Management Review 22* (3): 59–67.
KPMG. 2011. *International survey of corporate social responsibility reporting.* Retrieved from http://www.kpmg.com/PT/pt/IssuesAndInsights/Documents/corporate-responsibility2011.pdf
Lockett, A., J. Moon, and W. Visser. 2006. Corporate social responsibility in management research: Focus, nature, salience and sources of influence. *Journal of Management Studies* 43 (1): 115–136.
Mallin, C.A., and G. Michelon. 2011. Board reputation attributes and corporate social performance: An empirical investigation of the US best corporate citizens. *Accounting and Business Research* 41 (2): 119–144.
Martin, R.L. 2002. The virtue matrix: Calculating the return on corporate responsibility. *Harvard Business Review* 80 (3): 68–75.
McWilliams, A., and D. Siegel. 2001. Corporate social responsibility: A theory of the firm perspective. *Academy of Management Review* 26 (1): 117–127.
McWilliams, A., D.S. Siegel, and P.M. Wright. 2006. Corporate social responsibility: Strategic implications. *Journal of Management Studies* 43 (1): 1–18.
Michalos, A.C. 1997. Issues for business ethics in the nineties and beyond. *Journal of Business ethics* 16 (3): 219–230.
Nalband, N.A., and M.S. Al-Amri. 2013. Corporate social responsibility: Perception, practices and performance of listed companies of Kingdom of Saudi Arabia. *Competitiveness Review: An International Business Journal incorporating Journal of Global Competitiveness* 23 (3): 284–295.
Naser, K., A. Al-Hussaini, D. Al-Kwari, and R. Nuseibeh. 2006. Determinants of corporate social disclosure in developing countries: The case of Qatar. *Advances in International Accounting* 19: 1–23.
Norman, W., and C. MacDonald. 2004. Getting to the bottom of "triple bottom line". *Business Ethics Quarterly* 14 (02): 243–262.
Orij, R. 2010. Corporate social disclosures in the context of national cultures and stakeholder theory. *Accounting, Auditing & Accountability Journal* 23 (7): 868–889.

Patten, D.M. 1991. Exposure, legitimacy, and social disclosure. *Journal of Accounting and Public Policy* 10 (4): 297–308.

———. 2002. The relation between environmental performance and environmental disclosure: A research note. *Accounting, Organizations and Society* 27 (8): 763–773.

Porter, M.E. 1990. The competitive advantage of nations. *Harvard Business Review* 68 (2): 73–93.

Porter, M.E., and M.R. Kramer. 2006. Strategy and society: The link between competitive advantage and corporate social responsibility. *Harvard Business Review* 84 (12): 78–92.

Porter, M.E., J. Sachs, P.K. Cornelius, J.W. McArthur, and K. Schwab. 2002. *The global competitiveness report 2001–2002*, 16–25. New York: Oxford University Press.

Robertson, D.C. 2009. Corporate social responsibility and different stages of economic development: Singapore, Turkey, and Ethiopia. *Journal of Business Ethics* 88 (4): 617–633.

Schaltegger, S., and R.L. Burritt. 2010. Sustainability accounting for companies: Catchphrase or decision support for business leaders? *Journal of World Business* 45 (4): 375–384.

Tilt, C.A. 1994. The influence of external pressure groups on corporate social disclosure: Some empirical evidence. *Accounting, Auditing & Accountability Journal* 7 (4): 47–72.

Ullmann, A.A. 1985. Data in search of a theory: A critical examination of the relationships among social performance, social disclosure, and economic performance of US firms. *Academy of Management Review* 10 (3): 540–557.

Van der Laan Smith, J., A. Adhikari, and R.H. Tondkar. 2005. Exploring differences in social disclosures internationally: A stakeholder perspective. *Journal of Accounting and Public Policy* 24 (2): 123–151.

Van Marrewijk, M. 2003. Concepts and definitions of CSR and corporate sustainability: Between agency and communion. *Journal of Business Ethics 44* (2–3): 95–105.

WEF. 2015. The global competitiveness report 2014–2015. World Economic Forum. Geneva. Retrieved from http://www3.weforum.org/docs/WEF_GlobalCompetitivenessReport_2014-15.pdf

Xiao, J.Z., S.S. Gao, S. Heravi, and Y.C. Cheung. 2005. The impact of social and economic development on corporate social and environmental disclosure in Hong Kong and the UK. *Advances in International Accounting* 18: 219–243.

# 5

# Overcoming Institutional Barriers When Entering Brazil: A Legitimacy Perspective

Daniel Rottig, Jason A. Hoop, Nicholas J. Cid, and David M. Peterson

## Introduction

Despite ongoing political and economic challenges, Brazil remains a key emerging market and central trade and foreign direct investment destination for multinational corporations (MNCs) worldwide. Part of the BRIC (Brazil, Russia, India, and China) group of large emerging markets, Brazil constitutes the world's eighth biggest economy. The country's US$3.22 trillion purchasing power parity adjusted gross domestic product (GDP) (IMF 2018) exceeds the economic output of

D. Rottig (✉) • J. A. Hoop
Florida Gulf Coast University, Fort Myers, FL, USA
e-mail: DRottig@fgcu.edu

N. J. Cid
The Hertz Corporation, Estero, FL, USA

D. M. Peterson
FieldEdge, Fort Myers, FL, USA



W. Newburry et al. (eds.), *Contemporary Influences on International Business in Latin America*, AIB Latin America, https://doi.org/10.1007/978-3-319-98340-0_5

many developed countries, such as the United Kingdom and France. Yet, the country is characterized by continuous institutional challenges due to the volatile local political environment, systemic government corruption, and inward-oriented trade and investment policies (Bremmer 2014). Despite these challenges, which entail significant liabilities of foreignness for MNCs, Brazil offers considerable economic opportunities that make it a quite appealing market to enter.

In order to successfully enter Brazil, foreign MNCs need to understand the various institutional challenges in the country and learn how to overcome formal institutional barriers in order to gain local legitimacy in this market. Based on institutional theory, this chapter examines the local legitimacy pressures MNCs encounter when entering Brazil. More specifically, it discusses the formal political, economic, and legal institutional barriers when entering Brazil and examines strategies MNCs can use to manage these institutional challenges, and so establish local legitimacy in this market. To gain unique insights into the emerging market of Brazil and its idiosyncratic institutional environment and related legitimacy challenges for foreign MNCs, we employed a qualitative research approach that encompassed semi-structured interviews with executives of local firms as well as foreign MNCs operating in Brazil, and the analysis of company documents and media accounts.

## Legitimacy and Its Importance in the Context of Brazil

Legitimacy is defined as the acceptance, approval, and support of firms in a local environment (Suchman 1995). Legitimacy is the key productive resource for MNCs when entering different foreign institutional environments (Scott 2014), especially those of emerging markets (Rottig 2016). Legitimacy is based on the opinions and perceptions of specific constituencies that are able to grant or withdraw acceptance, approval, and support from organizations (such as MNCs) that are operating in an emerging market (Deephouse and Suchman 2008; Rottig 2016). Legitimacy, therefore, is a socially constructed attribute attached to MNCs that reflects an agreement between the actions and behaviors of

MNCs in a local institutional environment, and the perceptions of local constituencies that are able to grant or withdraw legitimacy. These constituencies include the general public, the media, the local government and regulators, and the financial community (Rottig and Reus 2009; Suchman 1995).

First, in the context of Brazil, becoming accepted, approved, and supported by the local population (i.e. general public) is one of the key factors for foreign MNCs to successfully enter and operate in this market. In one of our executive interviews, Jack Kahn, CEO Midwest Capital International, stated that "an important part of our business model was creating trust with the local people, and educating them on why we were here. Transparency breeds trust, and we focused on providing benefits to the local community, not just benefits for ourselves". When the general public in Brazil perceives a foreign MNC to benefit the local community, the MNC will more likely be accepted, approved, and supported, and thus legitimized. Such positive perceptions about a foreign MNC lead to a favorable attitude toward the MNC and facilitate the creation of trust and cooperation among locals that aid a foreign MNC to succeed in the market.

Another constituency that is of key importance to build legitimacy in Brazil is the local media, given its relevance in communicating crucial information about foreign MNCs. Sheafer (2001), for example, notes that an important resource in the area of communication is the attention the media gives to any organization, such as an MNC. The media has direct influence over the opinion formation of the local public through the coverage of the actions and behaviors of MNCs operating locally, and so provides important information (and the interpretation thereof) based on which the local public decides whether or not to accept, approve, and support foreign MNCs.

A third constituency to grant legitimacy comprises the local government and regulators, which determine whether foreign MNCs (as well as local companies) qualify to obtain, and deserve to maintain, a business license in a local market. This form of legitimacy is often referred to as political legitimacy. Alden and Vieira (2005) refer to legitimacy in the political realm as "recognition" or "economic realization". In the context of emerging markets, this type of legitimacy may be more difficult to obtain compared to developed counties in which political processes are typically independent and transparent. In many emerging markets, including Brazil, obtaining legal permission to operate a business locally, applying for licenses and permits, and obtaining information to be able to conduct business in that market may (at least partially) be affected by corrupt processes. These markets also have political systems that are either characterized by institutional voids (Khanna and Palepu 1997), in other words a lack or underdevelopment of local institutions in the form of "rules of the game" (North 1990) and the related processes to enforce them, or by institutional complexity (Torres de Oliveira and Rottig 2018), in other words a complicated set of institutions that make it difficult to successfully navigate local legitimacy demands by foreign MNCs.

The fourth key constituency able to grant legitimacy is the financial community. Finnemore (2009) refers to the financial operations of organizations as a strong indicator of their effectiveness in an international market. The author further asserts that the financial elite, which are very influential in political and financial circles especially in emerging markets, may influence the (financial) legitimacy of organizations. Financial legitimacy may take the form of an organization's ability to raise capital. Henisz and Zelner, for example, note that "formal structures do not grant credibility by virtue of their existence" (2005: 370) and further explain that organizations (such as MNCs) that source capital from local financial organizations can generate "legitimacy from a socially constructed standpoint" (2005: 370).

## Legitimacy Challenges in the Emerging Market of Brazil

A key barrier for MNCs aiming to enter the Brazilian market relates to high government taxes and tariffs. Brazil is a member of MERCOSUR, a customs union with Argentina, Paraguay, and Uruguay. (Venezuela is a full member but has been suspended since December 1, 2016 and still was at the time of this writing.) This agreement maintains high Common External Tariffs (CETs) on many countries including the United States. Brazil imposes high tariffs on many US imports affecting various industries such as automobiles, information technology, chemicals, plastics, textiles, and apparel. According to the Office of United States Trade Representative (2018), US firms exported US$30.3 billion worth of goods to Brazil in 2016, providing a large source of tax revenue for the Brazilian government in the form of import tariffs. In the same year, Brazil had a trade deficit in goods of US$4.1 billion with the United States, which does not give the Brazilian government an incentive to lower Brazil's high tariffs on imports from the United States.

Furthermore, taxes and tariffs are frequently manipulated to exploit MNCs, even if they have followed the rules of the game (Bremmer 2014; USTR 2018). The Economist (2011) provides an example from the automotive industry, in which Brazil increased the industrial product tax on cars by 30 percentage point. This tax was directly targeting importers, while manufactures in Brazil, the MERCOSUR countries, and Mexico were exempt. This policy was implemented in response to importers gaining a significant share within the local automotive industry, which is characterized by poor infrastructure leading to high costs associated with producing cars in Brazil. Another example can be found in tax breaks granted to local manufacturers of tablet computers, which discriminated against importers of these devices. In addition, the Economist (2011) reported that the Brazilian Development Bank (BNDES) has been accused of corrupt practices that resulted in selecting winners and losers. In addition, with more outstanding loans than the World Bank, the BNDES has funded several acquisitions of foreign firms by Brazilian companies and so directly intervened in the free market.

More recently, Brazil seems to have taken some small steps toward opening its economy to increase trade. During the final two years of the Great Recession of 2007–10 and in the aftermath of this financial and economic crisis, Brazil's currency has weakened significantly. While the Brazilian Real (BRL) traded at 1.56 to the United States Dollar (US$) in August of 2008, it weakened to more than 4 BRL per US$ by the third quarter of 2018. This significant depreciation of the Brazilian Real versus the US Dollar has greatly reduced the purchasing power of Brazilian firms that rely on imports as part of their supply chain. Brazil's government has therefore considered lowering import tariffs in an effort to reduce costs for local manufacturers that rely on imported parts and components, and use the opportunity of a weaker Real to focus on exports to counteract the recent trend of lower demand for Brazilian products in the country's largest trading partner, China.

However, these small steps toward opening the economy are not indicative of Brazil reversing its generally protectionist trade ideology. Instead, Brazil seems to continue focusing on, as Bremmer put it "zealously protecting local interests … pick[ing] the sectors in which they will allow capital investment, and select[ing] the local, often state-owned, companies they wish to promote" and thus implement trade and investment policies that are "slow-moving, selective, and with a heavy dash of nationalism and regionalism" (2014: 104). This can be exemplified by Brazil's lowered import tariffs that are applicable largely in the raw materials and industrial components sectors and so mostly benefit local manufacturers, and the fact that it selectively excludes products from other Latin American countries, such as Mexico in addition to its fellow MERCOSUR countries. Brazil has further raised import tariffs on products such as steel, petrochemicals, and pharmaceuticals to protect local manufacturers at the cost of foreign MNCs.

Furthermore, the Brazilian economic recession makes it difficult for foreign MNCs to generate profits in Brazil. Especially as the local currency remains weak, so does the purchasing power of local consumers demanding imported products. The former Vice President of Hertz Brazil, Roy Ritenour, mentioned in one of our interviews that the rental car industry is no exception to this trend. While the weaker Real has resulted in more foreign tourism in the country that led to an increased car rental volume in Brazil, each rental car transaction has become less valuable in US$ terms for the company, given that it charges consumers in local currency, but reports profits on its financial statements in US$ terms (i.e. the company faces translation exposure for its profits in Brazil) (Madura 2017). Furthermore, given the weakened economy in Brazil, the once rising middle class has struggled with decreasing discretionary income, which had a direct and negative effect on the local car leasing and car rental business.

Given the current formal institutional environment in Brazil, it seems that the high taxes and tariffs will remain in place. A large part of the local population remains poor and pays no or only minimal taxes, which allows politicians to increase tax rates without affecting the poor. These higher tax rates generate public revenues, yet stifle private investments in the economy. In addition, given that voting in elections is mandatory in Brazil, wealth transfer from the rich to the poor remains a popular strategy among politicians to secure votes, and so become (re-) elected. These wealth transfers (financed by tax revenues) tie up funds that could be used for investments in education, the healthcare system, as well as the local judicial system in order to fight the systemic level of corruption in the country.

While this lack of strong formal institutions has prevented Brazil from achieving the institutional development and stability needed to drive lasting economic growth that would create more and higher-paying jobs, and has made the country a risky and expensive market for MNCs to enter and navigate in the short term, the country has significant potential in the long term. The former Vice President of Hertz Brazil, Roy Ritenour, emphasized in one of our interviews that it would be a great time to invest in the Brazilian market for long-term oriented MNCs, despite the current institutional issues the country is facing. Such MNCs, therefore, need to gain a better understanding of what strategies to employ in order to establish local legitimacy.

## Strategies for MNCs to Establish Legitimacy in Brazil

When attempting to establish acceptance, approval, and support in Brazil, foreign MNCs need to understand that legitimacy is not unidimensional, but a multidimensional construct that consists of several facets. Thus, establishing and maintaining legitimacy in Brazil requires a combination of a proper foreign market entry strategy as well as proactive management of the four local legitimacy-granting constituencies in Brazil, which we discussed earlier in this chapter, once an MNC is operating locally. In the next section, we will discuss some strategies foreign MNCs may consider to establish legitimacy in Brazil, starting with entry-mode considerations. The formal institutional environment in Brazil allows foreign MNCs to enter the local market through both, non-equity and equity-based entry modes. We will discuss each category of entry modes and their respective types and legitimacy implications next.

## Non-equity-based Entry Mode Considerations

Non-equity-based entry modes include exporting, contractual agreements, and formal alliances with local business partners, community groups, and non-profit organizations.

### Exporting

While exporting is a commonly used foreign-market entry mode by MNCs, managers of MNCs need to be aware of and actively manage the unique, trade-related institutional environment in Brazil. As discussed earlier in this chapter, Brazil is characterized by an inward-oriented trade policy aimed at protecting local manufacturers at the cost of foreign competitors as well as selective and unexpectedly changing policies to protect local interests. Foreign MNCs, therefore, need to gain a better understanding about the specific trade policies and countries/regions that may receive favorable treatment. For example, the Mercosur countries and Mexico are generally exempt from Brazil's high import tariffs and MNCs with operations in these countries may be able to gain an advantage when exporting products to Brazil from these markets compared to those MNCs that are not present in these countries.

This notion can be illustrated by one of our interviews with Tarik Ayasun of Taray International, a company that specializes in exporting US-made products to more than 70 countries around the globe, including Brazil. In addition to Taray International's export business, the company also acts as a liaison between US businesses and customers in Brazil. During the interview, Mr. Ayasun provided insight into the intricacies of exporting to Brazil and emphasized the importance of gaining acceptance and support from the government and local public. Mr. Ayasun also pointed to the challenges due to the high tariffs and quotas on imported products from countries such as the United States, and the related need for foreign MNCs to develop unique and innovative approaches for successfully exporting to Brazil. One of these approaches to legally work around the system that Mr. Ayasun employs is to ship parts to Uruguay for assembly, and then transport them to Brazil. In so doing, the final products are "made in Uruguay" and so not subject to the high import tariffs given that Uruguay is a member of MERCOSUR.

MNCs unable to manufacture in countries that are exempt by Brazil's high import tariffs may develop other strategies to manage them. In one of our interviews, Roy Ritenour, former Vice President of Hertz Brazil, discussed some of Hertz' strategies for minimizing tariffs in the car rental industry. He noted that the key was to develop relationships with local car manufacturers. These relationships are particularly important in Brazil where long-term car leasing accounts for a large part of the car rental business. Sourcing its fleet of cars from local car manufacturers allowed Hertz to offer customers domestic car brands without passing on import costs, and also offer brands of global automakers that had set up plants in Brazil to avoid the considerable import tariffs. In so doing, Hertz was able to build local legitimacy by supporting local manufacturers. At the same time, Hertz offered foreign-made cars by marketing them as "specialty" vehicles, creating a premium image for these rentals that allowed the company to pass on the cost related to import tariffs to consumers. Foreign MNCs therefore need to understand the idiosyncrasies of the Brazilian, trade-related institutions and intricacies of working with (and around) the system to successfully export products to this market.

The aforementioned relationships with local business partners are also important in order to successfully operate in the local market. Tarik Ayasun of Taray International advised in one of our interviews that foreign MNCs that are able to develop strong personal relationships with their Brazilian clients are more likely to ensure that they "actually get paid, and those relationships can also springboard you towards other reliable clients". Relationship-based business is more common in Brazil than transaction-based business in developed countries, such as the United States, and managers of MNCs need to understand this important, context-specific feature of the Brazilian market in order to establish local legitimacy.

In addition, US-based MNCs may take advantage of services and safeguards offered by the US government to protect and mitigate the risk of export transactions. In one of our interviews, the Director of the US Export Assistant Center for the US Department of Commerce, Kenneth Mouradian, emphasized that US-based companies need to understand the specific institutional context of Brazil before entering the country through exports, and to solicit the help the US government offers to its companies. For example, the Export-Import Bank of the United States (EXIM) provides receivable insurance that helps exporters to curtail non-payment risk. Furthermore, the Overseas Private Investment Corporation (OPIC) provides insurance for some types of political risk. Foreign MNCs may also use local resources in Brazil, such as the services and information provided by the government-owned Serviço Brasileiro de Apoio às Micro e Pequenas Empresas (SEBRAE), which exists in every state in Brazil, an organization that conducts market research, assists in accounting matters, and connects foreign MNCs to potential, local customers. By tapping into these resources, MNCs will be able to better understand, more correctly interpret and, thus, more effectively navigate the Brazilian formal institutional environment and so are more likely to establish local legitimacy.

## Contractual Agreements and Local Alliances

Another type of non-equity-based entry modes available to MNCs to enter Brazil comprises contractual agreements in the form of franchising, licensing, turnkey projects, management/consulting contracts, research and development contracts, and co-marketing agreements. While these types of contractual agreements allow a foreign MNC to enter Brazil with relatively small investments and thus reduced overall financial risk, these entry modes inhere the strategic risk of creating and nurturing local competitors. Hence, foreign MNCs whose competitive advantage relies on proprietary knowledge and technology need to carefully consider the implications of potential intellectual property rights violations. In fact, starting in 2017, Brazil has been on the U.S. Trade Representative's Special 301 Watch List due to "significant concerns with respect to high levels of counterfeiting and piracy in Brazil, including Internet piracy, as well as concerns regarding the long delays in the examination of patents and trademarks (a reported average pendency of nearly two and a half years for trademarks and almost 11 years for patents)" (International Trade Administration 2017).

An additional option for foreign MNCs to enter Brazil through non-equity-based entry modes is the formation of formal alliances with local business partners, community groups, and non-profit organizations that are widely accepted, approved, and supported. These alliances with local partners allow foreign MNCs to develop valuable local social capital and gain access to location-specific knowledge and information needed to establish legitimacy (Rottig 2011). Furthermore, an alliance with a local partner entails an important signaling benefit for a foreign MNC given that it communicates to local regulators, the local financial community, and to the general public that the foreign MNC possesses the necessary local connections and experience by allying with a local partner, which alleviates local stakeholder uncertainty about the foreign MNC and so often leads to its ready endorsement (Rao et al. 2008). A local alliance also sends the important signal to local stakeholders that the foreign MNC has access to the necessary resources and capabilities to successfully operate in the market, including financial, marketing, research and development (scientific) resources, as well as shared learning capabilities and skills (Swaminathan and Moorman 2009). Such alliances, therefore, are particularly valuable for new ventures, entrepreneurial endeavors as well as new product introductions by foreign MNCs in order to readily establish legitimacy in a local market through gaining access to the local alliance partner's acceptance, approval, and support (Alon and Rottig 2013; Gans and Stern 2003). These benefits are referred to as legitimacy spill-overs and are particularly valuable in emerging markets, such as Brazil, which are generally hostile to foreign MNCs but favorable to firms that partner and ally with established, successful, local companies.

## Equity-based Entry-mode Considerations

Equity-based entry modes into Brazil include international joint ventures (i.e. equity-based strategic alliances), mergers and acquisitions, as well as Greenfield ventures.

## International Joint Ventures

International joint ventures (IJVs) constitute a double-edged sword for foreign MNCs when entering Brazil. On the one hand, IJVs comprise the same benefits as the afore-discussed, non-equity-based alliances with local partners in that they provide foreign MNCs with the opportunity to gain access to location-specific knowledge and information needed to establish legitimacy, build valuable social capital, and benefit from legitimacy spill-overs from local joint-venture partners that are accepted, approved, and supported in a local environment. Furthermore, joint ventures with local Brazilian firms provide foreign MNCs with the ability to mitigate their liability of foreignness through knowledge sharing, access to local resources, less discrimination by local government regulations, and the sharing of risk and technology.

In one of our executive interviews, Ian Webb, the Vice President of Sales and Marketing for B/E Aerospace, reflected on a joint venture with a local Brazilian firm that produces aviation components. Through B/E Aerospace's local partnerships, the company was able to readily enter the Brazilian market and expand its operations without facing significant public or government resistance. Furthermore, according to Transparency International, Brazil is considered one of the most corrupt countries, and creating strong relationships with local business partners in the form of a joint venture may facilitate foreign MNCs to successfully navigate this institutional environment. Ian Webb from B/E Aerospace also mentioned in one of our interviews that the partnership with a local Brazilian aviation components manufacturer has significantly helped his company to operate in Brazil and gain legitimacy in the market. The joint venture between the two companies exclusively employs local workers and has built valuable connections and rapport with key local stakeholders, and so gained the acceptance, approval, and support of the local government and general public.

On the other hand, IJVs also inhere the risk of developing and nurturing a local competitor which also characterizes the aforementioned types of non-equity-based contractual agreements, and so needs to be carefully managed, particularly given the high risk of intellectual property rights violation in Brazil. Successfully entering Brazil with an international joint venture, therefore, is very context specific and particularly requires careful execution in regard to controlling a local joint-venture partner, reducing partner conflict, building commitment, and pro-actively managing cultural differences (Reus and Rottig 2009).

## International Mergers and Acquisitions

Acquiring or merging with a local Brazilian company is another equity-based entry-mode option for foreign MNCs. Brazil constitutes the largest economy in Latin America and has been the top destination for cross-border merger and acquisition activity in the region from 2012 to 2017, with nearly US$150 billion in transaction value over this period (which is higher than the cross-border merger and acquisition value of the next two biggest economies in Latin America, Mexico and Chile, combined over the same period) (Baker and McKenzie 2018). In fact, in 2017, nine of the ten largest acquisitions by foreign companies in Latin America were conducted in Brazil. Foreign MNCs conducting international mergers or acquisitions in Brazil, however, need to be aware of the challenges and legitimacy consequences of the local institutional environment.

From a formal institutional perspective, the Brazilian regulatory environment is very bureaucratic and difficult to navigate for foreign investors, particularly for those aiming to gain ownership in local companies through an acquisition. A recent study of mergers and acquisitions in Brazil by Deloitte revealed that "In Brazil, due to the disconnect of all involved regulatory bodies needed in an integration or divestiture, the update or issuance of new regulatory licenses must start 3–6 months in advance of Day One, in order to ensure new entities are operational, and avoid potential disruption" (2017: 4). Hence, foreign MNCs that are considering entering Brazil through mergers or acquisitions need to carefully navigate the local formal institutional environment in order to be able to establish legitimacy in this market.

In cross-border acquisitions in general, and in the emerging market of Brazil in particular, foreign MNCs also need to understand and pro-actively manage informal institutional challenges. International mergers and acquisitions often result in cultural clashes of the combined management teams and workforces, leading to the turnover of key executives, managers, and key personnel of the acquired company resulting in the loss of key information, knowledge about the local institutional environment, and external relationships with customers, suppliers, the government and other stakeholders (Rottig and Reus 2018; Rottig et al. 2013). This, in turn, often lowers the acceptance, approval, and support of a foreign company in a local institutional environment.

In fact, such cultural clashes and related issues of integrating the business processes and acquired workforces have been mentioned as the greatest challenge related to post-acquisition integration in a recent survey of foreign acquirers in Latin America generally, and particularly in Brazil (Baker and McKenzie 2018). This finding can be illustrated by an interview with the finance director of a French insurance company, which acquired a Brazilian insurer, who noted that "Post-merger integrations are tough, and we faced problems with the culture of the target that affected operations … Our lack of understanding of the way employees worked created issues between the management and employees that took time to resolve" (Baker and McKenzie 2018: 19). These cultural issues not only affect non-Latin American acquirers in Brazil, but also acquirers from within the region given intra-Latin-American cultural differences. In fact, from a cultural perspective, Latin America should not be treated as a homogenous region as doing so would create the wrong perception among managers of MNCs that cultural differences, and the pro-active management thereof, are not important when merging with or acquiring companies in Brazil.

This notion can be illustrated by the merger between the Chilean LAN and Brazilian TAM airlines in 2010, which created LATAM, and the ensuing national and organizational cultural differences during the multi-year integration of the transaction. In one of our interviews, a Chilean executive of the combined LATAM, who was part of the post-merger integration process, mention that the Chilean LAN, for example, was much more cost-oriented and structured than the Brazilian TAM, which resulted in integration problems and the difference between the Chilean and Brazilian national cultures (including the different languages) further exacerbated the integration challenges of the transaction.

In sum, in order to establish local legitimacy when entering Brazil through mergers or acquisitions, foreign MNCs need to account for the institutional challenges in the country, anticipate the appropriate timeline for formal deal approval by local regulators and post-deal implementation, develop a context-specific integration approach, and particularly emphasize the sociocultural integration of the combined managerial team and workforces (Rottig 2007, 2013, 2017; Rottig et al. 2017).

## Greenfield Ventures

Lastly, Greenfield ventures are another alternative for foreign MNCs to enter Brazil, yet constitute a challenging enterprise given that this is the only equity-based entry mode that does not involve a local partner. Without the valuable location-specific knowledge and information, local connections, and guidance of a local partner, it becomes very difficult for foreign MNCs to navigate the complex and non-transparent formal local institutional environment in Brazil that is characterized by cumbersome and complex taxation laws, bureaucratic delays, and rigid labor laws. In fact, Brazil ranks 125 in the latest ranking of the World Bank's Doing Business Index (2018), which measures the impact of the local formal institutional environment on business activities (such as Greenfields by foreign MNCs) in the areas of starting a business, dealing with construction permits, getting electricity, registering property, obtaining credit, protecting minority investors, paying taxes, enforcing contracts, and resolving insolvency, in 190 economies. Brazil's ranking is second to last in South America (only Bolivia ranks lower) and one of the lowest in the entire Latin American region. This may be the reason why Greenfield ventures have declined over the past few years, from 363 ventures in 2014 to 287 in 2015 and 200 in 2016 (Banco Central do Brasil 2018).

In one of our interviews, we spoke with Marcelo Daciw, a Brazilian entrepreneur who operates businesses in Brazil as well as in the United States. Mr. Daciw mentioned that "the bureaucratic nature of Brazil is a nightmare and it is even worse for foreigners". As a local entrepreneur, it took him 5–6 months to open a business in Brazil, and he mentioned that this timeframe will be longer for foreign MNCs that do not have experience working within the bureaucratic Brazilian system. Mr. Daciw's recommendation for foreign MNCs considering entering Brazil through a Greenfield venture is to work with either the Chamber of Commerce or a private company that specializes in entering Brazil, otherwise foreign MNCs "may get lost in a sea of bureaucracy and (related) inability to gain acceptance".

Hence, in order to establish legitimacy after entering Brazil through a Greenfield venture, foreign MNCs need to possess considerable knowledge and information about local institutions and significant experience regarding how to effectively navigate the local institutional environment, or employ the assistance of local agencies and consultants.

## Pro-active Management of Legitimacy-granting Constituencies in Brazil

Foreign MNCs may establish legitimacy in Brazil by pro-actively managing the key constituencies in Brazil that are able to grant (and withdraw) legitimacy. These constituencies comprise the general public, the media, local government and regulators, and the financial community.

### The General Public

First, the general public controls critical resources on both the demand and supply side that are crucial for MNCs in order to establish local legitimacy in Brazil. On the demand side, the local public, as consumers, controls the spending power over the products and services offered by foreign MNCs and only purchases products and services from those MNCs that are accepted, approved, and supported. On the supply side, as the workforce, the local public controls the willingness to provide labor to foreign MNCs and only does so if an MNC possesses local acceptance, approval, and support. Hence, by pro-actively reaching out to the general public in Brazil—investing in the local community, localizing corporate social responsibility activities, and building trust and cooperation with key local community groups and stakeholders—MNCs may be able to establish local legitimacy. Such actions by MNCs are referred to as social adaptability (Rottig 2016), and MNCs that have a clear understanding about the key local social institutions and their effects on legitimacy will be better able to pro-actively manage the local public and, thus, establish local legitimacy. In addition, MNCs can influence the local public's opinion by pro-actively managing the second constituency that is able to grant and withdraw legitimacy in Brazil: the media.

## The Media

While the media does not control tangible resources directly (such as, for example, the general public through its purchasing power on the demand side and labor force on the supply side), it has considerable influence through its coverage and reporting of the actions and behavior of foreign MNCs. The media, therefore, influences the opinion of the general public and has the power to either endorse (and thus legitimate) or disapprove of foreign MNCs. Sheafer (2001), for example, notes that such media legitimacy often relies on organizations being able to effectively communicate their actions to the media, and so suggests that MNCs ought to pro-actively reach out and manage media coverage. Jack Kahn, CEO Midwest Capital International, substantiated this in one of our interviews by emphasizing that pro-actively working with the media in Brazil by providing information for press releases and granting interviews was an effective way to increase his company's exposure in the local market and convey a positive message to the local public that his company actively helped the local economy by turning around a failing (local) company and so saving existing jobs as well as creating new ones. Doing so facilitated the development of a considerable amount of goodwill among the local public and led to widespread local acceptance and support of his company. Investing time, resources, and financial capital into a deliberate media strategy (both traditional and social media) can, therefore, be a very productive and beneficial strategy for foreign MNCs to establish local legitimacy, particularly in the emerging market of Brazil where the general public relies heavily on media coverage.

## The Government and Regulatory Agencies

The third constituency in Brazil that MNCs need to pro-actively manage in order to establish legitimacy is the local government and regulators. This constituency controls critical resources in form of its political/regulatory power to grant business licenses to foreign MNCs without which these companies would not be able to enter and operate in the local market. Political and regulatory institutions in emerging markets, such as Brazil, are more complex than those in developed countries due to their often non-transparent, corrupt and (deliberately) difficult to navigate character (Torres de Oliveira and Rottig 2018). Hence, foreign MNCs need to understand the specific context (Khanna 2014) of each emerging market in which they operate and adapt their entry strategies and local operations by "understanding of the importance and influence of local governments and the need to adjust to the institutional demands of these governments in order to establish and maintain legitimacy" (Rottig 2016: 9).

In emerging markets with stable political environments, such 'political adaptability' (Rottig 2016) may require foreign MNCs to build strong ties and relationships with a local government (e.g. in China, where possessing *guanxi* with the local government is key to successfully operate in this market). In emerging markets with unstable and changing political environments, however, ties with the local government may constitute a liability. This is due to the fact that changes in government or polarized politics are common in such markets, and new governments typically sever ties with foreign MNCs that were affiliated with the previous government. In these latter emerging markets, of which Brazil is an example (as illustrated by the recent, October 2018 election), localizing their business operations and building ties and relationships with mid-level civil servants that actually "run" the country regardless of which political party controls the government may prove more beneficial in order to build local political legitimacy (Rottig 2016). In addition, localizing business operations, which involves hiring locals, contracting local suppliers, and tapping into local sources of financing, would send a strong signal that an MNC has a lasting stake in the local market and so substantiate the acceptance, approval and support by the local government.

### The Financial Community

The fourth constituency in Brazil that is able to bestow legitimacy on foreign MNCs is the local financial community. Although MNCs have the option to tap into international financial markets to secure funding for their foreign market entries and local operations around the world, working with local banks and financial institutions facilitates the establishment of legitimacy in Brazil. The local financial community, similar to the media, can influence public opinion on the economic solvency (and thus legitimacy) of foreign MNCs. The financial community also has lobbying power with the local government and so may help foreign MNCs whose operations are financed by local banks to obtain and maintain business licenses. Hence, by establishing ties and relationships with local financial institutions in Brazil, foreign MNCs will be better able to develop legitimacy. In doing so, foreign MNCs can also tap into local sources of funding that may facilitate financial transactions. An illustrative quote from one of our interviews exemplifies this notion. Jack Kahn, CEO Midwest Capital International, stated that "my company was severely lacking the ability to transfer funds and execute financial maneuvers because all of my financial assets were in the United States. One of the things that helped the most was coming to an agreement with a national bank in Brazil to help me legitimize my presence in Brazil. Working with the Brazilian bank made it much easier to operate in Brazil".

## Conclusion

While Brazil is open for international trade and investment, the country remains plagued by a rigid, non-transparent, and difficult to navigate formal institutional environment. A large number of slow bureaucratic processes inhibit entrepreneurship and the establishment of local operations by foreign investors. Onerous labor laws entail substantial costs for foreign MNCs operating in the market, and ownership restrictions in several local industries such as insurance/banking, aviation, and media discourage foreign direct investment. Foreign MNCs, therefore, have to navigate an uncertain, unstable, and risky political, regulatory, and economic environment which makes it difficult to establish local legitimacy.

Despite these institutional challenges, Brazil has become an important market for MNCs given its status as one of the key emerging countries around the globe and the fact that it constitutes the largest economy and most populous country in Latin America. Brazil possesses extensive raw materials, a diversified economy, and a large domestic market. With more than 200 million inhabitants, a large working-age population at all levels of education, and a (purchasing power adjusted) per capita GDP of US$15,500 in 2017, Brazil is an important market for MNCs from a resource/manufacturing as well as consumer perspective. Recent attempts to curtail the high level of systemic corruption in the country—e.g. Operação Lava Jato (Operation Car Wash), an anticorruption probe that started in 2014 and prosecuted executives from some of Brazil's largest companies, including Petrobras and Odebrecht, and the recent incarceration of former President Luiz Inácio Lula da Silva, who gave himself up to the police in April of 2018 to start serving a 12-year sentence on corruption charges—may constitute a positive development that may benefit foreign MNCs considering whether or not to enter and operate in Brazil in the long-run.

It remains to be seen how the recent, October 2018 election will affect Brazil's economy and foreign multinational corporations aiming to enter and operate in this market. The election has offered Brazilian voters two extreme political choices: Fernando Haddad of the left-wing Partido dos Trabalhadores (PT) party, supported by the popular former President Luiz Inácio Lula da Silva who campaigned for Fernando Haddad out of prison while serving his 12-year sentence, and Jair Bolsonaro of the Partido Social Liberal PSL, a right wing populist. The election of the latter as the new president, which resulted in a drastic shift of Brazilian politics to the right, raised both concerns and hope in the country. President Bolsonaro's populist campaign, which has widely been compared with the populist campaign and political rhetoric of U.S. President Donald J. Trump, and the selection of a far-right former army captain as Vice President who shares Mr. Bolsonaro's nostalgia for Brazil's military dictatorship from

1964–1985, are reasons for considerable concerns about a new wave of far-right, authoritarian-style government in the country as well as in Latin America (a wave that has also recently been evident in other parts of the globe). However, the country's moribund economy and systemically corrupt political environment called for a change in Brazil after nearly 15 years of left-wing rule. The new President's selection of a University of Chicago-trained free-market economist, Paulo Guedes, as his economic advisor and new finance minister is sending signals for hope that the long-needed economic and financial reforms will be realized, similar to the Milton Friedman-style free-market reforms that were implemented in Chile under General Augusto Pinochet, who came to power in 1973 after overthrowing socialist president Salvador Allende.

This chapter examined how foreign MNCs can successfully enter Brazil, analyzed the formal institutional legitimacy challenges in the country, and sketched out strategies MNCs can use to gain and maintain local legitimacy in this emerging market. We hope that this exploratory study and the initial insights it provides will encourage more work on the institutional environment of Brazil, and so contribute to a growing body of literature that studies the institution-based performance determinants of MNCs aiming to enter and operate in emerging markets.

## References

Alden, C., and M.A. Vieira. 2005. The new diplomacy of the South: South Africa, Brazil, India and trilateralism. *Third World Quarterly* 26 (7): 1077–1095.

Alon, I., and D. Rottig. 2013. Entrepreneurship in emerging markets: New insights and directions for future research. *Thunderbird International Business Review* 55 (5): 487–492.

Baker & McKenzie. 2018. *A buyer's guide to M&A in Latin America: How to overcome obstacles and boost market share in the world's most urbanized region.* Chicago: Baker & McKenzie Global Services.

Banco Central do Brasil. 2018. Historical series of the direct investment flows – Breakdowns by country or by sector. http://www.bcb.gov.br/ingles/economic/SeriehistFluxoInvDir_i.asp

Bremmer, I. 2014. The new rules of globalization. *Harvard Business Review* 92 (1): 103–107.
Deephouse, D.L., and M.C. Suchman. 2008. Legitimacy in organizational institutionalism. In *The SAGE handbook of organizational institutionalism*, ed. Royston Greenwood, Christine Oliver, Kerstin Sahlin, and Roy Suddaby. Thousand Oaks: SAGE.
Deloitte. 2017. *Latin America mergers & acquisitions study: Integration and divestiture best practices throughout the region*. London: Deloitte Touche Tohmatsu.
Finnemore, M. 2009. Legitimacy, hypocrisy, and the social structure of unipolarity. *World Politics* 61 (1): 58–85.
Gans, J.S., and S. Stern. 2003. The product market and the market for 'ideas': Commercialization strategies for technology entrepreneur. *Research Policy* 32 (2): 333–350.
Henisz, W.J., and B.A. Zelner. 2005. Legitimacy, interest group pressures, and change in emergent institutions: The case of foreign investors and host country governments. *Academy of Management Review* 30 (2): 361–382.
IMF. 2018. World economic outlook: Cyclical upswing, structural change. April.
International Trade Administration. 2017. Brazil – Protecting intellectual property. https://www.export.gov/article?id=Brazil-Protecting-Intellectual-Property
Khanna, T. 2014. Contextual intelligence. *Harvard Business Review* 92 (9): 59–68.
Khanna, T., and K. Palepu. 1997. Why focused strategies may be wrong for emerging markets. *Harvard Business Review* 75 (4): 41–51.
Madura, J. 2017. *International Financial Management*. 13th ed. Boston, MA: Cengage.
North, D.C. 1990. *Institutions, institutional change, and economic performance*. Cambridge: Cambridge University Press.
Office of the United States Trade Representative. 2018. US-Brazil trade statistics. https://ustr.gov/countries-regions/americas/brazil
Rao, R.S., R.K. Chandy, and J.C. Prabhu. 2008. The fruits of legitimacy: Why some new ventures gain more from innovation than others. *Journal of Marketing* 72 (4): 58–75.
Reus, T.H., and D. Rottig. 2009. Meta-analyses of international joint venture performance determinants: Evidence for theory, methodological artifacts and the unique context of China. *Management International Review* 49 (5): 607–640.

Rottig, D. 2007. Successfully managing international mergers and acquisitions: A descriptive framework. *International Business: Research Teaching and Practice* 1 (1): 103–126.

———. 2011. The role of social capital in cross-cultural M&As: A multinational corporation perspective. *European Journal of International Management* 5 (4): 413–431.

———. 2013. A marriage metaphor model for sociocultural integration in international mergers and acquisitions. *Thunderbird International Business Review* 55 (4): 439–451.

———. 2016. Institutions and emerging markets: Effects and implications for multinational corporations. *International Journal of Emerging Markets* 11 (1): 2–17.

———. 2017. Meta-analyses of culture's consequences for acquisition performance: An examination of statistical artifacts, methodological moderators and the context of emerging markets. *International Journal of Emerging Markets* 12 (1): 8–37.

Rottig, D., and T.H. Reus. 2009. Institutional distance, organizational legitimacy, and the performance of foreign acquisitions in the United States. In *Best paper proceedings of the sixty-ninth annual meeting of the academy of management*, ed. George T. Solomon: Academy of Management.

———. 2018. Research on culture and international acquisition performance: A critical evaluation and new directions. *International Studies of Management & Organization* 48 (1): 3–42.

Rottig, D., T.H. Reus, and S.Y. Tarba. 2013. The impact of culture on mergers and acquisitions: A third of a century of research. In *Advances in mergers and acquisitions*, ed. Cary Cooper and Sydney Finkelstein. Bingley: Emerald Group Publishing Limited.

Rottig, D., J. Schappert, and E. Starkman. 2017. Successfully managing the sociocultural integration process in international acquisitions: A qualitative analysis of Canon's acquisition of Océ. *Thunderbird International Business Review* 59 (2): 187–208.

Scott, W.R. 2014. *Institutions and organizations: Ideas, interests and identities*. 4th ed. Thousand Oaks: SAGE Publications.

Sheafer, T. 2001. Charismatic skill and media legitimacy: An actor-centered approach to understanding the political communication competition. *Communication Research* 28 (6): 711–736.

Suchman, M.C. 1995. Managing legitimacy: Strategic and institutional approaches. *Academy of Management Review* 20 (3): 571–610.

Swaminathan, V., and C. Moorman. 2009. Marketing alliances, firm networks, and firm value creation. *Journal of Marketing* 73: 52–69.

The Economist. 2011. Protectionism in Brazil: A self-made siege. http://www.economist.com/node/21530144

The World Bank. 2018. *Doing business in 2018: Reforming to create jobs*. Washington, DC: The World Bank Group.

Torres de Oliveira, R., and D. Rottig. 2018. Chinese acquisitions of developed market firms: Home semi-formal institutions and a supportive partnering approach. *Journal of Business Research* 93: 230–241.

USTR. 2018. Brazil trade report. https://ustr.gov/sites/default/files/Brazil_0.pdf

# 6

# Internationalization and the Tale of the Cabo Frio Beachwear Cluster

Beatriz Kury, Angela da Rocha, and Jorge Ferreira da Silva

## Introduction

Clusters, or industrial districts, can be described as concentrations of economic activity in a specific geographic location that show a certain level of specialization. Industrial clusters are characterized by a set of firms typically operating in the same or related industries, together with an array of suppliers of raw materials and parts, equipment manufacturers, as well as all types of public and private supporting institutions. Several authors have pointed out the relevance of industrial clusters. For example, Porter (1998, p. 77) claims that location has become even more important in a globalized world and sees clusters as "critical masses [...] of unusual competitive success in particular fields". Scott (1996, p. 391) suggests that clusters are the "regional motors of the global economy", a result of the emergence of global value chains and changes in world capitalism.

B. Kury (✉) • A. da Rocha • J. F. da Silva
Pontifical Catholic University of Rio de Janeiro, Rio de Janeiro, Brazil
e-mail: beatrizkury@terra.com.br; angelarocha@iag.puc-rio.br; shopshop@iag.puc-rio.br



W. Newburry et al. (eds.), *Contemporary Influences on International Business in Latin America*, AIB Latin America, https://doi.org/10.1007/978-3-319-98340-0_6

A substantial body of the literature on industrial clusters has addressed the question of the evolution over time of these territorial agglomerations of firms. According to a recent literature review by Martínez-Fernández, Capó-Vicedo, and Vallet-Bellmunt (2012), studies on cluster lifecycle are the second most frequent type of published research on the subject. However, fewer studies have looked specifically at the issue of a cluster's decline. Bergman (2008, p. 114) advocates the need for additional research to examine the process by which a cluster may prosper initially, "yet at the end exhibit fatal vulnerabilities". Zucchella (2006, p. 26) also indicates that the birth and growth of clusters has received substantial attention in the literature, but there are few studies on "their decline, crisis, and eventual renewal".

This study aims, therefore, at examining the lifecycle of a relatively small beachwear cluster of Cabo Frio, a seaside resort located in the northern coast of the state of Rio de Janeiro, Brazil. The research question that guided the study was: "Why did the beachwear cluster of Cabo Frio fail to serve international markets despite private and public efforts to develop export activity?"

## Literature Review

Becattini (1990, p. 39) defines a cluster (or industrial district) as "a socio-territorial entity [...] characterized by the active presence of both a community of people and a population of firms" in a given geographic location. The relevance of the community comes from social ties between individuals and families, as well as a common system of values and beliefs, leading to trust and cooperation. The firms in a cluster can be of various sizes, although a cluster typically encompasses a large number of small firms and, in some cases, one or a few larger firms. System interactions between actors in a cluster stimulate cooperation. In addition to the advantages associated with location of suppliers and institutions and the ability of a cluster to attract highly qualified customers, firms in a cluster cooperate because the advantages of cooperation outweigh the costs of coordination (Lorenzen 2001). Vertical cooperation is a fundamental feature of an industrial cluster, as well as horizontal competition (Becattini 1990; Paniccia 1998; Tomlinson and Jackson 2013).

## Cluster Evolution

Although the study of cluster lifecycle is not new in the extant literature, scholars have not yet reached an agreement as to which phases one should consider when examining a cluster lifecycle. In fact several proposals appear in the literature (Table 6.1). The examination of the proposed stages suggests that there are four possible phases: (1) Birth; (2) Take-off; (3) Growth; (4) Maturity; (5) Stagnation, or Decline. Of course, a specific cluster does not have to follow all these stages.

### Birth

A cluster can start spontaneously (e.g. in a location with given natural resources, or close to a port), or it can be induced (e.g. as a result of government actions, as in the case of most technology parks). In any case, for a cluster to emerge, several conditions seem to be necessary, including the formation of a local community that favors cooperation and sharing.

**Table 6.1** Cluster lifecycle stages

| Studies | Stage 1 | Stage 2 | Stage 3 | Stage 4 |
|---|---|---|---|---|
| Tichy (1998) | Creation | Growth | Maturity | Petrification |
| Swann (1998) | Critical mass | Take-off | Peak entry | Saturation |
| Fornahl and Menzel (2003) | Emerging | Growing | Sustaining | Stagnating |
| Wolter (2003) | Set-up | Growth | Change | Adaptation |
| Maskell and Kebir (2005) | Existence | Expansion | | Exhaustion |
| Lorenzen (2005) | Arise | Decline | Shift | |
| Maggioni (2004) | Birth/ take-off | Golden age | Maturity | |
| Bergman (2006) | Formative | Growth | Maturity | Petrification |
| Press (2006) | Emergence | | Endurance | Exhaustion |
| Bergman (2008) | Existence | Expansion | | Exhaustion |
| Menzel and Fornahl (2010) | Emergence | Growth | Sustainment | Decline |
| Shin and Hassink (2011) | Genesis | Development | Change | |

Adapted and enlarged from Bergman (2008, p. 116), Press (2006), Menzel and Fornahl (2010), and Shin and Hassink (2011)

Without this, there would not be a real cluster but merely a geographic agglomeration of firms. According to Scott and Garofoli (2007, p. 5), the emergence of a cluster does not necessarily rely on existing comparative locational advantages, but more often "on the basis of endogenously built competitive advantages". They are "social creations".

### Take-off

The next stage is characterized by a fast period of expansion. Some authors consider take-off an independent phase (e.g. Swann 1998), but Bergman (2008) suggests it is part of the growth stage. This stage can happen just after the birth of a cluster, or the cluster can hibernate for a substantial period of time before expansion. Take-off can result from the opening of national or international markets to the cluster's products.

### Growth

The growth of a cluster can be the result of traditional factors, such as favorable local conditions, diffusion of knowledge and innovation, attractiveness to investors, and so on (Iammarino et al. 2006). At this point, the cluster is already very attractive and brings together all kinds of support institutions (such as government agencies, universities and research centers, venture capitalists, etc.) and firms in related industries (such as suppliers of parts, equipment manufacturers, etc.). The emergence and consolidation of a local coordination system (e.g. manufacturers' associations) occurs in this phase. However the growth of a cluster is associated with demand conditions. Since many clusters are internationalized, their growth can be associated with the expansion of demand for the cluster's products in international markets. It has been claimed more recently, however, that due to the phenomenon of globalization "new diversified and 'idiosyncratic' patterns of [cluster] growth have been observed" (Guerrieri and Pietrobelli 2004, p. 899).

## Maturity

Maturity is technically reached when the rate of entry/exit of firms tends to stability. It can be associated with the stagnation of demand for local products, caused by exogenous factors, or by limits to the capacity of the cluster to increase supply (which could be a result of diseconomies of scale or full use of non-substitutable natural resources). The costs of additional growth may not be counterbalanced by the benefits (Swann 1998; Bergman 2008). Firms may face congestion costs, and new firms may not add to the competitive advantages of the cluster. It is also possible that the leading firms in the cluster do not show a desire to expand and rely on the advantages previously built up, instead of continuously searching for new advantages (Bergman 2008). Clusters can remain for a long period in the maturity stage, or they can stagnate, or even decline.

## Stagnation or Decline

Several endogenous and exogenous forces may cause a cluster to fall. Costs may rise substantially due to competition among firms for limited resources, such as the costs of specialized labor, or logistics. Even when a cluster is extremely successful, success itself may stimulate the emergence of new clusters, offering locational advantages compared to the old cluster. Another major reason for the decline of clusters is technological obsolescence. If a cluster faces a radical change in technology, it may not have the capabilities required to adopt the new technology (Trippl and Tödtling 2008). Changes in global supply chains may also have a strong impact on a cluster's development. In fact, risks and vulnerabilities are inherent to a cluster. Also, clusters may stagnate or decline due to changes in their industry. Yet Valdaliso, Elola, and Franco (2016) have shown that clusters can deviate from the trajectory of their industries. Recent studies of Italian industrial districts also throw some light on this issue. Trippl and Tödtling (2008, p. 213) argue that scholars have frequently ignored that clusters can be both "a blessing and a curse" to their regions. If the cluster fails, there is general impoverishment and unemployment, and diminishing returns for the region (Potter and Watts 2011).

Bergman (2008) claims that there may be another phase in a cluster's evolution—"renaissance"—in which readjustments and restructuring may take place, in such a way that the cluster creates new competitive advantages and reinvents itself. Martin (2010) also suggests that clusters can have periods of stagnation followed by recovery; they can also evolve continuously, in permanent adjustment to technological or other environmental changes. In fact, the author identifies several possible trajectories for a cluster, of which only one portrays the traditional lifecycle model (Fig. 6.1).

One of the risks faced by a cluster is path dependence (Dobusch and Schüßler 2012). Path dependence is generally understood as a factor that limits the potential strategic choices of firms, industries, or clusters. The mechanism of path dependence works as a chain of causal mechanisms that reinforce each other over a period of time. Vergne and Durand (2010, p. 737) define path dependence as "a property of a stochastic process which obtains under two conditions (contingency and self-reinforcement) and causes lock-in in the absence of external shock". The often-used term "history matters" indicates that previous knowledge influences future knowledge, present investments limit the alternatives

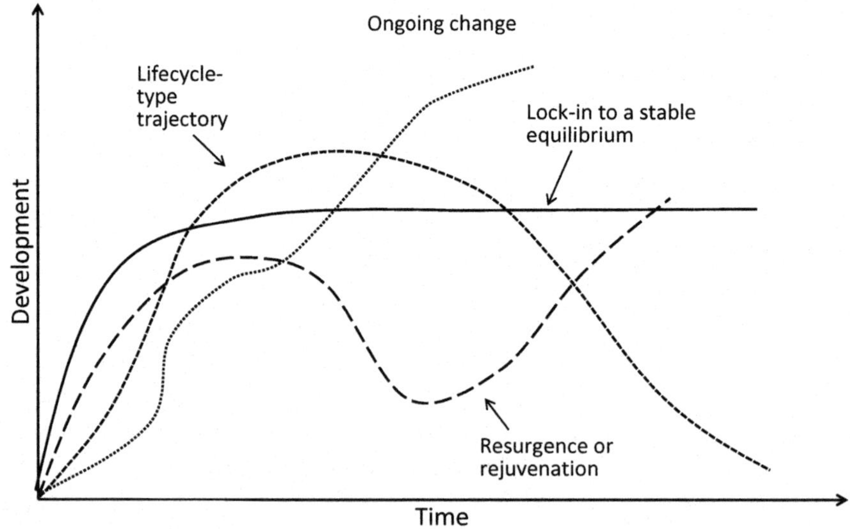


**Fig. 6.1** Alternative paths for a cluster. (Adapted from Martin 2010, p. 10)

for future investments, and organizational cultures shape future decisions. Lock-in is a potential outcome of path dependence.

Sydow, Schreyögg, and Koch (2009) suggest a process leading to path dependence. Initially, the firm would have a reasonable number of alternatives to follow. Once the firm chooses one or another alternative, the process of self-reinforcement would start, leading to the reduction of the number of options, making it difficult to change the original decisions. Finally, the path would become definite and non-reversible, leading to lock-in. Yet several authors caution against the supposed inevitability of the lock-in effect (e.g. Drahokoupil 2012; Greener 2002; North 1990), claiming that firms may reorient their paths by using fragments of experiences or knowledge that were not initially followed (Noda and Collis 2001; Schneiberg 2006).

Another potential threat to a cluster's success is isomorphic behavior (DiMaggio and Powell 1991), which is the tendency of the firms in a cluster to behave similarly, imitating the more successful ones. More heterogeneous clusters may find it easier to escape the lock-in effect (Martin 2010), since firms have followed alternative paths or alternative strategies in their history. In addition, governments may intervene by making available new resources (training, resources to invest in new technologies, legal mechanisms, etc.). Trippl and Tödtling (2008) suggest three possible forms of renewal of industrial clusters—incremental change, diversification, and radical change. Incremental change consists of small adjustments without modifying the path, but allowing the cluster to adjust to new conditions. Diversification implies the inclusion of new economic activities, without abandoning the original ones. Radical change would mean a drastic modification of the cluster's activities.

## Cluster Internationalization

Globalization may pose both threats and opportunities to a cluster's development. In fact, a number of studies have documented the impact of globalization on the cluster's lifecycle, including relocation and reconfiguration (e.g. Bertolini and Giovanetti 2006; Sammarra and Belussi 2006). The literature on industrial clusters and districts has been less concerned with the process by which a cluster internationalizes, focusing more on the impact of globalization. Other studies looked at whether the location in industrial districts creates locational advantages that boost internationalization (Catalan and Ramon-Muñoz 2013). Guerrieri and Petrobelli (2004) argue that to become internationalized, a cluster needs to develop and integrate local and global linkages and networks. Specifically, the authors point out the need to participate in global production networks and other global "systemic forms of integration" (p. 912). In the same vein, Zucchella (2006) claims that internationalization may play a relevant role in mature clusters. In these clusters, focal firms or key players may have international experience and act as gatekeepers, identifying potential threats and opportunities, and connecting the other firms with global supply chains and networks. The establishment of international linkages, however, may have a deleterious effect on local linkages (De Martino et al. 2006). Schmitz (1999a) also found that the development of alliances between key firms in the Sinos Valley footwear cluster in Brazil and global suppliers has weakened local cooperation among manufacturers. The author suggests that market failures faced by industrial clusters might be better solved by joint private action, rather than government action (Schmitz 1999b).

Several actors may play a role in triggering a cluster's internationalization process. Leading firms in a cluster may be the initiator of internationalization (Bacchiocchi et al. 2014; Ferreira et al. 2006; Mariotti et al. 2008). Also, international intermediaries may play a relevant role in connecting firms in a cluster, particularly small and medium-sized enterprises (SMEs), to global value chains (Ellis 2003). Private institutions may also be of paramount importance to start the internationalization process. For example, a recent study (Cannatelli and Antoldi 2012) showed that a manufacturers' association was able to promote joint export cooperative groups among SMEs in an Italian furniture cluster. The facilitator was responsible for identifying the opportunity and for inviting the firms to participate. But it is main role in the process was to act as a guarantor, in the absence of trust among the entrepreneurs, who had been fiercely competing with each other for decades. The authors indicate that network facilitators can play different roles during the process of establishing an export group. During the creation of the group, the facilitator can act as "pivot of the alliance". As the alliance progresses, facilitators can then act as mediators, to assure that relationships between alliance members are built. Finally, the facilitator becomes an advisor, at the same time the group is capable of choosing an internal leader.

The international business literature offers little insights on the internationalization of clusters. It is generally assumed in this literature that firms internationalize as sole actors, and joint action is largely ignored (Bonaccorsi 1992). Even network theory, although recognizing that firms are embedded in social networks and that internationalization happens in the context of these networks, still looks at the individual firm as the unit of analysis, not the network (e.g. Chetty and Holm 2000; Johanson and Mattson 1988; Johanson and Vahlne 2009, 2011; Sharma and Blomstermo 2003). This stream of research recognizes, however, that firms use networks to enter foreign markets, that the nature of ties and interactions among members of the network is relevant to internationalization, and that belonging to networks allows SMEs to advance faster in the global arena.

## Methods

This research uses the case study method of investigation. Case studies respond for approximately 7% of the studies on industrial clusters (Martínez-Fernández et al. 2012), and are predominant in cluster lifecycle studies. Case studies are often used in the international business literature to describe and analyze processes, and their use has been considered useful to foster the understanding of such processes (e.g. Jones and Khanna 2006). Following the tradition in the study of industrial clusters, the unit of analysis is the cluster. Specifically, we look at the trajectory of the beachwear cluster of Cabo Frio, Brazil.

Data sources were both secondary and primary. Secondary sources included several reports on the evolution of clusters by government and private institutions; other information available from the internet; academic studies; and articles in the business press. Primary data was gathered between 2014 and 2016, by means of: (1) in-depth personal interviews conducted with three entrepreneurs of leading firms in the cluster, one of which was also the head of the local industry association, and with a consultant to Sebrae; (2) telephone interviews with government agents involved in public actions in the cluster; (3) informal interviews in a business meeting organized by Sebrae under the auspices of the Interamerican Development Bank (IDB); and (4) informal interviews during several visits to the cluster. These eclectic data sources permitted us to get different perspectives, from different types of actors at different moments of time. They also made possible access to internal documents that helped to understand the cluster's history. Specifically, the participation in a large business meeting where the future of the cluster was being discussed helped us to understand the dynamics of social interaction among local actors, the efforts by institutions, and the problems faced by the firms in cooperating. The data collected was therefore both retrospective and real-time. In-depth interviews were taped and transcripts made. The researchers took notes during or after telephone interviews and informal conversations.

Data analysis was done in two steps. First, we developed a detailed descriptive account of the cluster's trajectory, confronting secondary and primary data collected for the study. The variety of sources, as well as of data collection methods, was also necessary for triangulation. This descriptive account was very important to put together the series of events and projects that shaped the trajectory of the cluster over time. The historical description was a critical step because of the large amount of different types of data gathered during the period of the study, and the need "to present an 'authentic' understanding of people's experience" (Ghauri 2004, p. 117). This is one of the most serious challenges faced by qualitative researchers. The historical analysis was not done at the end of data collection; rather, it happened along the data collection process. This was necessary because historical data was not easily available, and events that happened a long time before were already reinterpreted, and even their time limits changed from one person to another. The second step in data analysis was to organize the data in categories. In this chapter, we focused on the problems faced by the cluster to internationalize. The categories emerged from the data, but they were confronted with the literature as the analysis progressed.

# The Cabo Frio Beachwear Cluster

## The Context

The beachwear industry developed in Brazil to serve the country's large domestic market for these products. Three major factors explain the domestic demand for beachwear: a tropical climate, a long coastal line of beaches, and a culture of sensuality. By 2014, it was estimated that the beachwear industry's annual revenue was around US$2 billion dollars, of which only a very small portion (US$10.7 million) was exported. The main markets for Brazilian exports of beachwear were the United States, Portugal, France, Israel, and Paraguay (Simões 2015). Exports of beachwear peaked in 2005, but then declined in the following years (Fig. 6.1). The reduction in the volume exported by the industry was to a large extent due to the overvalued Brazilian currency, a situation that became more acute after 2005. Nevertheless, with the substantial devaluation of the Real in 2015, it was expected that the industry would be more price competitive in the near future.

The industry comprises more than 1300 firms, of which around 70% are small firms. There is also a large number of micro firms operating informally. A few large-sized firms, mostly located in the state of São Paulo, were responsible for a large percentage of exports in 2005, but this situation has changed since then. Firms that competed only on price were unable to meet the prices offered by Asian competitors, and therefore ceased to export. In fact, by 2015 firms that continued to export were located mostly in the cities of Rio de Janeiro and São Paulo. These firms, typically medium-sized, had established brand names and were able to export their products based on design and exclusivity, adopting a differentiation strategy. Nevertheless, they could only export small volumes, because of their size. As a result, the average unit price of exported beachwear products more than doubled (in US$) during the past decade.

The recent history of the industry also shows that imports have risen steadily, at the same time exports decreased, suggesting that the local industry lost price-competitiveness both in the domestic and international markets. Indeed, by 2014, imports of beachwear products have far exceeded exports. More than 90% of the imports of beachwear products came from China (Moiseichyk et al. 2012) (Fig. 6.2).

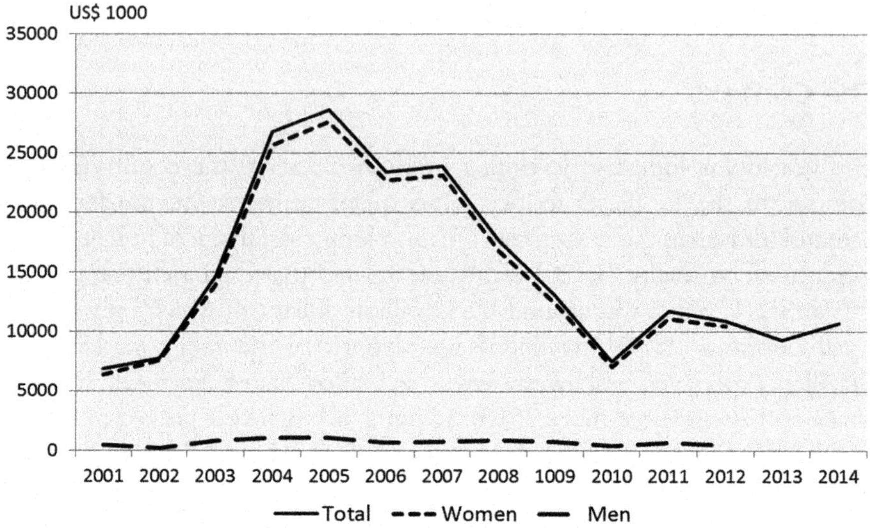


**Fig. 6.2** Evolution of Beachwear exports: Brazil

## The Cluster Lifecycle

The Cabo Frio beachwear cluster was responsible, in 2014, for 2% of the Brazilian production of beachwear products and employed 3000 people the whole year, and 10,000 during the summer season. The cluster can be classified as a Marshallian district, formed by small firms. It is estimated that presently between 150 and 200 firms are located in the cluster. The cluster followed the typical path predicted in the cluster lifecycle literature: birth, take-off, growth, and maturity.

### Birth

The Cabo Frio beachwear cluster has its origins in the 1950s, when a local entrepreneur started a business to serve the beach resort areas in the region. The business grew rapidly and was soon imitated by other entrepreneurs. Until 1970, however, almost all producers operated informally, and copied products of established brand name manufacturers and designers located in the city of Rio de Janeiro. Stores were typically established in the entrepreneur's home.

## Take-off

It was only in the 1980s that the cluster started to grow, with the inflow of entrepreneurs from the city of Rio de Janeiro, who recognized an opportunity to establish manufacturing units or brand name stores in the region (Cassiolato and Peixoto 2004; Peixoto 2005; Cardoso 2006). International sales started as tourists carried beachwear products to their countries of origin to resell, or to offer as gifts. Nevertheless, local firms did not adopt any specific strategy to increase foreign sales, but remained passive. Instead, they were contacted by foreign buyers and only served unsolicited foreign orders.

## Crisis and Growth

Local firms faced high seasonality, because a large percentage of their sales was associated with school vacations. However, an increase in the number of days in school in the second half of the 1990s caused a reduction of around 30% of the cluster's sales. The crisis prompted local government assistance programs to increase the cluster's competitiveness. Local government actions included providing better infrastructure to the area where the stores were located (known as the "Bikini Street"), and the establishment of a ferry service to serve the area, thus increasing attractiveness and facilitating access. These changes, in turn, helped to increase the flow of information and knowledge among local firms, attracted new firms to the cluster, and increased the cluster's size and influence. Innovation spread not only in relation to products, processes, and the adoption of new machinery, but also in the design of producers' local stores (Cardoso 2006; Pereira and Reis 2008). As the cluster developed, several institutions joined or were established in the region, including banks, a local college, as well as a manufacturers' association (ACIRB - Associação Comercial e Industrial da Rua dos Biquínis / Commercial and Industrial Association of Bikini Street). Efforts were made during the first half of the 2000s to develop export activities, especially the creation of an export consortium.

### Maturity

Due to the emergence of a "new" middle class in Brazil, and the attractiveness of Cabo Frio as a beach resort, the cluster was able to grow and mature. Although there is no consolidated data available concerning the number of firms that entered and exited the cluster, or the evolution of the cluster's sales (domestic or international), one can assume (based on the data collected) that, by 2016, the cluster had reached maturity, with a steady number of firms operating in the region. Sales were basically domestic with an insignificant volume being occasionally sold to other countries.

## The Pau Brazil Export Consortium (2003–2004)

Sebrae, a non-profit national organization financed by the Brazilian government and dedicated to support micro and small firms, had an important role in developing the cluster. In spite of an initial and unsuccessful attempt to create a joint-export marketing group, Sebrae's actions were directed toward changing the local mindset of the entrepreneurs, stimulating them to sell their products in other states of the country, as well as entering international markets. In addition, the organization also advised local entrepreneurs to diversify their product lines to other types of products that could be sold during the whole year. The aim was to reduce the high seasonality of the cluster's sales, a major obstacle to retaining qualified labor, and keeping high standards of quality.

Sebrae agents kept insisting to local entrepreneurs that joint efforts were the best path to overcome the problems faced by the cluster and to create a new development path. Specifically, exporting to countries in the Northern Hemisphere would counterbalance seasonality effects. There was, however, substantial resistance by local entrepreneurs to associative movements largely due to "the corporate culture of the region [...]: generally very individualistic, distrustful, with little strategic orientation, and unable to realize the competitive advantages that could come from cooperation" (Pereira and Reis 2008, p. 42). Moreover, the previous unsuccessful experience with an export consortium had negatively impacted any new cooperation initiatives.

In spite of the obstacles, an opportunity triggered the internationalization of the cluster. In 2003, Sebrae, the Federation of Industries of the State of Rio de Janeiro (FIRJAN), and several other organizations launched Rio Fashion Business, an event parallel to Rio Fashion Week, aimed at creating an opportunity for the Rio de Janeiro entrepreneurs to meet foreign buyers. Efforts were made by the organizers to stimulate all the fashion clusters located in the state to participate. To prepare for the event, Sebrae decided to establish and support a new export marketing group, named "Consórcio de Exportação Pau Brasil" (the Pau Brazil Export Consortium).

The choice of firms to participate in the group was unilaterally made by Sebrae, causing several local entrepreneurs that were not invited to complain (Cardoso 2006; Pereira and Reis 2008). Eight firms were selected to enter the consortium, most of them with international experience. Sebrae also hired a designer to develop a collection for the consortium, as well as a historian to search for local cultural design elements. Accordingly, the new collection, named Tupinambás, reflected elements of the culture of Indian tribes that had lived in the region (Pereira and Reis 2008). There was, however, some criticism regarding the absence of elements typically used by local beachwear manufacturers, such as shells and beads (Cardoso 2006).

The initiative did generate some sales, but there is substantial controversy regarding the results. The firms were able to get in contact with several potential buyers from Spain, Italy, and France; most of the sales were to Spain. According to an executive of a local association, the firms were unable to cooperate: "a [foreign] buyer came, and one firm got the order; another buyer came, and another firm got the second order. The orders were not shared. And then the consortium started to collapse". In addition, four out of the eight firms that participated in the consortium went bankrupt. Having developed a product line to serve international markets, but one not adequate to the preferences and tastes of the domestic market, they were unable to sell their production internally, and could not export all their output. The other four firms were larger and were able to keep two product lines, one aimed at the domestic market and the other at the international market (Cardoso 2006).

Several other issues contributed to the failure in exporting. Insufficient or inadequate financing was another obstacle. In fact, most of the financing came from Banco do Brasil, the largest state bank in the country. Banco do Brasil had developed a special line of credit for small firms established in clusters, but due to its highly centralized structure and national coverage, the Cabo Frio branch was unable to offer customized support to local firms (Villela and Soares 2009). This inability to offer specialized services to the cluster was more critical when it came to financing export activities. In addition, local firms had made limited use of marketing to promote their products either to the domestic or to the international market. According to Brazilian Internet Steering Committee (2012), only 13% of the firms used the internet to display and promote their products. In spite of this, some business people were aware of the potential advantages of marketing efforts, but there had been no joint efforts to promote the cluster.

At a certain point, Sebrae admitted that the strategy used to develop the cluster and to promote exporting had been unsuccessful. It was concluded that instead of promoting export cooperation, it would be better to help individual firms to export. Nevertheless, the consortium was not terminated, but remained as a symbol of the cluster's export activities, mostly for public relations purposes. It was also decided that Sebrae would focus on supporting any local firm interested in exporting. An executive of a local association explained: "After the consortium ended, there were still some international sales. But slowly the volume went down, and finally came to zero. One firm withdraw [from exporting], then another, and then exports were not interesting anymore, and basically everybody discontinued exporting".

## The Strategic Plan (2005–2008)

A management consulting firm was hired by a pool of government and private non-profit associations, under the leadership of Sebrae, to develop a strategic plan for the cluster, covering the period from 2005 to 2008. The plan aimed at developing a culture of cooperation within the cluster, increasing firm competitiveness in global markets, and improving firm profitability (Sebrae 2005). There were eight programs designed to improve the development of competencies, to facilitate market access, to strengthen the cluster's institutional image, to improve customer relationship management, to improve the products, to stimulate social and environmental responsibility, to develop a local service center, and to manage information and knowledge. Within each program, several actions were envisaged to be initially carried out by the supporting institutions—such as Banco do Brasil (a state bank), Senac (a non-profit organization dedicated to the training of workers), Correios (the post office service), and a local university, among others—but with the intention of later transferring the responsibility for implementation to the local firms. Yet the entrepreneurs claimed that they did not have the time to perform these activities (Cardoso 2006). As time passed the results appeared to be quite modest and the initiative ended. In fact, a study conducted by Sebrae (2008) during 2008 with 55 local firms showed that cooperative efforts were still embryonic. International activities were limited, the attitude was reactive (25% gave as the main reason for not exporting the lack of foreign orders), most firms (72%) had no quality control activities, and the availability of information systems was still quite limited.

## The IDB Project (2011–2017)

In spite of the experiences and the problems faced, efforts to develop the cluster by supporting institutions were not discontinued. By 2011, the Interamerican Development Bank, Sebrae, the Secretary of Economic Development (SEDEIS) of the State of Rio de Janeiro, in partnership with the federal government and other institutions, agreed and signed a project to develop two clusters in the state of Rio de Janeiro, one of which was the Cabo Frio beachwear cluster. The final purpose was to transfer to the state government a methodology to develop clusters located in the state of Rio de Janeiro. The project did not intend specifically to develop international activities, but internationalization was still seen as a major strategy to reduce seasonality, and to face the serious downturn in the domestic market since 2015.

The project recognized the two main problems faced by the Cabo Frio cluster: (1) the lack of an effective structure of collective governance; and (2) "an enormous skepticism among company owners towards the effectiveness of collective actions" (IDB 2015, p. 2). To a large extent, this skepticism was the result of failed previous experiences, but also an obstacle to the implementation of new actions. Apparently, the emphasis on developing new governance mechanisms was not fully appreciated by entrepreneurs, and the IDB report mentioned the need to offer shorter-term benefits to maintain firms' interest in and support of the project. In addition, according to a state government agent interviewed for the present study, the lack of local leaders or a flagship firm capable of mobilizing and providing direction to the cluster was one of the most serious problems encountered. In addition, there was a major concern regarding the end of the project (at the beginning of 2017) and its impact on the cluster. If until then, the cluster was unable to overcome resistance to cooperation and to establish new mechanisms of governance, there were substantial doubts as to whether the results would be enduring. In order to help deal with these problems, Sebrae hired two outside consultants to work on the project, with the purpose of sensitizing the entrepreneurs to the need for cooperation, and organized work groups in order to develop and implement short- and long-term actions. A major understanding among the support institutions, at this point, was that they should in fact only provide support, but that the firms in the cluster had to lead the process.

A meeting organized by Sebrae in 2016 gathered a large group of local entrepreneurs to discuss the actions implemented to support the cluster, and the need to organize for the future, after the end of the project ("What will happen when the IDB grant ends?"). Interestingly, the most revealing aspects of the interaction within the cluster became apparent during the debates in this business meeting. On this occasion, representatives of the institutions involved with the cluster urged the entrepreneurs to cooperate in order to take advantage of the substantial grant made available by the IDB ("no other cluster in Brazil received as much money"). The participants seemed to be roughly divided into two groups, based on old and new leaderships that appeared to be emerging. There was also a third group in the cluster, comprising entrepreneurs who did not attend the meeting, although they had been invited. The climate of the meeting could be described as somewhat aggressive, in some cases bitter, in others indifferent. A major issue openly discussed was the difficulty faced by the cluster in implementing collective actions. One entrepreneur mentioned the lack of firm participation in the local association, "because they [the entrepreneurs] do not understand what it means to act collectively". Other entrepreneurs also mentioned the lack of support by the city government in implementing actions that could improve the local infrastructure. Representatives of institutions repeatedly pointed out the importance of collective action: "you need to believe in your potential and in the collectivity"; "crises serve to show that together we are stronger"; and "it is more satisfying and feels better to act together than independently". In addition, the representatives of the support institutions presented specific actions that were underway, such as the development of an internet portal for the cluster, a printed catalogue of firms, and an exhibition during the Olympic Games in Rio de Janeiro. One of the actions included bringing foreign buyers to visit the cluster during the Olympic Games.

### Problems Identified by Local Entrepreneurs

The problems faced by the cluster in exporting are still present in 2016. Table 6.2 shows the problems identified as limiting international activities faced by firms in the cluster. Although the exchange rate was a serious obstacle to exporting, our data suggests that support institutions failed in terms of preparing the firms for export. In fact, it seems that local firms have not acquired the necessary knowledge to start and remain exporting.

## Discussion and Conclusions

### Discussion

The results of this study show how local firms and supporting institutions failed to take advantage of the typical benefits of being located in a cluster, due to the inability to cooperate. As mentioned by Wolfe and Gertler (2004, p. 1074), "the key assets that determine the viability of a cluster are firm-based". Undoubtedly, the potential to cooperate is one of the key competitive advantages of small firms located in the same region, and

**Table 6.2** Problems associated with international activities reported by the entrepreneurs

| Problems | Extracts |
|---|---|
| *Price-related* | |
| Lack of price competitiveness | "To sell outside Brazil became difficult. We cannot sell at these prices to foreign customers. This is the first problem. Labour costs have risen, all our costs have gone up, taxes increased, energy prices also increased… And today, out there, they want to pay less for the cheapest bikini than they did ten years ago. So today it is a problem to export beachwear"<br>"But the deal has not been closed. I believe the problem is the price, but I am not sure. Because everything else was fine, the product has good quality"<br>"The cost is a major impediment. Because the price they want to pay [for the product] does not cover the costs" |
| Low export profitability | "There is no advantage in selling without a profit. There must be a profit. But now, if you want to export, you will not get anything from it, so nobody wants to export"<br>"Uncertainty is a problem. You have to invest in order to export. And you wonder whether there will be any return. And then you don't go forward" |
| *Marketing-related* | |
| Lack of knowledge of export channels | "I tried to use *Exporta Fácil*[a] but it was not easy. I sent the merchandise, but it took six months to arrive. And then the guy there [the foreign buyer] could not get the package, there were some documents missing. The product was sent back to Brazil. The guy asked us to dispatch again. It took four months to arrive…"<br>"The government stimulated the use of *Exporta Fácil*, but there were several problems. And the merchandise was not delivered. And we had to send a lot of documents…" |
| Lack of knowledge of exporting procedures | "It is very difficult, and we have little information on how to export. Our costs are high, and we cannot afford to hire a specialist to take care of all the required procedures for us" |

(*continued*)

**Table 6.2** (continued)

| Problems | Extracts |
|---|---|
| Lack of market knowledge | "We really need a study to understand how export markets work, what the benefits are, what we need to do"<br>"There are places where they use the Brazilian bikini, but not in others. For example, they use the Brazilian bikini in Portugal, France, Spain, Greece. Now, I have sold to the US, to California. But their requirements are different" |
| Need for product adaptation | "Some foreign buyers contact us to ask whether we would be interested in exporting. We say yes, but only if they do not require changes in our products" |
| Lack of conformity to international market standards | "We do have quality products in Brazil. We try to make our products with high standards of quality, the best way possible, but the requirements there are much more. Not only concerning how to make the product, but also regarding issues such as labels"<br>"We need to know what type of information should come in the product, labels, sizes" |
| *Behavioral* | |
| Attractiveness of the domestic market/ Lack of interest in exporting | "It is much easier to sell to the cities nearby, or other states, than to foreign markets"<br>"We have invested here, in the domestic market"<br>"We prefer to supply the stores here, even to serve a wholesaler in Brazil. We sell to other states of Brazil, to other stores that carry our brand. [...] Exporting is not a target, but I am not saying it is not an option" |
| Lack of cooperative orientation | "We have an association, but the problem here is that people are disunited. Businessmen do not participate in meetings, do not act together..."<br>"The entrepreneurs here are still not united"<br>"The association does not receive any support from the local businessmen. Only a few seemed interested in cooperating. I do not understand why they do not cooperate. I guess they get too involved with their own business and forget the collective" |

[a]Government program aimed at exporting using the post office service

producing similar products, since they can overcome liabilities of size and gain joint economies of scale. Therefore, the lack of cooperation among local firms in the Cabo Frio beachwear cluster severely impacts the cluster's ability to expand its sales.

The failure to develop international activities is clearly connected to the fact that firms in the cluster have not learned to cooperate in order to achieve a common goal. Although one cannot dismiss the deleterious effects of the overvalued Brazilian currency on the cluster's foreign trade, the history of the cluster clearly points to a lack of cooperative action from the beginning, even at a time when the exchange rate was favorable to exporting. Indeed, to escape price competition from Chinese and other Asian competitors, the only strategic choice later available was differentiation, a path that can only be pursued by small firms acting together, because of the marketing costs that need to be incurred (such as branding, development of channels of distribution, promotion, etc.). In fact, medium-sized firms in the city of Rio de Janeiro have successfully followed this path.

Interestingly, there was substantial consensus among the participants of the Cabo Frio cluster (entrepreneurs, consultants, and representatives of support institutions) that the main problem was lack of cooperation among cluster members. This difficulty in cooperating has already been identified in certain Brazilian industrial clusters, where "an extremely non cooperative business culture emerged" (e.g. Meyer-Stamer 1998, p. 1495). Similar results were obtained in a recent study (Deboçã and Martins 2015, p. 1025) of two furniture clusters located in different states of Brazil, in which "the behavior of entrepreneurs … tends strongly towards individualism". Furthermore, the main relational benefits associated with belonging to a cluster identified by firms were only "location (proximity to large consumer centers) and access to roads" (p. 1040).

The intriguing question is then: "Why have Brazilian firms located in clusters not learned to cooperate?" Meyer-Stamer (1998) suggested that the roots of this lack of cooperation were threefold: (1) a long-term tradition of market protection and, as a result, a lack of international competition in the domestic market; (2) an inability to plan for the long-term, probably due to decades of chronic high inflation rates or hyperinflation; and (3) as a consequence, internalization of activities within each firm, leading to excessive vertical integration. In spite of this, the author pointed out that, faced with severe threats in the 1990s, certain Brazilian clusters had undergone a substantial change in firms' behavior toward "competition and internal efficiency" (p. 1496). Change, however, could only happen as certain preconditions emerged, particularly the existence of change agents and role models within the clusters. Deboçã and Martins (2015) explain the failure to cooperate in Brazilian furniture clusters as a result of "lack of coordination", leading to the offer of competitive, and not complementary, products, which in turn stimulates competition, rather than cooperation. In an early study on the formation of export consortia in Brazil, Da Rocha (1988) indicated that these organizations rarely succeeded, for several reasons, including lack of trust among members, lack of a governance structure, and resistance to cooperate.

In the case of the Cabo Frio beachwear cluster, change agents, particularly Sebrae, have tried to introduce new practices and attitudes toward cooperation in the cluster, but failed to do so, in opposition to the experience reported by Cannatelli and Antoldi (2012) in a furniture industrial district in Italy. In addition, the absence of flagship firms in the cluster (Zucchella 2006) did not provide a local role model that could potentially serve to show new alternative paths. Another reason might be the fact that firms essentially offer similar products, therefore they have little incentive to cooperate and adopt a competitive attitude *vis-à-vis* the other firms, as reported in other studies. Furthermore, the fact that several experiences of internationalization and cooperation in the cluster have failed created resentment and distrust among members and between members and support institutions.

## Conclusions

The Cabo Frio beachwear cluster has followed the traditional stages in a cluster's lifecycle, having reached maturity in the late 2000s. However, the cluster is currently at a crossroads, as the Brazilian economy faces a severe downturn. The cluster faces a combination of the weakening of demand for the cluster's products in the domestic market and the failure to enter international markets, a situation that has been envisaged in the literature as leading to decline (De Propris and Lazzeretti 2009). The cluster seems to be following a path-dependent trajectory, and it faces the risk of lock-in. Most firms are not interested in exporting or, worse still, see exporting as a non-alternative, because of perceived uncertainty and risk. In addition, failed experiences of internationalization have the potential to halter future initiatives in export cooperation, due to resistance and disbelief in positive results.

As domestic sales fall, and since the cluster has failed to develop international markets, will it change its path and promote a new cycle of innovation or will it face stagnation or decline? As proposed by Martin (2010), clusters have essentially two alternative paths: one leads to a stable state (and potentially, but not necessarily, to decline); and the other consists of a dynamic process of change and adaptation. Will the Cabo Frio beachwear cluster be able to face the present challenges and follow a new path, or "renaissance" (Bergman 2008), or will it be locked-in?

This study presents several limitations. First, it examines only one beachwear cluster. Other clusters may show different paths than the one examined here. Second, the cluster studied suffered several interventions from government and non-government support agencies that have had an impact on the behavior of local entrepreneurs. Third, we mainly had to rely on secondary sources to describe the cluster's history. More longitudinal research is needed to explore the reasons for this lack of cooperation among firms in Brazilian industrial clusters.

## References

Bacchiocchi, E., M. Florio, and A. Giunta. 2014. Internationalization and industrial districts: Evidence from the Italian automotive supply chain. *International Review of Applied Economics* 28 (1): 1–21.

Becattini, G. 1990. The Marshallian industrial districts as a socio-economic notion. In: *Industrial Districts and Inter-Firm Cooperation in Italy*, 37–51. Geneva: International Institute for Labour Studies.

Bergman, E.M. 2006. The sustainability of clusters and regions at Austria's accession edge. In *The environment and sustainable development in the New Central Europe*, 59–77. New York: Berghahn Books.

Bergman, E.M. 2008. Cluster life-cycles: An emerging synthesis. *Handbook of Research on Cluster Theory* 1: 114–132.

Bertolini, P., and E. Giovannetti. 2006. Industrial districts and internationalization: The case of the agri-food industry in Modena, Italy. *Entrepreneurship & Regional Development* 18 (4): 279–304.

Bonaccorsi, A. 1992. On the relationship between firm size and export intensity. *Journal of International Business Studies* 23 (4): 605–635.

Brazilian Internet Steering Committee. 2012. *ICT microenterprises 2010 – Survey on the use of information and communication technologies in Brazilian microenterprises*. São Paulo. isbn:978-85-60062-50-8.

Cannatelli, B., and F. Antoldi. 2012. The role of network facilitators in fostering trust within strategic alliances: A longitudinal case study. *Journal of Small Business & Entrepreneurship* 25 (1): 19–33.

Cardoso, F. S. 2006. A Influência da Exportação no Desenvolvimento de Arranjos Produtivos Locais de Moda no Estado do Rio de Janeiro. Rio de Janeiro, Fundação Getúlio Vargas, EBAPE. Unpublished MBA thesis.

Cassiolato, J. E., and F. Peixoto 2004. O Pólo de Moda Praia de Cabo Frio/RJ. Programa de Financiamento de Bolsas de Mestrado Vinculadas à Pesquisa "Micro e Pequenas Empresas em Arranjos Produtivos Locais no Brasil". Rio de Janeiro: SEBRAE/UFSC/NEITEC/FEPESE.

Catalan, J., and R. Ramon-Muñoz. 2013. Marshall in Iberia. Industrial districts and leading firms in the creation of competitive advantage in fashion products. *Enterprise and Society* 14 (02): 327–359.

Chetty, S., and D.B. Holm. 2000. Internationalisation of small to medium-sized manufacturing firms: A network approach. *International Business Review* 9 (1): 77–93.

Da Rocha, A. 1988. Os consórcios como alternative para exportação. In *Gerência de Exportação no Brasil,* ed. Rocha, A. (org.), 181–190. Rio de Janeiro: UFRJ; São Paulo: Atlas.

De Martino, R., D. Mc Hardy Reid, and S.C. Zygliodopoulos. 2006. Balancing localization and globalization: Exploring the impact of firm internationalization on a regional cluster. *Entrepreneurship and Regional Development* 18 (1): 1–24.

De Propris, L., and L. Lazzeretti. 2009. Measuring the decline of a Marshallian industrial district: The Birmingham jewellery quarter. *Regional Studies* 43 (9): 1135–1154.

Deboçã, L.P., and R.S. Martins. 2015. Competitive advantages from horizontal relationships in productive agglomerations: Perceptions of local agents. *Revista Brasileira de Gestão de Negócios 17* (56): 1025.

DiMaggio, P.J., and W.W. Powell. 1991. The iron cage revisited? Institutional isomorphism and collective rationality in organizational fields. In *The new institutionalism in organizational analysis*, 5–28. Chicago: The University of Chicago Press.

Dobusch, L., and E. Schüßler 2012. Theorizing path dependence: A review of positive feedback mechanisms in technology markets, regional clusters, and organizations. *Industrial and Corporate Change 22 (3): 617–647.*

Drahokoupil, J. 2012. Beyond lock-in versus evolution, towards punctuated co-evolution: On Ron Martin's 'rethinking regional path dependence'. *International Journal of Urban and Regional Research* 36 (1): 166–171.

Ellis, P. 2003. Are international trade intermediaries catalysts in economic development? A new research agenda. *Journal of International Marketing* 11 (1): 73–96.

Ferreira, M.P., A.T. Tavares, and W. Hesterly. 2006. Evolution of industry clusters through spin-offs and the role of flagship firms. In *Multinationals, clusters and innovation*, 87–106. London: Palgrave Macmillan.

Ghauri, P. 2004. Designing and conducting case studies in international business research. In *Handbook of qualitative research methods for international business*, 109–124. Cheltenham: Edward Elgar.

Greener, I. 2002. Theorising path-dependency: How does history come to matter in organizations? *Management Decision* 40 (6): 614–619.

Guerrieri, P., and C. Pietrobelli. 2004. Industrial districts' evolution and technological regimes: Italy and Taiwan. *Technovation* 24 (11): 899–914.

Iammarino, S., F. Sanna-Randaccio, and M. Savona. 2006. Obstacles to innovation and multinational firms in the Italian regions: Firm-level evidence from the third community innovation survey. In *Multinationals, clusters and innovation*, 63–83. London: Palgrave Macmillan.

IDB – Interamerican Development Bank. 2015. Reporte de estado del proyecto. BID, Fondo Multilateral de Inversiones. Internal document ATN/ME-13075-BR, June 2015.

Johanson, J., and L.G. Mattson. 1988. Internationalization in industrial systems – A network approach. In *The Internationalization of the Firm: A Reader*, 303–321. London: Academic Press.

Johanson, J., and J.E. Vahlne. 2009. The Uppsala internationalization process model revisited: From liability of foreignness to liability of outsidership. *Journal of International Business Studies* 40 (9): 1411–1431.

———. 2011. Markets as networks: Implications for strategy-making. *Journal of the Academy of Marketing Science* 39 (4): 484–491.

Jones, G., and T. Khanna. 2006. Bringing history (back) into international business. *Journal of International Business Studies* 37 (4): 453–468.
Lorenzen, M. 2001. Ties, trust, and trade: Elements of a theory of coordination in industrial clusters. *International Studies of Management & Organization* 31 (4): 14–34.
Lorenzen, M. 2005. Why do clusters change? *European Urban and Regional Studies* 12 (3): 203–208.
Maggioni, M.A. 2004. The rise and fall of industrial clusters: technology and the life cycle of region. IEB – Institut d'Economia de Barcelona Working Paper, 2004/6, Barcelona.
Mariotti, S., M. Mutinelli, and L. Piscitello. 2008. The internationalization of production by Italian industrial districts' firms: Structural and behavioural determinants. *Regional Studies* 42 (5): 719–735.
Martin, R. 2010. Roepke lecture in economic geography – Rethinking regional path dependence: Beyond lock-in to evolution. *Economic Geography* 86 (1): 1–27.
Martínez-Fernández, M.T., J. Capó-Vicedo, and T. Vallet-Bellmunt. 2012. The present state of research into industrial clusters and districts. Content analysis of material published in 1997–2006. *European Planning Studies 20* (2): 281–304.
Menzel, M.P., and D. Fornahl. 2010. Cluster life cycles – Dimensions and rationales of cluster evolution. *Industrial and Corporate Change* 19 (1): 205–238.
Meyer-Stamer, J. 1998. Path dependence in regional development: Persistence and change in three industrial clusters in Santa Catarina, Brazil. *World Development* 26 (8): 1495–1511.
Moiseichyk, A.E., T.M.M. Brum, C.H.A. Veiga, and D.B. Veiga. 2012. Desempenho importador do segmento de moda praia brasileiro: uma proposta de analise. *The Internext* 7 (2): 70–88.
Noda, T., and D.J. Collis. 2001. The evolution of intraindustry firm heterogeneity: Insights from a process study. *Academy of Management Journal* 44 (4): 897–925.
North, D.C. 1990. *Institutions, institutional change and economic performance.* Cambridge: Cambridge University Press.
Paniccia, I. 1998. One, a hundred, thousands of industrial districts. Organizational variety in local networks of small and medium-sized enterprises. *Organization Studies* 19 (4): 667–699.
Peixoto, F. 2005. *Local e os Sistemas de Inovações em Países Subdesenvolvidos: O caso do arranjo produtivo de moda praia de Cabo Frio/RJ.* Doctoral dissertation, Dissertação (Mestrado), Instituto de Economia da Universidade Federal do Rio de Janeiro, Rio de Janeiro.

Pereira, C.A.M., and P. Reis 2008. Comunicação, cultura e sustentabilidade: desenvolvimento sustentável nos APLs de Cabo Frio e Santo Antônio de Pádua. Editora E-papers.

Porter, M.E. 1998. Cluster and the New Economics of Competition. *Harvard Business Review* 76 (6):77–90

Potter, A., and H.D. Watts. 2011. Evolutionary agglomeration theory: Increasing returns, diminishing returns, and the industry life cycle. *Journal of Economic Geography* 11 (3): 417–455.

Press, K. 2006. *A life cycle for clusters?: The dynamics of agglomeration, change, and adaptation*. Heidelberg: Physica-Verlag/Springer Science & Business Media.

Sammarra, A., and F. Belussi. 2006. Evolution and relocation in fashion-led Italian districts: Evidence from two case-studies. *Entrepreneurship and Regional Development* 18 (6): 543–562.

Schmitz, H. 1999a. Global competition and local cooperation: Success and failure in the Sinos valley, Brazil. *World Development 27* (9): 1627–1650.

———. 1999b. Collective efficiency and increasing returns. *Cambridge Journal of Economics 23* (4): 465–483.

Schneiberg, M. 2006. What's on the path? Path dependence, organizational diversity and the problem of institutional change in the US economy, 1900–1950. *Socio-Economic Review* 5 (1): 47–80.

Scott, A.J. 1996. Regional motors of the global economy. *Futures* 28 (5): 391–411.

Scott, A.J., and G. Garofoli. 2007. The regional question in economic development. In *Development on the ground: Clusters, networks and regions in emerging economies*, 3–22. London: Routledge.

Sebrae/RJ. 2005. Plano estratégico – Pólo de moda praia de Cabo Frio e Região. Internal document, fevereiro de 2005.

———. 2008. Diagnóstico das empresas do projeto: Polo de confecção de Cabo Frio e Região. Rio de Janeiro: Sebrae, Área de Estratégias e Diretrizes. Internal document.

Sharma, D.D., and A. Blomstermo. 2003. The internationalization process of born globals: A network view. *International Business Review* 12 (6): 739–753.

Shin, D.H., and R. Hassink. 2011. Cluster life cycles: The case of the shipbuilding industry cluster in South Korea. *Regional Studies* 45 (10): 1387–1402.

Simões, K. 2015. Marcas apostam em coleções de luxo. *Valor*, 30.01.2015, p. F2.

Swann, G.P. 1998. Towards a model of clustering in high-technology industries. In *The dynamics of industrial clustering*, 52–76. Oxford: Oxford University Press.

Sydow, Jörg, Georg Schreyögg, and Jochen Koch. 2009. Organizational path dependence: Opening the black box. *Academy of Management Review* 34 (4): 689–709.

Tichy, G. 1998. Clusters: Less dispensable and more risky than ever. In *Clusters and regional specialisation*, 226–237. London: Pion Limited.

Tomlinson, P.R., and I. Jackson. 2013. Cooperative ties and the impact of external factors upon innovation in an industrial district: Some insights from the North Staffordshire table and giftware sector. *Regional Studies* 47 (4): 580–596.

Trippl, M., and F. Tödtling. 2008. 12 cluster renewal in old industrial regions: Continuity or radical change? In *Handbook of research on cluster theory*, vol. 1, 203.

Valdaliso, J.M., A. Elola, and S. Franco. 2016. Do clusters follow the industry life cycle? Diversity of cluster evolution in old industrial regions. *Competitiveness Review* 26 (1): 66–86.

Vergne, J.P., and R. Durand. 2010. The missing link between the theory and empirics of path dependence: Conceptual clarification, testability issue, and methodological implications. *Journal of Management Studies* 47 (4): 736–759.

Villela, L.E., and L.C. Soares. 2009. Gestão participativa, informação e acesso a financiamentos no Banco do Brasil S/A, na percepção de atores locais e de empresários de micro e pequenas empresas dos APLs de Cabo Frio – RJ e Nova Friburgo – RJ. *Administração Pública e Gestão Social* 1 (3): 274–293.

Wolter, K. 2003. A life cycle for clusters? The dynamics governing regional agglomerations. Proceedings of the Conference on Clusters, Industrial Districts and Firms: The Challenge of Globalization, Modena.

Wolfe, D.A., and M.S. Gertler. 2004. Clusters from the inside and out: Local dynamics and global linkages. *Urban Studies* 41 (5–6): 1071–1093.

Zucchella, A. 2006. Local cluster dynamics: Trajectories of mature industrial districts between decline and multiple embeddedness. *Journal of Institutional Economics* 2 (01): 21–44.

# 7

# Investigating the Export Behavior of Family SMEs from Chile

Constanza Bianchi

## Introduction

Family firms represent the majority of all businesses worldwide (IFERA 2003; Shanker and Astrachan 1996). Likewise, several studies report that family small and medium-sized enterprises (SMEs) represent the majority of SMEs worldwide (Casillas et al. 2007; IFERA 2003). In fact, about 85 percent of all the firms in the European Union (EU) and the United States, and an even a greater proportion in emerging countries, are family-owned (IFERA 2003). Furthermore, they account for an enormous percentage of the employment, revenue, and gross domestic product (GDP) of most capitalist countries (Sharma et al. 1997).

Family firms have the ability to adapt to changing environments, launch products, and enter markets that investor-controlled or managerially led firms are unable to address (Dyer and Whetten 2006). Family firms have also been found to sustain more profitable businesses than

C. Bianchi (✉)
Universidad Adolfo Ibáñez, Santiago, Chile
e-mail: constanza.bianchi@uai.cl



W. Newburry et al. (eds.), *Contemporary Influences on International Business in Latin America*, AIB Latin America, https://doi.org/10.1007/978-3-319-98340-0_7

firms with other ownership structures under adverse economic conditions (Sirmon and Hitt 2003).

Furthermore, it has recently been recognized that a substantial number of family SMEs are active in the international arena (Casillas and Acedo 2005). It is this recognition that has led to family business internationalization becoming an important research area (Fernandez and Nieto 2006; Graves and Thomas 2006, 2008). In fact, among family businesses, internationalization has become a strategy for growth, and sometimes even for survival (Kontinen and Ojala 2010). However, despite the importance of family SMEs to local economies, there is limited research and very little is known about the international expansion process of family SMEs (Kontinen and Ojala 2010).

Previous research on SME internationalization has focused on industry conditions and competitive forces (Zahra 2003). Subsequently, recent research has also stressed the need to identify and examine the unique resources and capabilities attributed to family ownership that may lead to competitive advantage in family SMEs (e.g., George et al. 2005; Sciascia and Mazzola 2008; Zahra et al. 2008). Furthermore, many family SMEs belong to emerging countries. Emerging economies have had rapid growth and transformation in the past two decades, and firms from these markets are accelerating in their efforts to integrate into the global economy (Hoskisson et al. 2000). Emerging market contexts are characterized by institutional turbulence and lower levels of economic development compared to developed nations (Welsh et al. 2006). In addition, emerging markets are heterogeneous in their level of development and environmental surroundings. This can lead to differences in resources and capabilities required for the export process of emerging market firms.

Emerging market SMEs must seek to identify such resources and leverage them through capabilities in the foreign market. Firm-specific resources and capabilities are derived from managerial assets, inter-firm networks, and redeployment of resources (Eisenhardt and Martin 2000; Luo 2003). Country-specific resources are derived from the resource endowments of countries, including country of origin image and their institutional environment (Elango and Pattnaik 2007; Javalgi and White 2002). Thus, in the international context, emerging market SMEs will have a combination of firm-specific and country-specific resources and capabilities.

Specifically, firm-level and managerial factors that may increase or deter export levels for emerging-market, family-owned SMEs have not yet been addressed thoroughly and there is a specific need to gain a better understanding of the differences in firm and managerial level factors between exporters and non-exporters. Furthermore, Chile is a country market that has been under-researched, especially in relation to its family owned exporters. Thus, an important goal of this research is to identify perceived barriers to exports as well as firm and managerial capabilities that differentiate family exporters from non-exporters. Overall, the objective of this study is to identify key factors differentiating between exporters and non-exporters for Chilean family SMEs.

The findings of this study contribute to strengthen and extend traditional theories of family SME internationalization and export marketing to an emerging market context. The findings also have important implications for export promotion agencies, governments, and family businesses because they identify factors stimulating firms' exports and the barriers they face entering and operating in foreign markets (Leonidou 2004). In addition, this is in line with a recent call for more research on emerging markets such as Eastern Europe, Central Asia and Latin America (Leonidou et al. 2010).

The remainder of the chapter is organized as follows; the next section will look at the literature surrounding exporting behavior and emerging markets. Following this, the chapter will address the research method and then present the results from the findings. The chapter will end with a discussion of the findings and some concluding remarks.

## Literature Review

Drawing on Fernandez and Nieto (2006), a family SME can be conceptualized as a small or medium-sized enterprise that belongs to a family with one or more members in managerial positions and is also viewed by the firm as a family SME. The feature that makes a family business different from a non-family business is the involvement of the family in the ownership and management of the firm; a family business is a combination of the reciprocal economic and non-economic values created through a combination of the family and the business systems in place (Habbershon and Williams 1999).

Furthermore, the growing economic globalization provides new opportunities for family SMEs to internationalize (Menéndez-Requero 2005). Family SMEs are found to internationalize their businesses after consolidating their positions in their domestic markets (Fernandez and Nieto 2006; Graves and Thomas 2006, 2008). Operating in overseas markets allow firms to gain economies of scale and scope, as well as a prestigious image that will assist in the domestic market (Lages and Montgomery 2004).

Exporting represents the most popular, fastest, and easiest way for many companies from emerging markets to internationalize (Leonidou et al. 2007). Exporting has been used as a strategy by firms for market development by achieving economies of scale, and enabling them to become more competitive in the wider marketplace (Chitakornkijsil 2009). There is vast research conducted on the export behavior of firms (Katsikeas et al. 1996; Leonidou and Katsikeas 1996; Leonidou et al. 2002; Rialp et al. 2005). These studies have focused on different aspects of the firm's export performance such as: firm and managerial characteristics that impact on export performance (e.g., Leonidou et al. 1998), the impact of firm size and age (Williams 2011; Zou and Stan 1998), and factors that stimulate the decision to initiate export (Bilkey 1978), among other issues.

The different factors that may influence family SME exporting decisions have been studied by a number of family business scholars (e.g., Casillas and Acedo 2005; Crick et al. 2006; Davis and Harveston 2000; Fernandez and Nieto 2006; Gallo and Pont 1996; Graves and Thomas 2006, 2008; Okoroafo 1999; Sciascia and Mazzola 2008; Zahra 2003). However, there has been mixed results with regard to the determinant factors in internationalization of family SMEs as mentioned earlier (Sciascia and Mazzola 2008). When we examine the influence of ownership on internationalization, this study suggests that we may need to look beyond the level of ownership possession and utilization of resources that are attributed to family ownership and that led to competitive advantages (Sirmon and Hitt 2003; Zahra 2003).

Family involvement in management has been seen as an important factor in the internationalization processes of family firms (Bell et al.

2004; Claver et al. 2008; Kontinen and Ojala 2010). According to George et al. (2005), owners generally appear to be risk averse, which negatively affects the scale and scope of internationalization. Further, the entry of external owners, such as venture capitalists, is found to significantly increase the scale and scope of internationalization (Graves and Thomas 2004). The factors enhancing the internationalization of family firms include a general long-term orientation, and speed in decision making. In addition, it has been found that family businesses that are likely to be more successful in international expansion are those with a willingness to use information technology, a capability for innovation, and a commitment to internationalization (Kontinen and Ojala 2010). Generally speaking, the entry on the scene of new generations has been seen as having a positive influence on internationalization, although generational change has sometimes had no influence, or even a negative influence, on internationalization (Graves and Thomas 2008).

## Theoretical Framework

Theoretical approaches to internationalization have predominantly focused on firms located in developed markets, especially the United States, Europe, and Japan, with less knowledge about firms from the emerging markets (e.g., Katsikeas et al. 1996; Luo and Peng 1999). Emerging markets are generally defined as low-income, rapid-growth countries using economic liberalization as their primary engine of growth (Hoskisson et al. 2000; Peng and Luo 2000). These market contexts are characterized by institutional turbulence and lower levels of economic development compared to developed nations (Welsh et al. 2006). Thus, firms from emerging markets are not known for having the most innovative technology, and they also experience shortages of financial capital, which hinders the implementation of marketing strategies in international markets (Arnold and Quelch 1998; Wright et al. 2005). For example, although Chile is one of the most developed and competitive countries in Latin America, it has a relatively small domestic market and lower levels of competitiveness than more developed markets.

This study draws on the theoretical perspective of the resource-based view (RBV) (Barney 1991; Wernerfelt 1984), which views firms as unique bundles of resources that provide the basis upon which a competitive advantage can be pursued (Barney 1991). A firm's resources include all assets, capabilities, organizational processes, information, and knowledge controlled by the firm that enables the implementation of successful relationships. According to RBV, firms that possess resources that are valuable, rare, inimitable, and non-substitutable can achieve a sustainable competitive advantage by implementing value-creating strategies that are difficult for competitors to duplicate (Barney 1991).

Furthermore, while possessing resources is important, RBV suggests that capabilities are a source of inimitable and sustainable competitive advantage to the firm because they transform resources into products and services superior to those of competitors (Amit and Schoemaker 1993; Makadok 2001). Capabilities enable firms to create economic rent more effectively than rivals by enhancing the productivity of firm resources (Amit and Schoemaker 1993). Research suggests that activities such as acquiring, coordinating, and integrating resources from external and partner organizations can enhance firm performance (Ethiraj et al. 2005; Teece et al. 1997). Thus, capabilities are defined as the firm's abilities to absorb, integrate, and transform internal and external resources into sustainable competitive advantages that, in turn, drive superior performance (Amit and Schoemaker 1993; Sirmon et al. 2007; Teece et al. 1997).

Several studies have identified that export development is more likely to occur in a firm possessing certain firm-specific and managerial attributes than in one lacking them (Aaby and Slater 1989; Cavusgil and Naor 1987). Other studies have identified the importance of managerial attitudes in developing internationalization strategies (Andersson 2000; Calof and Beamish 1995). For example, senior management with a foreign market orientation has been considered an important factor in explaining the export growth of firms (Cavusgil and Nevin 1981). Furthermore, management attributes such as language skills and knowledge have been found to aid top managers to compete successfully in international markets (Chadee and Kumar 2001). Similarly, Brooks and Rosson (1982) find that the type and level of education is important for international growth. Ethnic background (Simmonds and Smith 1968), command of foreign language(s) (Swift 1991), and the age of the manager (Bilkey 1978) are also found to be positively correlated with exporting.

Other important managerial attributes identified are managerial perceptions of benefits and costs (Forsgren and Hagström 2007) and knowledge in export matters (Cavusgil and Zou 1994). Research has also found that domestically oriented managers were more risk averse than internationally oriented managers (Shaw and Darroch 2004).

Overall, the theoretical premise of the study is that exporting for emerging market firms is largely dependent on the resources and capabilities developed and acquired by these firms, in order to expand their source of competitive advantage to new international markets. The literature proposes that market knowledge, networks with home and host actors, and government support may generate unique capabilities for firms from emerging markets and help them compete against more resourceful firms from developed nations.

Although the previous literature does a good job of identifying the general drivers and factors that may increase exporting, there is a need to understand more specifically firm-level variables and managerial characteristics that affect export behavior of family SMEs from an emerging market. Thus, based on the above literature review the following research questions can be formulated: (1) *what factors are perceived to aid or inhibit export market expansion for family SMEs from emerging markets?* (2) *What firm-level factors and managerial capabilities differentiate Chilean family SME exporters from non-exporters?*

## Methods

An online survey was applied to family SMEs from Chile between September and November, 2013. The sample frame was derived from the largest directory of Chilean companies (http://www.sofofa.cl/Net/DirectorioIndustrial), which publishes a list of more than 2000 firms and their detailed contact information. Managers of these companies were contacted through email to solicit their participation in the survey and also to identify the key informants and make sure that the firm was a family business. A pre-tested Chilean version of the questionnaire was sent to the participants. A two-stage e-mail sent out with follow-up telephone calls yielded a total of 89 responses. After eliminating two surveys with missing data, a total of 87 responses were used for the data analysis.

The key informants for the study were the owners or managers responsible for the export decisions of the firm. In this sample, a total of 87 percent of the informants were top managers of the firms, while the remainder of the respondents were senior and professional employees involved with the firm's decision process to export or not to export.

The questionnaire was pre-tested by a small number of exporters in Chile to refine the wording, readability, and clarity of the measures before conducting the final survey. To reduce the common method bias, we use semantic differential scales and 5-point Likert-type scales (Podsakoff et al. 2003). The questionnaire examines the year of establishment, number of employees, and exporting status (Philp 1998). Furthermore, measures of managerial perceptions/experiences regarding general benefits derive from Sullivan and Bauerschmidt (1991); managerial perceptions regarding barriers were adopted from Leonidou and Katsikeas (1996); and the measure of costs were adopted from Sullivan and Bauerschmidt (1991) and Katsikeas and Morgan (1994). Finally, measures associated with exporting and management profile were adopted from Li (2001). The key informant was the manager most responsible for the decision to export or not to export within the firm. The results of the study are presented using a frequency distribution and t-test analysis using SPSS software.

## Findings

In this section, the findings of the study are discussed. These findings report the summary statistics and the following indicators: length of time within the industry, number of employees, international markets, perceived benefits and advantages of exporting, factors inhibiting export activity, firm and management commitment, and managerial characteristics.

### Descriptive Information of Participating Firms

The results of the survey show that the average age of family SMEs was 23.5 years. Only two firms have been in existence for over 100 years, 63 percent have been in existence for less than 20 years, and 33 percent of the firms have been in existence less than 10 years. The data also shows a significant difference in the average length of time within the industry between exporters (30.9 years) and non-exporters (13.6 years). Secondly, the survey showed that 17 percent had more than 100 employees, while 78 percent had less than 50 employees, and 49 percent had 10 or less employees. In addition, there was a significant difference between established exporters and the size of the firm, with the larger firms playing a dominant role in exporting.

More than 79 percent of the respondents had an Internet site that was initially used for marketing their products or services. The findings of this study also show that the first international markets were identified as United States (29 percent), Peru (6 percent), Mexico (6 percent), and the UK (6 percent), which includes two distant markets as opposed to neighboring countries in the South American region. The most recently entered overseas markets listed by the survey respondents were the Chinese, US, and Peruvian markets. The results of the survey also indicate that these firms on average derived 53 percent of their revenue from international markets. Nearly 28 percent of the exporters within the respondents derived more than 90 percent of their income from international sales. This is possibly an indication of the high reliance on export markets due to the limited market and the relatively low prices in Chile.

## Benefits of Exporting

Respondents were asked to indicate what they considered to be the benefits of exporting as a marketing strategy. The most important benefits of exporting identified by the participant firms were to *diversify markets*, *increase profitability*, *exploit economies of scale*, and *overcome a limited home market*. There were no significant differences between exporters and non-exporters on the benefits of exporting; although overall scores were higher for exporters than non-exporters. Table 7.1 summarizes the findings of this question.

**Table 7.1** Benefits of exporting

| Benefits of exporting (Sullivan and Bauerschmidt 1991) | Mean (sd.) exporters ($n = 47$) | Mean (sd.) non-exporters ($n = 40$) | t-test for equality of means (sig/t.) |
|---|---|---|---|
| Diversify its markets | 4.64<br>(0.560) | 4.63<br>(0.568) | 0.915<br>(−0.107) |
| Utilize excess production capacity | 3.83<br>(1.14) | 3.64<br>(0.987) | 0.413<br>(0.823) |
| Reduce the impact of a domestic economic turndown | 4.00<br>(1.02) | 3.77<br>(1.05) | 0.315<br>(1.011) |
| Overcome a limited home market | 4.15<br>(0.935) | 4.21<br>(1.02) | 0.774<br>(−0.289) |
| Add to its overall profitability | 4.53<br>(0.693) | 4.51<br>(0.621) | 0.913<br>(0.109) |
| Gain a prestigious image which would help its domestic performance | 4.20<br>(0.947) | 4.09<br>(0.855) | 0.563<br>(0.580) |
| Exploit economies of scale | 4.20<br>(0.947) | 4.19<br>(0.924) | 0.967<br>(0.041) |

Means significantly different between exporters and non-exporters, t-values in brackets: results significant at $*p < 0.05$, $**p < 0.001$

## Firm Resource and Capabilities

In the second section of the questionnaire, respondents were asked to indicate the importance of 11 "firm-specific" factors that were perceived by managers to enhance their firm's export activity. As seen in Table 7.2, the three firm-specific factors are *the high quality of products*, *long-term relationships with business partners*, and *the ability to embrace new business ideas or management methods*. There was a significant difference between exporters and non-exporters on one factor: product's price—where evaluations were significantly higher for exporters.

## Factors Inhibiting Export Activity

The third section of the survey contained a set of questions designed to investigate managerial perceptions regarding inhibitors of export activity. Respondent firms identified dealing with *exchange rate variability*, *selecting a reliable foreign distributor*, and *limited government support to encourage*

**Table 7.2** Firms resources and capabilities

| Resources and capabilities (Sullivan and Bauerschmidt 1991) | Mean (sd.) exporters (*n* = 47) | Mean (sd.) non-exporters (*n* = 40) | t-test for equality of means (sig/t.) |
|---|---|---|---|
| Products' price | 4.11<br>(0.840) | 3.50<br>(1.36) | **0.013***<br>**(−2.543)** |
| Perceived high quality of products | 4.68<br>(0.783) | 4.58<br>(0.813) | 0.539<br>(−0.617) |
| Unique technology/ know-how | 3.87<br>(0.969) | 3.45<br>(1.19) | 0.073<br>(−1.818) |
| Quality packaging | 3.70<br>(0.931) | 3.55<br>(1.01) | 0.467<br>(−0.730) |
| Marketing skills | 3.66<br>(0.915) | 3.80<br>(0.939) | 0.483<br>(0.705) |
| Innovative production skills | 3.96<br>(0.779) | 3.78<br>(1.07) | 0.362<br>(−0.916) |
| Well-established networks of distributors | 4.09<br>(0.855) | 3.78<br>(1.27) | 0.180<br>(−1.352) |
| Well-established online sales | 2.89<br>(1.32) | 3.33<br>(1.35) | 0.136<br>(1.503) |
| Extensive range of products | 3.02<br>(1.03) | 2.90<br>(1.17) | 0.609<br>(−0.531) |
| Brand identity | 3.94<br>(0.870) | 4.05<br>(1.05) | 0.579<br>(0.557054) |
| Long-term relationships with business partners | 4.57<br>(0.617) | 4.43<br>(0.675) | 0.284<br>(−1.079) |
| Ability to embrace new business ideas/management methods | 4.23<br>(0.666) | 4.28<br>(0.716) | 0.783<br>(0.276) |
| Well-established company credo or mission statement | 3.91<br>(0.996) | 3.83<br>(1.10) | 0.691<br>(−0.399) |
| Close relationship with the founding family | 3.66<br>(1.05) | 3.45<br>(1.06) | 0.358<br>(−0.924) |

Means significantly different between exporters and non-exporters, t-values in brackets: results significant at $*p < 0.05$, $**p < 0.001$

*exports* as the major inhibitors to exporting. This is possibly a reflection of the recent appreciation of the peso or the decline of the United States dollar (USD) which has strongly affected their profitability. There were significant differences between exporters and non-exporters on several factors inhibiting export activity. Non-exporters scored the following factors significantly higher: management's lack of knowledge and experience, lack of financial resources, legal and regulatory barriers, unfamiliar foreign business practices, difficulties collecting payments from foreign markets, problem in selecting a reliable foreign distributor, and inaccurate market information. These results suggest that non-exporters perceive the same inhibitors as exporters, but they seem much stronger and more difficult to overcome by non-exporters which are usually smaller in size. The responses to these questions are listed in Table 7.3.

For the following section, responses from 11 questions helped gauge possible costs that could inhibit exporting activities. The most important costs identified by the overall sample of firms were; *financing new plant capacity*, *employing managers with international expertise*, and *labor cost in Chile*. There were significant differences between exporters and non-exporters on several costs as inhibitors of exporting, with non-exporters rating significantly higher the following factors: compliance with export regulations, financing new plant capacity, employing managers with export experience, and export documentation and procedures. The evaluation scores are listed in Table 7.4.

## Managerial Factors Driving Export Activity

This question asked respondents their perceptions regarding managerial factors enhancing export activity. Respondents identified the following: *responding to changing needs of customers through close regular contacts*, *constantly looking to develop new business, products and services,* and *maintaining good relationships with current business partners* as the major enhancing factors for export activity. There were no significant differences between exporters and non-exporters.

## Characteristics of Managers

Finally, the last section of the survey identified the characteristics of a firm's main decision maker. This information was collected by focusing on managerial attributes as outlined in Table 7.5. The data shows (Table 7.6) that most respondents were male, and 100 percent of the managers were tertiary educated. In addition, firms that were exporting had managers that were much more skilled in export matters, and also

**Table 7.3** Factors inhibiting export activity

| Our firm's export activity is or could be inhibited by: Scale adopted from Leonidou and Katsikeas (1996) | Mean (sd.) exporters (*n* = 47) | Mean (sd.) non-exporters (*n* = 40) | t-test for equality of means (sig/t.) |
|---|---|---|---|
| Low priority afforded to export market developments | 2.45 (1.34) | 2.80 (1.34) | 0.226 (1.220) |
| Management's lack of knowledge and experience | 2.53 (1.43) | 3.58 (1.38) | **0.001**** **(3.454)** |
| The limited quantities of stocks for market expansion | 2.85 (1.20) | 3.13 (1.24) | 0.299 (1.045) |
| The lack of financial resources | 3.19 (1.36) | 4.00 (1.17) | **0.004*** **(2.936)** |
| Limited government support to encourage exports | 3.45 (1.28) | 3.83 (1.17) | 0.158 (1.425) |
| Extremely low prices required to gain volume sales | 3.26 (1.15) | 3.63 (1.25) | 0.156 (1.433) |
| Extensive legal and regulatory barriers | 3.28 (1.28) | 3.68 (1.16) | 0.135 (1.508) |
| Exchange rate variability | 4.02 (0.967) | 3.93 1.07 | 0.661 (−0.440) |
| Unfamiliar foreign business practices | 3.11 (1.10) | 3.65 (1.14) | **0.027*** **(2.246)** |
| Difficulties collecting payments from foreign markets | 3.09 (1.26) | 3.75 (1.10) | **0.011*** **(2.589)** |
| Problems in selecting a reliable foreign distributor | 3.40 (1.09) | 4.18 (1.13) | **0.002**** **(3.222)** |
| Risks involved in selling abroad | 3.43 (1.06) | 3.70 (1.11) | 0.242 (1.177) |
| Inadequate or inaccurate market information | 3.28 (1.02) | 3.73 (1.22) | 0.065 (1.872) |
| The lack of demand for the types of products we produce | 2.57 (1.17) | 2.98 (1.21) | 0.122 (1.564) |
| Our firm's lack of cultural understanding | 2.62 (1.05) | 2.88 (1.18) | 0.285 (1.077) |
| The impact of the global crisis | 3.04 (1.12) | 3.23 (1.25) | 0.475 (0.711) |

Means significantly different between exporters and non-exporters, t values in brackets: results significant at $*p < 0.05$, $**p < 0.001$

**Table 7.4** Cost factors inhibiting exports

| Our firm's export activity is inhibited by the high cost of: Scale adopted from Katsikeas and Morgan (1994) | Mean (sd.) exporters (*n* = 47) | Mean (sd.) non-exporters (*n* = 40) | t-test for equality of means (sig/t.) |
|---|---|---|---|
| Labor in Chile | 3.47 | 3.38 | 0.743 |
| | (1.21) | 1.43 | (−0.329) |
| Domestic transport | 3.15 | 3.33 | 0.517 |
| | (1.16) | 1.37 | (0.650) |
| International shipping/airfreight | 3.21 | 3.48 | 0.319 |
| | (1.22) | 1.22 | (1.002) |
| Raw materials | 3.47 | 3.10 | 0.142 |
| | (1.02) | 1.30 | (−1.482) |
| Public utilities | 3.47 | 3.23 | 0.338 |
| | (1.06) | 1.29 | (−0.964) |
| Domestic government charges | 2.96 | 3.10 | 0.571 |
| | (1.16) | 1.17 | (0.568) |
| Insurance associated with exports | 2.94 | 3.23 | 0.249 |
| | (1.07) | 1.25 | (1.160) |
| Compliance with stringent export regulations | 3.00 | 3.45 | 0.079 |
| | (1.10) | 1.26 | (1.776) |
| Financing new plant capacity | 3.43 | 3.95 | **0.048*** |
| | (1.13) | 1.30 | **(2.007)** |
| Employing managers with stringent export skills/experience | 3.13 | 3.78 | 0.010 |
| | (1.17) | 1.09 | (2.643) |
| Export documentation and procedures | 3.04 | 3.70 | **0.007*** |
| | (1.17) | 1.02 | **(2.759)** |

Means significantly different between exporters and non- exporters, t-values in brackets: results significant at $*p < 0.05$, $**p < 0.001$

had more experience in exporting than that of non-exporters. This is an important finding, as it indicates that export promotion agencies can help develop commitment to exporting by providing appropriate training and information on export matters.

## Discussion and Conclusions

This study attempts to examine and identify the key factors perceived by family SME from Chile as enhancing or inhibiting the export activities of their firms as well as the key characteristics of the decision makers within the Chilean marketplace. In addition, the objective of this study was to

**Table 7.5** Firm factors as drivers of exports

| Our firm's export activity is enhanced by: Scale adopted from Katsikeas and Morgan (1994) | Mean (sd.) exporters (*n* = 47) | Mean (sd.) non-exporters (*n* = 40) | t-test for equality of means (sig/t.) |
|---|---|---|---|
| Our tradition and being cautious about business expansion | 3.60 (0.970) | 3.88 (0.822) | 0.155 (1.434) |
| Building a consistent brand image | 4.23 (0.865) | 4.50 (0.679) | 0.119 (1.574) |
| Sharing the company history and philosophy with employees | 4.04 (0.658) | 4.23 (0.832) | 0.257 (1.142) |
| Constantly looking to develop new business, products and services | 4.47 (0.620) | 4.55 (0.597) | 0.534 (0.625) |
| Accumulating unique new technology/know-how | 4.11 (0.759) | 4.18 (0.984) | 0.715 (0.367) |
| Protecting and strengthening our own technologies/know-how | 4.13 (0.679) | 4.15 (1.09) | 0.908 (0.116) |
| Keeping up to date/modernizing management/methods/processes | 4.30 (0.657) | 4.18 (0.931) | 0.474 (−0.719) |
| Developing new business partners (suppliers and distributors) | 4.34 (0.635) | 4.38 (0.807) | 0.528 (−0.634) |
| Maintaining good relationships with current business partners | 4.51 (0.505) | 4.43 (0.747) | 0.958 (−0.053) |
| Responding to changing needs of customers through close regular contacts | 4.53 (0.620) | 4.53 (0.599) | 0.274 (1.101) |
| Not making radical changes to core products | 3.62 (0.922) | 3.85 (1.05) | 0.104 (1.643) |
| Having succession planning to keep the business within the family (or privately-held) | 3.26 (1.09) | 3.65 (1.15) | .0.687 (0.405) |
| Participating in international trade shows | 4.15 (0.834) | 4.23 (0.920) | **0.037*** **(2.115)** |

Means significantly different between exporters and non- exporters, t values in brackets: results significant at $*p < 0.05$, $**p < 0.001$

compare and identify factors differentiating exporters and non-exporters. This study makes several contributions to the fields of SME internationalization and family business. The findings of this study mainly contribute by identifying key firm and managerial characteristics that distinguish exporters from non-exporters in Chile, which has not been addressed by previous research.

**Table 7.6** Characteristics of respondents

| Scale adopted from Li (2001) | Mean (sd.) exporters (*n* = 47) (%) | Mean (sd.) non-exporters (*n* = 40) (%) | t-test for equality of means (sig/t.) |
|---|---|---|---|
| Male | 91.5 | 75.0 | 0.958 (–0.053) |
| Female | 8.5 | 25.0 | |
| Completed tertiary education | 100 | 100 | – |
| Received training in exporting | 82.9 | 52.5 | **0.004* (2.925)** |
| Fluency in a foreign language/s | 91.5 | 65.0 | **0.002* (3.178)** |
| Previously worked for a company that exported | 57.4 | 35.0 | **0.037* (2.120)** |
| Person born abroad | 10.6 | 10.0 | 0.924 (0.096) |
| Has lived abroad | 61.7 | 40.0 | **0.044* (2.044)** |
| Have family abroad | 57.4 | 50.0 | 0.493 (0.688) |

Means significantly different between exporters and non- exporters, t-values in brackets: results significant at $*p < 0.05$, $**p < 0.001$

According to Czinkota and Johnston (1981) a high level of proactive export commitment is crucial, otherwise stagnation and sometimes even setbacks and failures occur when exporting. Proactive motivations refer to motivations that are aimed toward strategic change, such as profit advantage, unique products, technological advantage, and economies of scale, as opposed to reactive motivations that include competitive pressures, over-production and excess capacity, and declining domestic markets or saturated markets. According to the data, Chilean managers show a proactive attitude toward exporting indicated by the main benefits of exporting perceived by them. Proactive exporters perform better in terms of sales volume, follow more cohesive export marketing strategies, and obtain more monetary firm sales that seek information-seeking activities (Czinkota and Johnston 1981; Katsikeas and Piercy 1993).

Three major barriers for non-exporters were the lack of financial resources, problems in selecting a reliable foreign distributor, and limited government support to encourage exports. These results are consistent with previous research on exporting which suggests that main barriers for exporters, especially for firms from developing markets, include lack of experience in foreign markets, deficiencies in managerial skills, and narrow product lines that preclude their taking advantage of economies of scale and scope

(Arteaga-Ortiz and Fernandez-Ortiz 2010; Aulakh et al. 2000; Leonidou 2004; Leonidou and Katsikeas 1996). Furthermore, inhibiting factors found in international studies (e.g., the cost of transport, raw materials and other inputs) are not significant barriers within the Chilean industry, possibly due to a more competitive economic environment that is emerging in Chile. Another constraint that was identified by respondents was the high cost of financing new plant capacity and the rise of labor costs.

This study makes a significant contribution to the literature in terms of understanding the export orientation of the Chilean industry focusing on management perceptions and firm characteristics. While there is evidence for a staged approach—to export market development through a first expansion strategy within Chile prior to targeting international markets—the first international markets were not physically close markets as has been reported in other studies. The largest markets for Chilean exporters were physically distant markets.

While there was a general agreement between exporters and non-exporters on the benefits of exporting and the factors enhancing firm competitiveness, there were significant differences between both groups in terms of the main inhibitors of exporting. Unlike some of the earlier international studies which identified cost of labor, transport, raw materials and other inputs as inhibiting factors for internationalization, this study did not identify them as any serious cost-based inhibitors. Although both groups perceive the same inhibitors of exporting, such as selecting a reliable distributor, lack of financial resources, and management's lack of knowledge and experience, the inhibitors are perceived as being much more relevant and difficult to overcome by non-exporters. Particularly, financing a new plant capacity and employing managers with export experience were considered as extremely relevant for non-exporters and main cost inhibitors for internationalization.

Overall, the data suggests that non-exporters mainly lack financial and managerial resources and capabilities to begin the export process, rather than confronting environmental constraints. The data suggests that there appears to be very few domestic barriers for export market development for Chilean firms possibly due to a more competitive economic environment that is prevailing in Chile. Moreover, most of the barriers are related to firm and managerial characteristics.

## Managerial Contribution

The major findings of this study point to a positive outlook with regard to internationalization of the industry based on positive managerial perceptions of exporting. Even the majority of non-exporters indicated their need and desire to develop export markets. In order to assist these companies to begin exporting, an important suggestion for governmental bodies and public policy is to provide resources and training for export related matters, such as funding and developing contacts with reliable distributors. Exporters were significantly less concerned about these issues than non-exporters. This was one of the key attributes that differentiated the exporters and the non-exporters. Therefore, there is scope for export promotion agencies to provide professional development courses in export management to assist novice exporters. It is also possible for government and industry-related agencies to facilitate mentoring of managers within smaller firms by some of the experienced managers within the Chilean industry. In addition, international managerial experience can provide additional capabilities for non-exporter firms. Finally, universities and other organizations can provide professional development courses in export management to assist novice exporters, or there is scope to provide mentoring to smaller firms by forming a network of cooperatives (Giuliani et al. 2010).

## Limitations and Future Research

Like many other studies examining the export orientation of firms, there is a bias toward respondents from companies that have internationalized. This study has provided a better understanding of the factors perceived to inhibit or enhance export expansion within the Chilean industry. However, given the limited sample size, the next step is to undertake follow-up interviews to probe in-depth factors identified in this study as aiding or inhibiting the export process. In addition, a suitable model of export behavior for emerging market firms can be developed.

## References

Aaby, N.E., and S.F. Slater. 1989. Management influences on export performance: A review of the empirical literature 1978–1988. *International Marketing Review* 6 (4): 7–26.

Amit, R., and P.J. Schoemaker. 1993. Strategic assets and organizational rent. *Strategic Management Journal* 14 (1): 33–46.

Andersson, S. 2000. The internationalization of the firm from an entrepreneurial perspective. *International Studies of Management & Organization* 30 (1): 63–92.

Arnold, D.J., and J.A. Quelch. 1998. New strategies in emerging markets. *MIT Sloan Management Review 40* (1): 7.

Arteaga-Ortiz, J., and R. Fernández-Ortiz. 2010. Why don't we use the same export barrier measurement scale? An empirical analysis in small and medium-sized enterprises. *Journal of Small Business Management* 48 (3): 395–420.

Aulakh, P.S., M. Rotate, and H. Teegen. 2000. Export strategies and performance of firms from emerging economies: Evidence from Brazil, Chile, and Mexico. *Academy of Management Journal* 43 (3): 342–361.

Barney, J. 1991. Firm resources and sustained competitive advantage. *Journal of Management* 17 (1): 99–120.

Bell, J., D. Crick, and S. Young. 2004. Small firm internationalization and business strategy an exploratory study of 'knowledge-intensive' and 'traditional' manufacturing firms in the UK. *International Small Business Journal* 22 (1): 23–56.

Bilkey, W.J. 1978. An attempted integration of the literature on the export behavior of firms. *Journal of International Business Studies* 9 (1): 33–46.

Brooks, M.R., and P.J. Rosson. 1982. A study of export behavior of small and medium-sized manufacturing firms in three Canadian provinces. In *Export management: An international context*, 39–54. New York: Praeger.

Calof, J.L., and P.W. Beamish. 1995. Adapting to foreign markets: Explaining internationalization. *International Business Review* 4 (2): 115–131.

Casillas, J.C., and F.J. Acedo. 2005. Internationalisation of Spanish family SMEs: An analysis of family involvement. *International Journal of Globalisation and Small Business* 1 (2): 134–151.

Casillas, J.C., F.J. Acedo, and A.M. Moreno. 2007. *International entrepreneurship in family businesses*. Cheltenham: Edward Elgar Publishing.

Cavusgil, S.T., and J. Naor. 1987. Firm and management characteristics as discriminators of export marketing activity. *Journal of Business Research* 15 (3): 221–235.

Cavusgil, S.T., and J.R. Nevin. 1981. Internal determinants of export marketing behavior: An empirical investigation. *Journal of Marketing Research* 18: 114–119.

Cavusgil, S.T., and S. Zou. 1994. Marketing strategy-performance relationship: An investigation of the empirical link in export market ventures. *The Journal of Marketing* 58: 1–21.

Chadee, D., and R. Kumar. 2001. Sustaining the international competitive advantage of Asian firms: A conceptual framework and research propositions. *Asia Pacific Journal of Management* 18 (4): 461–480.

Chitakornkijsil, P. 2009. SMEs, entrepreneurship and development strategies. *International Journal of Organizational Innovation (Online)* 1 (4): 127.

Claver, E., L. Rienda, and D. Quer. 2008. Family firms' risk perception: Empirical evidence on the internationalization process. *Journal of Small Business and Enterprise Development* 15 (3): 457–471.

Crick, D., R. Bradshaw, and S. Chaudhry. 2006. "Successful" internationalising UK family and non-family-owned firms: A comparative study. *Journal of Small Business and Enterprise Development* 13 (4): 498–512.

Czinkota, M.R., and W.J. Johnston. 1981. Segmenting US firms for export development. *Journal of Business Research* 9 (4): 353–365.

Davis, P.S., and P.D. Harveston. 2000. Internationalization and organizational growth: The impact of Internet usage and technology involvement among entrepreneur-led family businesses. *Family Business Review* 13 (2): 107–120.

Dyer, W.G., and D.A. Whetten. 2006. Family firms and social responsibility: Preliminary evidence from the S&P 500. *Entrepreneurship Theory and Practice* 30 (6): 785–802.

Eisenhardt, K.M., and J.A. Martin. 2000. Dynamic capabilities: What are they? *Strategic Management Journal* 21 (10–11): 1105–1121.

Elango, B., and C. Pattnaik. 2007. Building capabilities for international operations through networks: A study of Indian firms. *Journal of International Business Studies* 38: 541–555.

Ethiraj, S.K., P. Kale, M.S. Krishnan, and J.V. Singh. 2005. Where do capabilities come from and how do they matter? A study in the software services industry. *Strategic Management Journal* 26 (1): 25–45.

Fernández, Z., and M.J. Nieto. 2006. Impact of ownership on the international involvement of SMEs. *Journal of International Business Studies* 37 (3): 340–351.

Forsgren, M., and P. Hagström. 2007. Ignorant and impatient internationalization? The Uppsala model and internationalization patterns for Internet-related firms. *Critical Perspectives on International Business* 3 (4): 291–305.

Gallo, M.A., and C.G. Pont. 1996. Important factors in family business internationalization. *Family Business Review* 9 (1): 45–59.

George, G., J. Wiklund, and S.A. Zahra. 2005. Ownership and the internationalization of small firms. *Journal of Management* 31 (2): 210–233.

Giuliani, E., A. Morrison, C. Pietrobelli, and R. Rabellotti. 2010. Who are the researchers that are collaborating with industry? An analysis of the wine sectors in Chile, South Africa and Italy. *Research Policy* 39 (6): 748–761.

Graves, C., and J. Thomas. 2004. Internationalisation of the family business: A longitudinal perspective. *International Journal of Globalisation and Small Business* 1 (1): 7–27.

———. 2006. Internationalization of Australian family businesses: A managerial capabilities perspective. *Family Business Review* 19 (3): 207–224.

———. 2008. Determinants of the internationalization pathways of family firms: An examination of family influence. *Family Business Review* 21 (2): 151–167.

Habbershon, T.G., and M.L. Williams. 1999. A resource-based framework for assessing the strategic advantages of family firms. *Family Business Review* 12 (1): 1–25.

Hoskisson, R.E., L. Eden, C.M. Lau, and M. Wright. 2000. Strategy in emerging economies. *Academy of Management Journal* 43 (3): 249–267.

International Family Enterprise Research Academy (IFERA). 2003. *Family Businesses Dominate* 16 (4): 235–240.

Javalgi, R.G., and D. Steven White. 2002. Strategic challenges for the marketing of services internationally. *International Marketing Review* 19 (6): 563–581.

Katsikeas, C.S., and R.E. Morgan. 1994. Differences in perceptions of exporting problems based on firm size and export market experience. *European Journal of Marketing* 28 (5): 17–35.

Katsikeas, C.S., and N.F. Piercy. 1993. Long-term export stimuli and firm characteristics in a European LDC. *Journal of International Marketing* 1 (3): 23–47.

Katsikeas, C.S., N.F. Piercy, and C. Ioannidis. 1996. Determinants of export performance in a European context. *European Journal of Marketing* 30 (6): 6–35.

Kontinen, T., and A. Ojala. 2010. The internationalization of family businesses: A review of extant research. *Journal of Family Business Strategy* 1 (2): 97–107.

Lages, F., and D.B. Montgomery. 2004. Export performance as an antecedent of export commitment and marketing strategy adaptation: Evidence from small and medium-sized exporters. *European Journal of Marketing* 38 (9/10): 1186–1214.

Leonidou, L.C. 2004. An analysis of the barriers hindering small business export development. *Journal of Small Business Management* 42 (3): 279–302.

Leonidou, L.C., and C.S. Katsikeas. 1996. The export development process: An integrative review of empirical models. *Journal of International Business Studies* 27 (3): 517–551.

Leonidou, L.C., C.S. Katsikeas, and N.F. Piercy. 1998. Identifying managerial influences on exporting: Past research and future directions. *Journal of International Marketing* 6: 74–102.

Leonidou, L.C., C.S. Katsikeas, and S. Samiee. 2002. Marketing strategy determinants of export performance: A meta-analysis. *Journal of Business Research* 55 (1): 51–67.

Leonidou, L.C., C.S. Katsikeas, D. Palihawadana, and S. Spyropoulou. 2007. An analytical review of the factors stimulating smaller firms to export: Implications for policy-makers. *International Marketing Review* 24 (6): 735–770.

Leonidou, L.C., B.R. Barnes, S. Spyropoulou, and C.S. Katsikeas. 2010. Assessing the contribution of leading mainstream marketing journals to the international marketing discipline. *International Marketing Review* 27 (5): 491–518.

Li, L. 2001. Networks, transactions, and resources: Hong Kong trading companies' strategic position in the China market. *Asia Pacific Journal of Management* 18 (3): 279–293.

Luo, Y. 2003. Industrial dynamics and managerial networking in an emerging market: The case of China. *Strategic Management Journal* 24 (13): 1315–1327.

Luo, Y., and M.W. Peng. 1999. Learning to compete in a transition economy: Experience, environment, and performance. *Journal of International Business Studies* 30 (2): 269–295.

Makadok, R. 2001. Toward a synthesis of the resource-based and dynamic-capability views of rent creation. *Strategic Management Journal* 22 (5): 387–401.

Menendez-Requejo, S. 2005. Growth and internationalisation of family businesses. *International Journal of Globalisation and Small Business* 1 (2): 122–133.

Okoroafo, S.C. 1999. Internationalization of family businesses: Evidence from Northwest Ohio, USA. *Family Business Review* 12 (2): 147–158.

Peng, M.W., and Y. Luo. 2000. Managerial ties and firm performance in a transition economy: The nature of a micro-macro link. *Academy of Management Journal* 43 (3): 486–501.

Philp, N.E. 1998. The export propensity of the very small enterprise (VSE). *International Small Business Journal* 16 (4): 79–93.

Podsakoff, P.M., S.B. MacKenzie, J.Y. Lee, and N.P. Podsakoff. 2003. Common method biases in behavioral research: A critical review of the literature and recommended remedies. *Journal of Applied Psychology 88* (5): 879.

Rialp, A., J. Rialp, and G.A. Knight. 2005. The phenomenon of early internationalizing firms: What do we know after a decade (1993–2003) of scientific inquiry? *International Business Review* 14 (2): 147–166.

Sciascia, S., and P. Mazzola. 2008. Family involvement in ownership and management: Exploring nonlinear effects on performance. *Family Business Review* 21 (4): 331–345.

Shanker, M.C., and J.H. Astrachan. 1996. Myths and realities: Family businesses' contribution to the US economy—A framework for assessing family business statistics. *Family Business Review* 9 (2): 107–123.

Sharma, P., J.J. Chrisman, and J.H. Chua. 1997. Strategic management of the family business: Past research and future challenges. *Family Business Review* 10 (1): 1–35.

Shaw, V., and J. Darroch. 2004. Barriers to internationalisation: A study of entrepreneurial new ventures in New Zealand. *Journal of International Entrepreneurship* 2 (4): 327–343.

Simmonds, K., and H. Smith. 1968. The first export order: A marketing innovation. *European Journal of Marketing* 2 (2): 93–100.

Sirmon, D.G., and M.A. Hitt. 2003. Managing resources: Linking unique resources, management, and wealth creation in family firms. *Entrepreneurship Theory and Practice* 27 (4): 339–358.

Sirmon, D.G., M.A. Hitt, and R.D. Ireland. 2007. Managing firm resources in dynamic environments to create value: Looking inside the black box. *Academy of Management Review* 32 (1): 273–292.

Sullivan, D., and A. Bauerschmidt. 1991. The basic concepts of international business strategy: A review and reconsideration. *MIR: Management International Review* 31: 111–124.

Swift, J.S. 1991. Foreign language ability and international marketing. *European Journal of Marketing* 25 (12): 36–49.

Teece, D.J., G. Pisano, and A. Shuen. 1997. Dynamic capabilities and strategic management. *Strategic Management Journal* 18: 509–533.

Welsh, D.H., I. Alon, and C.M. Falbe. 2006. An examination of international retail franchising in emerging markets. *Journal of Small Business Management 44* (1): 130.

Wernerfelt, B. 1984. A resource-based view of the firm. *Strategic Management Journal* 5 (2): 171–180.

Williams, D.A. 2011. Industry sector and export performance of small, locally-owned firms. *Allied Academies International Conference. Academy for Studies in International Business. Proceedings* 11 (2): 21. Jordan Whitney Enterprises, Inc.

Wright, M., I. Filatotchev, R.E. Hoskisson, and M.W. Peng. 2005. Strategy research in emerging economies: Challenging the conventional wisdom. *Journal of Management Studies* 42 (1): 1–33.

Zahra, S.A. 2003. International expansion of US manufacturing family businesses: The effect of ownership and involvement. *Journal of Business Venturing* 18 (4): 495–512.

Zahra, S.A., J.C. Hayton, D.O. Neubaum, C. Dibrell, and J. Craig. 2008. Culture of family commitment and strategic flexibility: The moderating effect of stewardship. *Entrepreneurship Theory and Practice* 32 (6): 1035–1054.

Zou, S., and S. Stan. 1998. The determinants of export performance: A review of the empirical literature between 1987 and 1997. *International Marketing Review 15* (5): 333–356.

# 8

# Acculturation Process in Cross-border M&A: A Case Study of a Brazilian Automobile Firm

Bruno de Oliveira Carvalho
and Mário Henrique Ogasavara

## Introduction

Mergers and acquisitions (M&A) are an increasingly common practice in the global market (Caiazza and Nueno 2014). M&A are considered a strategic tool that seeks to increase the growth and internationalization of firms (Dikova et al. 2010); an important mechanism to access new kinds of resources and strategic assets (Deng 2009); and a strategy to improve the poor performance of acquired companies (Angwin and Meadows 2012).

However, it should be noted that the M&A process provides great impact and expectancy of change on firms (Cartwright and Cooper 2012), which have to adapt to the modifications at all organizations levels (Stahl and Voigt 2005).

B. de Oliveira Carvalho (✉)
Unifanor Wyden, Fortaleza, Brazil
e-mail: bcarvalho@unifanor.edu.br

M. H. Ogasavara
ESPM (Escola Superior de Propaganda e Marketing), São Paulo, Brazil
e-mail: mario.ogasavara@espm.br



W. Newburry et al. (eds.), *Contemporary Influences on International Business in Latin America*, AIB Latin America, https://doi.org/10.1007/978-3-319-98340-0_8

For instance, Papadakis and Thanos (2010) measure the performance of post-merger integration and found that due to difficulties, the growth of the new firm is not significant enough to justify many changes or high investments in the M&A process. Some possible reasons for achieving poor performance are: (i) some M&A are driven by non-maximizing motives (Cartwright and Schoenberg 2006); (ii) poor choice of strategic partners (Rogan and Sorenson 2014); (iii) inappropriate prior analysis (Shrivastava 1986); (iv) lack of a careful diversification strategy (Adams and Neely 2000); (v) and lack of integration between firms involved (Schuler and Jackson 2001).

All these reasons have been extensively investigated over the past decades (Gomes et al. 2013). However, some inconsistencies exist with regard to the performance measurement of M&A in the literature, as there is no consensus on what key factors should be considered when measuring it (Papadakis and Thanos 2010).

Following this perspective of M&A performance, it emerges as a research field that links the success of M&A with the ability of acculturation of the involved firms (Nahavandi and Malekzadeh 1988; Stahl and Voigt 2008; Bajaj 2009; Sarala 2010). The M&A process comprises two types of "transformational" changes, with employees exposed to a different culture and a different way of doing things (Bajaj 2009).

According to Stahl and Voigt (2008), these cultural differences can become major obstacles to achieve the benefits of company integration. In the same vein, Weber et al. (2011) even claim that the clash between two national cultures is comparable to the clash between two organizational cultures. Barkema et al. (1996) and Shimizu et al. (2004) mentioned the term "double-layered acculturation", which is the process of the acquirer firm adapting not only to the national culture that is unfamiliar, but also dealing with a new organizational culture.

This kind of culture shock in the M&A process was observed in companies around the world among different industry sectors. It might affect the country's economy, depending on the strength of the industry. One of the sectors that has a significant share of the M&A process is the automotive industry. It ranks sixth in the manufacturing sector in terms of value of cross-border M&A purchases in the period 1990–2013 (UNCTAD

2014). In order to increase competitiveness, various automaker brands have gone through the process of M&A. For instance, Fiat acquired part of Ferrari in 1969; Volkswagen purchased Audi in the mid-sixties; Daimler-Mercedes merged with Chrysler in 1998; the acquisition made by Indian Tata Motors of Land Rover and Jaguar from Ford in 2008; Chinese Geely acquired Swedish Volvo in 2010, and so on (Jürgens 2002; Badrtalei and Bates 2007; Johnson et al. 2008; Balcet et al. 2012).

It seems that the M&A process is motivated by several factors. In the case of Geely/Volvo, for instance, the Chinese company bought the Swedish one in order to learn how to make safer and higher quality cars (Xiaohui and Haiyan 2011). Numerous other cases might be reported, each having its own special features. However, all cases have one thing in common: the process of acculturation post-M&A needs to be better examined.

During the process of M&A, regardless of how it occurs, acculturation happens to a greater or lesser degree. Berry (1997) defines acculturation as the general processes and impacts (both cultural and psychological) of intercultural contact. Back to the example of the Volvo acquisition, Xiaohui and Haiyan (2011) explained the cultural gap between both firms. While Volvo had an operating philosophy based on people and development, Geely focused on cost control and profitability.

In Brazil, the automotive industry also experienced a number of M&A transactions. Some examples include the case of Autolatina in 1987, the merger of the Brazilian operations of Volkswagen with Ford (Santana 2003), and the acquisition of Brazilian Troller by Ford (Quadros and Cansoni 2008). In addition to the rise of M&A transactions, new foreign competitors' entry in the market resulted in increased competition in the automotive sector (Scavarda et al. 2005). The automobile industry is very important to the Brazilian economy as it represented almost 25 percent of industrial gross domestic product (GDP) and 5 percent of total Brazilian GDP in 2013, reaching over US$100 billion in revenue (Anfavea 2014). In terms of global market, Brazil ranks as the fourth largest domestic market and the seventh largest producer of vehicles in the world (OICA 2014). However, it should be noted that there is a lack of studies that examine the stress involved in the acculturation process of M&A, providing an interesting field to be further researched.

Based on this context, we intend to answer the following two-part research question: how and which modes of acculturation are involved in the post-acquisition process in the automotive industry in an emerging market; and what are the cultural differences and difficulties? The aim of this study is to verify the process of acculturation considering integration and stress based on the framework proposed by Nahavandi and Malekzadeh (1988). To our knowledge, although their work is commonly cited in the literature, there is no study that empirically tests or validates this model.

This chapter develops a case study based on the acquisition process of a Brazilian firm by an American multinational company in the car industry. The data collection was obtained from in-depth interviews with managers who experienced the pre- and post-acquisition periods. A content analysis was performed in order to examine the acculturation process.

This study intends to contribute to the literature of acculturation by increasing knowledge about the cross-border M&A process involving a multinational company from a developed country, acquiring an emerging market firm in an industry sector that is well represented in the global market. It also intends to empirically test a framework that is well cited in the literature but has not been tested yet, and see its applicability in a real case. In terms of practical implications, this study intends to point out ways to prevent and reduce the stress that occurs in this change procedure, contributing to the increased performance of the M&A process.

The chapter is structured as follows. After contextualization in this introductory section, the next section will discuss the M&A process, acculturation, and presents Nahavandi and Malekzadeh's (1988) framework. In the third section, we describe the methodological procedures, following by the results and discussion. Finally, we present the conclusion, as well as some limitations and suggestions for future research.

# Theoretical Development

## Mergers and Acquisitions

The processes of merger and acquisitions (M&A) have increased in the domestic and international context and are related to economic, strategic, and financial aspects. Along with strategic alliances, M&A is an external alternative to develop innovative competencies (Hagedoorn and Duysters 2002).

M&A have attracted much interest from scholars who tried to explain and predict business results. There are a number of empirical studies analyzing M&A from diverse perspectives and paradigms, using different methods and examining different units of analysis (Cartwright and Schoenberg 2006; Meglio and Risberg 2010).

A review of the literature in the past decades shows that M&A waves follow business cycle fluctuations. In the late 1990s and early 2000s, M&A were more internationalized in their general scope, involving companies from more than one country, and they were focused on the merger of companies in the same industry segment. This movement explains many M&A within the automotive and IT industries in this period (Oberg and Holtström 2006).

With regard to Brazil, foreign companies are increasingly interested in investing in the Brazilian market through M&A. According to a KPMG survey on M&A (Motta and Coimbra 2012), foreign firms' involvement in M&A transactions surpassed that of domestic firms in 2012, representing 58 percent of such operations, particularly from the United States. In this way, foreign companies gained a strong presence in Brazil, including sectors that were traditionally dominated by Brazilian firms.

Recently, a research area in the M&A literature began to gain relevance by emphasizing the interaction between organizational cultures involved in this cross-border process (Mendenhall 2005; Teerikangas and Very 2006). According to these studies, cultural differences should be viewed with caution. Due to the number of changes that M&A bring to the organization, the adaptation of employees to the new reality takes time (Nikandrou and Papalexandris 2007) and can affect employees' behavior, which may determine the success or failure of the M&A transactions (Appelbaum et al. 2000).

According to DeCenzo, Robbins, and Verhulst (2010), culture has many functions in an organization: defining borders; creating distinctions between one organization and another; providing a sense of identity to members; making people commit themselves to collective individual interests; stimulating the stability of the social system, among others. Thus, culture is important because it unifies and maintains cohesive organization. In other words, culture defines the rules of the game and it is often deeply embedded in the company.

Therefore, acculturation has been a significant aspect to be examined in M&A deals (Sarala 2010). It collaborates in the success of the transactions by internalizing or integrating different national and organizational cultures (Shimizu et al. 2004).

## Post-acquisition Acculturation Process and Framework for Analysis

The term acculturation is defined as the set of phenomena that results from a continuous and direct contact between groups of individuals from different cultures which causes changes in the cultural initial models (patterns) of one or both groups (Cuche 1996).

Addressing the topic of post-acquisition acculturation is relevant as most research on M&A has focused on strategic and financial alignment between the acquired and acquirer firms (Nahavandi and Malekzadeh 1988) and little is known about the process of organizational acculturation that occurs post-acquisition (Sarala 2010).

Weber et al. (2011) analyzed the combined effect of corporate culture and national culture among the various integration studies in the post-acquisition period. They developed a theoretical model based on a multidisciplinary approach using strategic management, international management, and anthropology literatures. In addition, they also examined how the five dimensions of national culture proposed by Hofstede (1991) impact the post-acquisition integration process.

In a later study, Weber and Tarba (2012) focused on the analysis of organizational culture and presented a framework for conducting a review of organizational culture during the various stages of the M&A process.

As mentioned earlier, M&A transactions are widely applied in the automobile industry. Xiaohui and Haiyan (2011) examined the acculturation process by making a comparison of Chinese Geely and Swedish Volvo. They identified institutional culture, material culture, and spiritual culture, and proposed a method that integrates these three aspects.

Among the few studies of acculturation in post-acquisition processes (Very et al. 1998; Larsson and Lubatkin 2001; Teerikangas and Very 2006; Lakshman 2011), we highlight the research carried out by Nahavandi and Malekzadeh (1988), who proposed a framework of acculturation based on the characteristics of the two companies involved in the M&A process, as can be seen in Fig. 8.1.

According to Nahavandi and Malekzadeh's (1988) framework (hereafter the NM framework), the degree of congruence between the modes of acculturation of the acquirer and acquired firms affect the level of acculturation stress. It implies that the success or failure of the M&A process is directly associated with the level of stress. They proposed four modes of acculturation: assimilation, integration, separation, and deculturation.

In the assimilation mode the process is unilateral, where members of the acquired firm leave their corporate culture and adopt the acquirer culture. Employees tend to have a high attractiveness perception of the acquirer culture and show a detachment to their own culture. Compared to assimilation, the integration mode is less unilateral and more balanced.

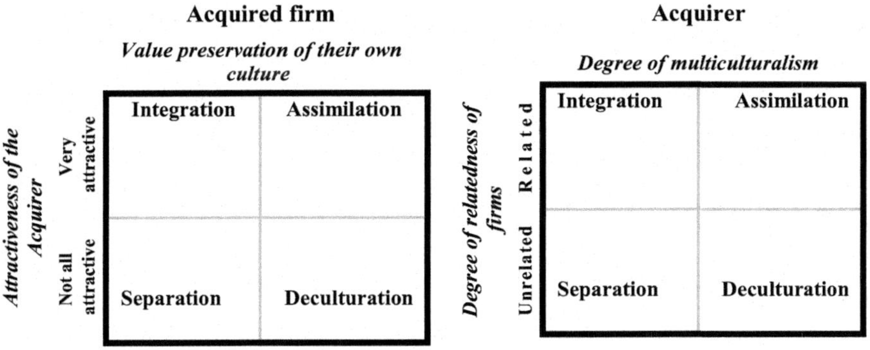


**Fig. 8.1** Modes of acculturation: acquired firms (left) and acquirer (right). (Source: Adapted from Nahavandi and Malekzadeh 1988, pp. 83–84)

Although the acquired firm implements cultural and organizational practices of the acquirer, it still guarantees an organizational identity. The acquired firm has a degree of freedom and independence to maintain its culture, though it is part of the financial and legal structure of the acquirer.

Separation is a mode of acculturation and involves minimal cultural exchange between both firms. The acquired company strives to keep separate, especially its cultural elements and operating practices. In general, the acquired firm has a strong culture and the desire to remain separate from the buyer. Moreover, the acquirer presents more multicultural features and there is a poor connection between the businesses of both firms.

Finally, in the deculturation mode, the culture of the acquired firm is weak, but its leaders and members are not able to accept the acquirer's culture. In addition, the acquirer firm has unicultural features and there is a weak relationship between business enterprises.

Therefore, the NM framework is based on the view of both the acquirer and acquired firms. For the acquired company (left side of Fig. 8.1), the model is based on the perception of acquirer attractiveness and how the acquired company members intend to preserve their own culture. For instance, if the acquirer firm is very attractive, but the perception is low for the acquired culture, there is a trend of assimilation among two cultures. As for the acquirer (right side of Fig. 8.1), the model is based on the degree of multiculturalism and its strategy of diversification.

It should be noted that the research of Nahavandi and Malekzadeh (1988) is quite relevant in the literature based on a high number of citations. Most of these studies cited NM work to argue the importance of acculturation or the modes of acculturation in M&A processes. To our knowledge there is no study that empirically tests and validates this framework. In addition, it considers both sides of the M&A process (i.e. acquirer and acquired firms). Thus, it will be interesting to apply and analyze it in a real M&A process, which is explained in the next section.

## Methods

This chapter develops a qualitative analysis based on a case study of a M&A transaction in the automobile industry in Brazil. The case deals with the acquisition of a Brazilian car company by a large foreign multinational firm, which was chosen for the following reasons: (i) impact on the media about the significant amount involved in this cross-border M&A transaction in the automobile industry; (ii) the acquirer is a traditional multinational firm in the industry; (iii) characteristics of the acquired firm, which is a genuine Brazilian company that produces and develops cars in a niche market segment; (iv) large cultural difference between the two companies in terms of nationality, processes, and products involved; (v) time spent to integrate and leverage the new subsidiary operation; and (vi) no prior empirical study investigated this M&A process using the lens of the acculturation literature.

Although the acquirer is a large American multinational firm that has more than a century of operating in the car industry and experience in a number of countries, it had difficulty leveraging its performance after the M&A transaction. The multinational firm still suffers to gain market share with the acquired brand. It is noteworthy that when the M&A process concluded, the acquired Brazilian company had good financial health and there was no reason to believe that the acquirer, with its strong brand and large international experience, could not leverage the local brand in the short term. The acquirer firm has taken a number of measures to reverse the situation. For instance, it updated and modernized the acquired plant, remodeled processes, increased production, and tried to adapt the acquired firm to international standards. However, the new company has not yet achieved a good result. Thus, it seems that acculturation needs to be considered in this post-acquisition process and further examined in this case study.

In order to better understand the object of study, first we reviewed the literature on M&A and acculturation. In addition, we collected real information about this specific M&A transaction from secondary sources such as business magazines, newspapers, and company and industry reports. Based on the academic literature and real data, we prepared a guideline for a structured qualitative interview to be used for in-depth interviews with key managers. The interview guideline is divided into two parts: (i) introductory questions to know more about the interviewees (department, length of service, and experience in the pre-acquisition period); and (ii) questions related to the acculturation process based on the NM framework.

We made a pre-selection of the interviewees based on the following criteria: (i) they should hold leadership positions (coordination, supervision, and management) in the department; (ii) they should have worked in the acquirer or acquired company during the pre-acquisition period; and (iii) have at least three years of work experience in the acquired firm.

A pre-test was conducted in January, 2013 with the Project Management Supervisor in order to test the structured interview guideline. After this interview, we noted that only few adjustments were necessary. A total of 14 in-depth interviews were done during January to March, 2013. Seven interviewees had worked in the acquired company in the pre-acquisition period and the other seven in the acquirer firm. All interviews were done by one interviewer (researcher), which is in accordance with the limits established by Gaskell and Bauer (2000). It should be noted that due to confidentiality reasons, neither the companies involved in the M&A transaction nor the names of the respondents were identified in this study. Respondents were coded as E1–E14 (Table 8.1).

**Table 8.1** Interviewees' general information

| #ID | Years of experience | Department | Job title | Workplace previous to acquisition | Interview time |
|---|---|---|---|---|---|
| E1 | 3 | Engineering | Chief Engineer | Acquirer | 60 min |
| E2 | 3 | Engineering | Project Management Supervisor | Acquirer | 37 min |
| E3 | 15 | Engineering | Environmental Engineering Supervisor | Acquired | 44 min |
| E4 | 8 | Engineering | Body and Electrical Engineering Supervisor | Acquired | 36 min |
| E5 | 6 | Manufacturing | General Plant Manager | Acquirer | 54 min |
| E6 | 5 | Logistics | Logistics Supervisor | Acquirer | 54 min |
| E7 | 7 | Logistics | Lean Manufacturing Manager | Acquired | 24 min |
| E8 | 12 | Quality Control | Quality Control Supervisor | Acquired | 34 min |
| E9 | 13 | Purchasing | Purchasing Supervisor | Acquired | 34 min |
| E10 | 8 | Marketing | Marketing Coordinator | Acquired | 34 min |
| E11 | 7 | Information Technology | IT Supervisor | Acquired | 42 min |
| E12 | 5 | Human Resource | Human Resource Supervisor | Acquirer | 31 min |
| E13 | 6 | Finance | Finance Supervisor | Acquirer | 55 min |
| E14 | 3 | Finance | Project Finance Manager | Acquirer | 34 min |
| | | | | Total | 9h 36 min |

**Table 8.2** Codes for mode of acculturation

| Acquired firm | Acquirer firm |
|---|---|
| *Acquirer attractiveness* | *Culture* |
| M&A—Perception of the acquirer attractiveness (low) | M&A—Degree of multiculturalism (unicultural) |
| M&A—Perception of the acquirer attractiveness (high) | M&A—Degree of multiculturalism (unicultural) |
| *Own value preservation* | *Diversification* |
| M&A—Perception of the own culture value (low) | M&A—Degree of relatedness of firms (low) |
| M&A—Perception of the own culture value (high) | M&A—Degree of relatedness of firms (high) |

All interviews were fully recorded with the respondents' permission, which result in a total of nine hours and 36 minutes of recording, and 200 pages of transcription. We perform a content analysis (Bardin 1977) and analyzed our data using the software Atlas.ti version 5.2. This software allowed us to search, categorize, organize, and register the interpretations. We created eight codes for the acculturation process based on the NM framework (see Table 8.2). The following section will discuss our findings.

## Results and Discussion

### Mode of Acculturation: Acquired Firm

Based on the NM framework, two points must be analyzed in the interview related to the acquired company: the perception of its own cultural values and the attractiveness of the acquirer.

According to the respondents, the employees of the acquired firms consider the acquirer very attractive, but they still have very strong ties to their own culture. For instance, interviewee E9 mentioned his admiration for the acquired company. He believes that some pre-acquisition characteristics must be preserved in the new company. He affirms that old employees who still work in the new firm are very courageous people. Another respondent (E11) shows a lot of nostalgia for the old regime and, in his opinion, some of the cultural traits must be maintained. Interviewee E10 summarizes this point:

> *In terms of culture, the acquiring company has many things to add, but it related to the structure processes. But we must be careful with this point. I think that it is good to bring the acquirer concepts, but not the process itself that includes all bureaucracy.* (E10)

Interviewee E4 believes that the acquirer firm is quite attractive and mentioned it with some excitement. He seems to be well integrated and satisfied with the acquisition. This shows the power of multinational companies in the automotive industry in Brazil (Motta and Coimbra 2012).

> *The buyer has much to add to us. The acquirer gives a lot of attention to the employees' health condition around the world. This is also coming here. I'm feeling that something is changing here! What I saw before and I am seeing now is that employees are more satisfied. They speak with pride about the acquirer.* (E4)

It should be noted that the acquirer firm is perceived as very attractive, but still has concerns about the applicability of procedures. It means that the cultural traits of the acquired company are still strong in its perception. Adding to this evidence, interviewee E10 reports:

> *I believe that some cultural traits must be maintained. There is much cool stuff in the acquired firm. A very good thing is that employees like the acquired firm's brand, like what you are doing, and know that you are making a difference in the company. I think this is an interesting cultural trait to be kept.* (E10)

Hence, first we found from the interviews that the buyer has many points to add to the acquired company. Second, the interviewees consider that some cultural aspects of the acquired firm should be kept. Applying these two aspects to the NM framework, the mode of acculturation perceived by respondents is *integration*. It implies that both cultures must coexist in the organization.

Conversely, there is another group of respondents who have attained a high perception of the acquirer and low attachment to their own culture. Interviewee E7 mentions that the acquired firm's practices should be abandoned:

> *The culture of [the acquired firm] no longer fits. It is not because it should or should not be maintained, although it could be even more efficient than today, but it does not fit anymore [...]. The dimension between both styles is very different. The actual process of the factory is very different than the way that [the acquired firm has] done [things] in the past.* (E7)

This view is reinforced by another respondent who states that everyone should assimilate the best practices of the acquirer (E8) and others who believe that some features of the acquired firm no longer fit in the current automobile industry:

> *This special car produces a very strong feature of [the acquired firm], but in our current market, where safety and quality are more important, this characteristic does not return to [the acquired firm], there is no way for that.* (E4)

Thus, there are also some interviewees from the acquired firm who perceived the mode of acculturation as *assimilation*. It means that the acquired company must assimilate the culture of the buyer.

## Mode of Acculturation: Acquirer Firm

With regard to the acquirer firm's respondents, two points are considered in the NM framework: the degree of multiculturalism and the degree of relatedness of firms. The findings are described as follows. In general, interviewees mention that the acquirer has a high degree of multiculturalism:

> *[The acquirer] encourages multiculturalism from the moment that starts encouraging diversity. The firm diversity is not only related to different cultures, countries, and races, but also religion, color, creed ... everything! So what [the buyer] believes when you have such diversity is that you can add the best of your culture with the best of the other.* (E2)

In the same vein, interviewee E5 states that the acquirer is an organization that supports and encourages multiculturalism and diversity. This cultural complementarity is a competitive advantage for the firm:

> *I would say that [the buyer] is a multicultural company. I think that the word diversity means that you have multiple people with different thoughts and may contribute differently to the business. It is a way to have new eyes, new thoughts, and different ways of thinking about business.* (E5)

In terms of the degree of relatedness of firms, the interviewees perceived that the products of the companies are quite different. Customers of the acquired firm use the product for other purposes, which is different from the acquirer:

> *With regards to the use of the products, I would say that they are different. Today the use of the product of [the acquired firm] is different from the product of [the buyer]. I would say that 80% of the usage of our car is very specific, it is a niche. It is another world […] It demands other requirements, other needs that are entirely different. I think that [the buyer] has much to add to [the acquired firm].* (E5)

This is in accordance with respondent E12 who reinforces the low degree of relatedness of firms, and another interviewee (E2) who states the business complementarity:

> *Both companies are in the same market, but they do not compete for the same customers. The profiles are totally different. While you are here in [the acquired firm] the car is used for more adventure, [the buyer] product is to have a passenger car.* (E12)

> *Both companies manufacture cars, but they are competing in distinct markets. The acquirer is more about passenger cars and trucks. While the acquired firm focused on [the] sports segment, which is a very specific market. The markets are different and they (acquired and acquirer) do not compete for the same customers, but they complement each other.* (E2)

Summarizing the buyers' respondent views, there is a consensus that the acquirer encourages multiculturalism and shows a low degree of relatedness of firms involved in M&A. Thus, the perceived mode of acculturation is separation. It means that the organizational cultures are distinct and must remain independent (Nahavandi and Malekzadeh 1988). The cultures of the two companies should not be "dissolved" and the business relationship should be complementary.

In addition to the content analysis, we built the netviews using Atlas.ti software. Figure 8.2 shows all categories mentioned in Table 8.2. It is possible to see that each of the encodings have two numbers in brackets. The first is the number of citations related to that code, and the second refers to the number of links with other codes. By considering only the codes that were related to a quote, we made a link with the perceived acculturation mode.

It becomes clear that all respondents of the acquirer believe that the company is multicultural and there is low relatedness between firms. According to Fig. 8.2, there are ten quotes related to the code "M&A – Degree of Multiculturalism (multicultural)" and eight quotes with "M&A – Degree of relatedness between firms (low)". Hence, the mode of acculturation is predominantly perceived as *separation*.

The alignment between the thoughts of all respondents is related to at least two important facts disclosed during the interviews. First, the "campaign" that has been made over the past few years by the firm in order to encourage diversity. Second, the strategy of market diversification of the acquirer that refers to adding a new product to its portfolio leads respondents to believe in a low level of relatedness of firms.

The analysis of the mode of acculturation based on the view of the acquired firm was not as homogeneous as the acquirer. In Fig. 8.3, three quotes are linked to the "M&A—Perception of own cultural value (low)", five to the "M&A—Perception of own culture value (high)", eight to the "M&A—Perception of the attractiveness of the acquirer (high)" and one to the "M&A—Perception of the attractiveness of the acquirer (low)". Thus, there are three modes of acculturation: *integration, assimilation*, and *separation*.

Figure 8.3 summarizes the findings based on the interviews transcriptions and netviews in terms of the mode of acculturation based on the NM framework.

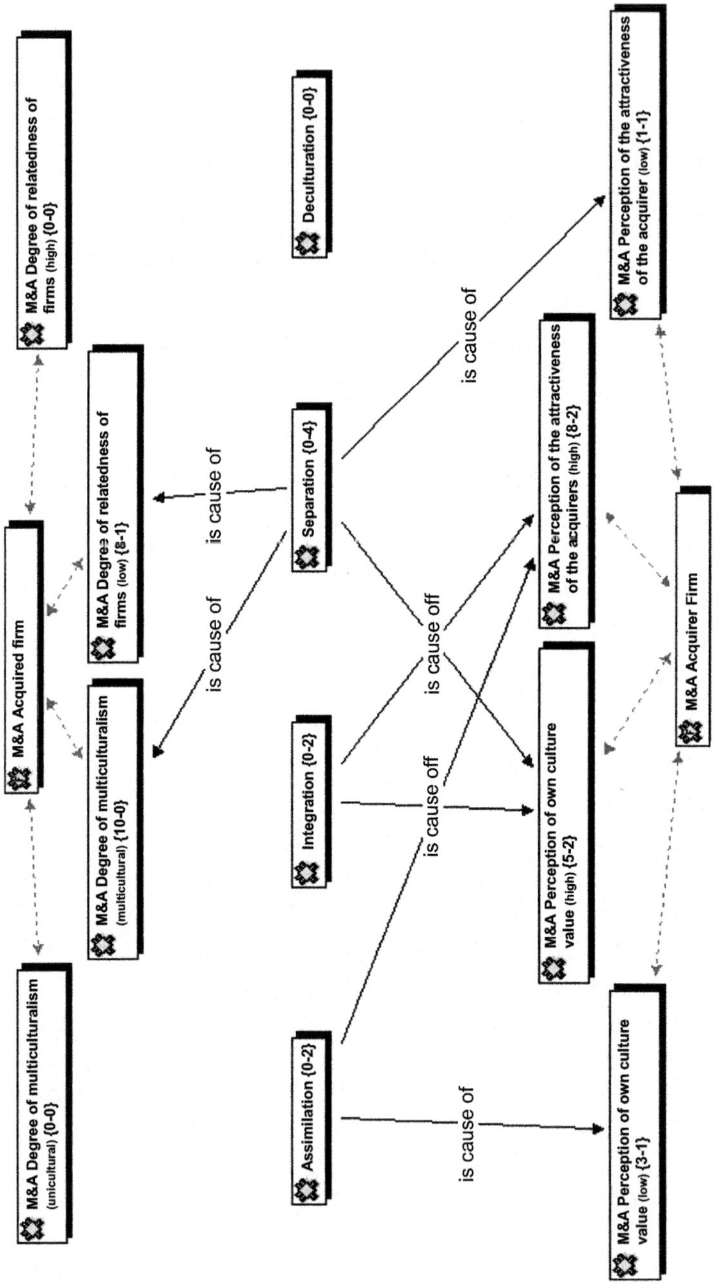


**Fig. 8.2** Perceived mode of acculturation based on *netviews*

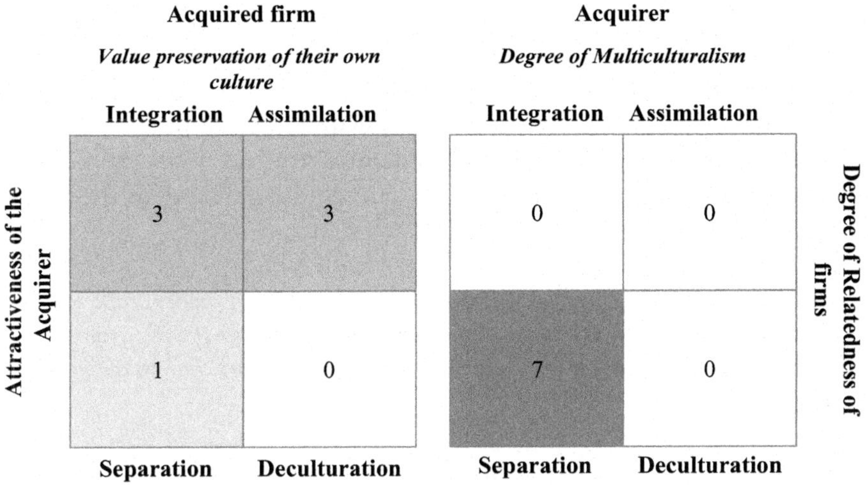


**Fig. 8.3** Perceived mode of acculturation based on the interviews

## Cultural Differences Between Firms

The first important cultural difference mentioned during the interviews was the formality or informality of the processes. In the acquired firm, the activities are performed informally, without following formal processes or procedures, while the acquirer has all diagramed processes, and these are formally documented.

> *Before it is like this example: What is this piece on the windshield? It had to have a "snorkel" there. How will we put the "snorkel"? They answered: "ordered change". There was no formalization of the changes. Now, it seems that there is a formalization of processes. It is due to a more structured process.* (E10)

> *There are still a lot of informal meetings. There is no culture of formalizing meetings... or people writing during the meetings. So this is something that we are asking people to do. I think the main difference between [the acquirer and acquired firm] is not only the absence of a structured system, but the informality of information.* (E2)

Another finding is related to the difference in organizational structure. The acquired company presented a more vertical structure, in which there was only one person making decisions: the owner. It was characterized as a family business. By contrast, the acquirer has a more horizontal structure, where the organizational functions are better structured and decision making occurs indirectly. We can see this in some of the statements in the interviews:

> *Before, in the acquired company, it was not easy to get to the owner of the company. Now we have direct access to the person who manages the resources and takes the risk. So, it helps a lot in decision making and in any changes along the process.* (E10)

It should be noted, however, that cultural differences impact not only on people themselves, but also on the processes that directly affect the results. Hence, in the M&A process, integration of culture must not only collaborate with sociocultural adaptation, but it is also an essential aspect to transfer tasks, and in the sharing of resources and learning (Stahl and Voigt 2008).

## Difficulties in the Process of Acculturation

Among the various difficulties faced during the post-acquisition acculturation process, two of them are more evident during the interviews: the difficulty of implementing procedures and processes, and the paradigm shift of the acquired company.

One respondent argues that the great difficulty in implementing processes and procedures in the acquired firm is due to the differences in company size and the market segment. As the buyer has a much larger organizational structure and formal processes, it is perceived to be more structured and robust, as noted in the following quotation:

> *So, there are things that work very well in the [acquirer]. [The acquirer firm] has more people, more car to sell and it works. But it has to be structured for that. Now, with a lean structure that we have, it is not feasible. I think it is good to bring the concepts of [the acquirer], but not the processes themselves. It is what we need to improve … taking directly from [the acquirer].* (E10)

Paradigm shifts in the acquired company are the most difficult aspect during the process of acculturation. One of the interviewees, who previously worked at the acquirer firm, describes his perception:

> *Paradigms are broken; and it is difficult to have a paradigm shift ... it is a culture that has existed for a long time, but we have this challenge to break paradigms. We need to bring this product development system, which is not only from the [buyer], but it is a global one. What we need to do is ... the word that I am going to use is quite strong, but ... transform an industry that was handmade for a high-tech industry, which is changing [the acquired firm].* (E2)

Difficulties will occur during the M&A process to a greater or lesser extent, and provide positive or negative results that are difficult to predict. According to Teerikangas and Very (2006), this process is related to the acculturation stress that occurs after the acquisition. Therefore, the NM framework contributes to identifying the mode of acculturation and the main problems and difficulties related to the post-acquisition process. It could help firms to avoid stress during the M&A process, which could lead to the successful implementation and integration of both firms.

## Conclusion

This chapter developed a case study analysis using a theoretical lens of acculturation to examine the post-acquisition process of a domestic firm by a foreign multinational company in the automotive industry in Brazil. Based on in-depth interviews with key managers involved in pre- and post-acquisition processes, we empirically applied the proposed framework of Nahavandi and Malekizadeh (1988) to see whether this model could be applied to identify and provide tools to reduce stress in acculturation in M&A processes.

According to the NM framework, we found that employees of the acquired firm perceived well the acculturation as *integration* and *assimilation*, while the acquirer saw it as *separation*.

This implies that at the same time that there is a perception of attractiveness of the acquirer, the managers of the acquired company enhance their own cultural values. The greater the divergence between the modes of acculturation experienced by these two companies in the M&A process, the greater the acculturation stress (Nahavandi and Malekizadeh 1988). In particular, when managers invest more time in the acquired company, it seems that the company values are stronger; this may be related to the sense of belonging. In other words, there is a feeling of company identity that these managers help to build. This is a way for the firm to protect its own identity. Hence, although the good features of the acquirer are recognized, the acquired company still keeps its own cultural values.

In addition, there are some organizational and cultural differences that have to be taken into account, with specific regard to the formality and informality of processes. There is still resistance in implementing and adapting some of the new procedures. Although it is important to formalize and standardize the procedures, some informal aspects need to be considered, particularly in terms of personal relationships or other cultural dimensions that are important to keep. Conversely, the new structure of the firm promotes a more decentralized decision-making process, which is not focused on the owner's decision (centralized). Sometimes, it takes more time to reach a decision, but there is a feeling of participation in the decision process.

Some difficulties still remain, particularly the aspects relating to the paradigm shift. There is a need to break the image of a small company and create a feeling of being part of a large and international corporation. The domestic perspective needs to change to a global mindset.

In terms of managerial implications, the findings show that the acculturation process needs to be analyzed in-depth, and the NM framework could help firms to better examine these factors. Thus, it is possible for business managers who are going through similar processes to prepare themselves using measures that seek to mitigate the impact of cultural differences and make the process less traumatic for employees without negatively impacting the results.

Nevertheless, there are some limitations to be considered in this research. First, it relates to the confidentiality aspect, which make it difficult to use historical data in the empirical analysis as evidence for evolution of the M&A process. Second, due to time constraints it was difficult to access all managers of the firm to conduct interviews. Finally, this study analyzed one specific case of the acquisition process, which does not make possible its generalization. However, it should be noted that we did not have access to other cases of acquisition.

Although limitations exist in this study, there is a great opportunity for future research in this area. First, further investigation could identify and use the company's historical data in order to highlight and relate the findings during the interviews. Second, future work could try to interview all staff levels, in addition to managers, to see if the perception about the mode of acculturation is homogeneous in all levels of the firm. Finally, further research could examine the applicability of the NM framework in other cases of acquisition within the automobile industry and even in other industry sectors. An interesting investigation could be the comparison of the acquisition process involving the same company or other companies in a different context (countries). Thus, there is a number of possibilities to extend this research and contribute to the literature of acculturation in the M&A process.

## References

Adams, C., and A. Neely. 2000. The performance prism to boost M&A success. *Measuring Business Excellence* 4 (3): 19–23.

Anfavea. 2014. *Brazilian automotive industry yearbook 2014*. Brasília: Anfavea (Associação Nacional dos Fabricantes de Veículos Automotores – Brazilian Automotive Industry Association).

Angwin, D., and M. Meadows. 2012. Acquiring poorly performing companies during a recession. *Journal of General Management* 38 (1): 1.

Appelbaum, S.H., J. Gandell, B.T. Shapiro, P. Belisle, and E. Hoeven. 2000. Anatomy of a merger: Behavior of organizational factors and processes throughout the pre-during-post-stages (part 2). *Management Decision* 38 (10): 674–684.

Badrtalei, J., and D.L. Bates. 2007. Effect of organizational cultures on mergers and acquisitions: The case of DaimlerChrysler. *International Journal of Management* 24 (2): 303.

Bajaj, H. 2009. Organizational culture in bank mergers & acquisitions. *Indian Journal of Industrial Relations* 45: 229–242.

Balcet, G., H. Wang, and X. Richet. 2012. Geely: A trajectory of catching up and asset-seeking multinational growth. *International Journal of Automotive Technology and Management* 12 (4): 360–375.

Bardin, L. 1977. *Análise de conteúdo*. Lisboa: Edições 70.

Barkema, H.G., J.H. Bell, and J.M. Pennings. 1996. Foreign entry, cultural barriers, and learning. *Strategic Management Journal* 17 (2): 151–166.

Berry, J.W. 1997. Immigration, acculturation, and adaptation. *Applied Psychology* 46 (1): 5–34.

Caiazza, R., and P. Nueno. 2014. Corporate strategies of automotive firms: How to become global leaders. *Competitiveness Review* 24 (2): 119–123.

Cartwright, S., and C.L. Cooper. 2012. *Managing mergers acquisitions and strategic alliances*. London. Routledge.

Cartwright, S., and R. Schoenberg. 2006. Thirty years of mergers and acquisitions research: Recent advances and future opportunities. *British Journal of Management* 17 (S1): S1–S5.

Cuche, D. 1996. *La notion de culture dans les sciences sociales*. Vol. 19. Paris: la Découverte.

DeCenzo, D.A., S.P. Robbins, and S.L. Verhulst. 2010. *Fundamentals of human resource management*. New Jersey. Wiley.

Deng, P. 2009. Why do Chinese firms tend to acquire strategic assets in international expansion? *Journal of World Business* 44 (1): 74–84.

Dikova, D., P.R. Sahib, and A. Van Witteloostuijn. 2010. Cross-border acquisition abandonment and completion: The effect of institutional differences and organizational learning in the international business service industry, 1981–2001. *Journal of International Business Studies* 41 (2): 223–245.

Gaskell, G., and M.W. Bauer. 2000. Towards public accountability: Beyond sampling, reliability and validity. In *Qualitative researching with text, image and sound*, 336–350. London: Sage.

Gomes, E., D.N. Angwin, Y. Weber, and S. Yedidia Tarba. 2013. Critical success factors through the mergers and acquisitions process: Revealing pre-and post-

M&A connections for improved performance. *Thunderbird International Business Review* 55 (1): 13–35.

Hagedoorn, J., and G. Duysters. 2002. External sources of innovative capabilities: The preferences for strategic alliances or mergers and acquisitions. *Journal of Management Studies* 39 (2): 167–188.

Hofstede, G. 1991. *Cultures and organizations. Intercultural cooperation and its importance for survival. Software of the mind.* London: McGraw-Hill.

Johnson, G., K. Scholes, and R. Whittington 2008. *Exploring corporate strategy: Text and cases.* London. Pearson Education.

Jürgens, U. 2002. *Corporate governance, innovation, and economic performance: A case study on volkswagen* (No. FS II 02-205). Social Science Research Center Berlin (WZB).

Lakshman, C. 2011. Postacquisition cultural integration in mergers & acquisitions: A knowledge-based approach. *Human Resource Management* 50 (5): 605–623.

Larsson, R., and M. Lubatkin. 2001. Achieving acculturation in mergers and acquisitions: An international case survey. *Human Relations* 54 (12): 1573–1607.

Meglio, O., and A. Risberg. 2010. Mergers and acquisitions – Time for a methodological rejuvenation of the field? *Scandinavian Journal of Management* 26 (1): 87–95.

Mendenhall, M.E. 2005. *Mergers and acquisitions: Managing culture and human resources.* Stanford: Stanford University Press.

Motta, L., and P. Coimbra. 2012. *Pesquisa de Fusões e Aquisições 2012 KPMG.* São Paulo: KPMG.

Nahavandi, A., and A.R. Malekzadeh. 1988. Acculturation in mergers and acquisitions. *Academy of Management Review* 13 (1): 79–90.

Nikandrou, I., and N. Papalexandris. 2007. The impact of M&A experience on strategic HRM practices and organisational effectiveness: Evidence from Greek firms. *Human Resource Management Journal* 17 (2): 155–177.

Öberg, C., and J. Holtström. 2006. Are mergers and acquisitions contagious? *Journal of Business Research* 59 (12): 1267–1275.

OICA – International Organization of Motor Vehicle Manufacturers. 2014. *OICA website.* Available at: http://www.oica.net. Accessed 10 July 2014.

Papadakis, V.M., and I.C. Thanos. 2010. Measuring the performance of acquisitions: An empirical investigation using multiple criteria. *British Journal of Management* 21 (4): 859–873.

Quadros, R., and F. Consoni. 2008. Innovation capabilities in the Brazilian automobile industry: A study of vehicle assemblers' technological strategies and policy recommendations. *International Journal of Technological Learning, Innovation and Development* 2 (1–2): 53–75.

Rogan, M., and O. Sorenson. 2014. Picking a (poor) partner a relational perspective on acquisitions. *Administrative Science Quarterly* 59 (2): 301–329. https://doi.org/10.1177/0001839214531719.

Santana, M.A. 2003. Trabalhadores e indústria automobilística em tempos de reestruturação. *Revista Brasileira de Ciências Sociais* 18 (51): 174–178.

Sarala, R.M. 2010. The impact of cultural differences and acculturation factors on post-acquisition conflict. *Scandinavian Journal of Management* 26 (1): 38–56.

Scavarda, L.F., T.P.W. Barbosa, and S. Hamacher. 2005. Comparação entre as tendências e estratégias da indústria automotiva no Brasil e na Europa. *Gestão & Produção, São Carlos* 12 (3): 361–375.

Schuler, R., and S. Jackson. 2001. HR issues and activities in mergers and acquisitions. *European Management Journal* 19 (3): 239–253.

Shimizu, K., M.A. Hitt, D. Vaidyanath, and V. Pisano. 2004. Theoretical foundations of cross-border mergers and acquisitions: A review of current research and recommendations for the future. *Journal of International Management* 10 (3): 307–353.

Shrivastava, P. 1986. Postmerger integration. *Journal of Business Strategy* 7 (1): 65–76.

Stahl, G.K., and A. Voigt. 2005. Impact of cultural differences on merger and acquisition performance: A critical research review and an integrative model. *Advances in Mergers and Acquisitions* 4: 51–82.

———. 2008. Do cultural differences matter in mergers and acquisitions? A tentative model and examination. *Organization Science* 19 (1): 160–176.

Teerikangas, S., and P. Very. 2006. The culture–performance relationship in M&A: From yes/no to how. *British Journal of Management* 17 (S1): S31–S48.

UNCTAD – United Nations Conference on Trade and Development. 2014. *World investment report 2014*. Geneva: United Nations Publication.

Very, P., M. Lubatkin, and R. Calori. 1998. A cross-national assessment of acculturative stress in recent European mergers. In *De Gruyter studies in organization*. De Gruyter. 85–110.

Weber, Y., and S. Yedidia Tarba. 2012. Mergers and acquisitions process: The use of corporate culture analysis. *Cross Cultural Management: An International Journal* 19 (3): 288–303.

Weber, Y., S.Y. Tarba, and A. Reichel. 2011. A model of the influence of culture on integration approaches and international mergers and acquisitions performance. *International Studies of Management & Organization* 41 (3): 9–24.

Xiaohui, C., and L. Haiyan 2011. *Study on enterprise cultural integration after Geely's acquisition of Volvo*. School of Management-Wuhan University of Technology.

# 9

# Exploring the Relationship Between International Service Performance and Personal Characteristics in the Latin American Context

Leonardo Liberman and David Kimber C.

## Introduction

Multinational corporations (MNCs) are organizations that span national borders, behave as social communities and count with productive knowledge that is a source of comparative advantage (Kogut and Zander 1996). Because of their scope, MNCs are characterized by a large amount of intercultural interactions, service exchanges and transactions among employees, customers and suppliers originating from different countries and cultures.

If these interactions are well managed, individuals' performance within these companies might improve, as might the performance of the MNC as a whole. Conversely, inattention to these interactions, exchanges and transactions can create important hurdles that can have a negative effect

L. Liberman (✉)
Libens Research and Development, Santiago, Chile

D. Kimber C.
Universidad de los Andes, Santiago, Chile
e-mail: dkimber@uandes.cl



W. Newburry et al. (eds.), *Contemporary Influences on International Business in Latin America*, AIB Latin America, https://doi.org/10.1007/978-3-319-98340-0_9

on performance. If not properly managed, they can become the source of predicaments that might go undetected until they have already caused important harm (Brett et al. 2006). Even though the focus has increased on personality traits of service employees (Teng and Liu 2014), these studies have not taken cross-cultural interactions into account. In this vein, we contend that there are general personal characteristics that influence these regular intercultural contacts and that affect the performance of individuals. Based on a literature review, in the current study, we assessed the influence of ethnocentrism, cultural intelligence and emotional intelligence on the overall service performance of employees. Following that, we present previous research in the area and state some hypotheses.

## Theoretical Development

There is a considerable body of research dealing with the nature and characteristics of ethnocentrism. Ethnocentrism is understood as a view in which one's own group is the center of everything, and all others are scaled and rated with reference to it (Sumner 1906). Ethnocentrism is an inflexible in-group out-group distinction that comprises antagonistic and stereotyped attitudes and behaviors with regards to out-groups (Adorno et al. 1950). It also involves having positive, submissive and stereotyped views and attitudes toward the in-group. Extant research suggests that in intercultural work contexts, ethnocentrism has a negative effect on interpersonal perceptions within the organization. Ethnocentrism has been found to be negatively related to social attraction, competence, character, and hiring endorsements. It has also been studied with regard to its influence on the perceptions of managerial attraction, credibility and effectiveness in a manager-subordinate conflict situation (Adorno et al. 1950; Neuliep et al. 2005; Sumner 1906).

According to Caligiuri and Tarique (2011), lower levels of ethnocentrism have been identified as one of the characteristics that predict performance among expatriate executives (Shaffer et al. 2006). Lower levels of ethnocentrism have also been found to be associated with intercultural knowledge absorption (Kayes et al. 2005), and have been considered one of the essential attributes of global leaders (Maznevski and DiStefano 2000). Based on the above-mentioned findings, we suggest that ethnocentrism will be negatively associated with the performance of employees working for a MNC.

Another characteristic that might be related to performance is cultural intelligence. Cultural intelligence (CQ) is the individual's ability to effectively behave and manage interactions in culturally heterogeneous situations (Earley 2002, Ang and Van Dyne 2008). It is a particular form of intelligence that is different from general, emotional and social intelligence (Earley and Ang 2003) since CQ is focused on intercultural settings. CQ is also a multidimensional construct that has four different facets: a cognitive, a metacognitive, a motivational and a behavioral one. The *cognitive* facet refers to the level of cultural knowledge that a person has attained about similarities with, and differences from, other cultures. This knowledge is acquired through education and personal experience and considers facts, practices, conventions, norms and beliefs of different cultures (Ang and Van Dyne 2008; Bandura 1999). Besides, the metacognitive facet refers to the mental processes carried out by individuals to attain cultural knowledge. It involves the capacity to question cultural assumptions, to adjust the mental schemes during and after relevant experiences (Ang and Van Dyne 2008). This particular facet enables individuals to adjust their strategies to achieve desired outcomes in cross-cultural encounters. Further, the motivational facet is related to the drive to engage in culturally diverse interactions. It defines the energy, direction and persistence when learning and working in cross-cultural situations (Crowne 2006). Finally, the behavioral facet is the ability to acquire or adapt behaviors, and to exhibit suitable verbal and nonverbal behaviors in international contacts. This facet implies having a behavioral repertoire to respond appropriately in situations with people from other cultures and the flexibility to adjust behaviors according to the specifics of each cultural contact (Ang and Van Dyne 2008).

There are a number of studies dealing with the relationship between CQ, cultural adaptation and/or effectiveness. For example, in a study involving global professionals in Singapore, Templer, Tay and Chandrasekar (2006) analyzed the relationship between motivational CQ and three types of cross-cultural adjustments (general, work and interaction adjustment). They found that emotional CQ was related to these three variables, and that employees with a high motivational CQ tended to adjust better to work, life and social demands in foreign environments. This led them to conclude that CQ was a valid, applicable and generalizable construct.

Ang et al. (2007) also found evidence supporting the validity of cultural intelligence over general intelligence, emotional intelligence (EQ) and other variables. They found that the explained variance of cultural adaptation increased by 4 percent in a sample of US undergraduates and 3 percent in a sample of undergraduates from Singapore, when adding this variable to the equation. They also found that metacognitive and behavioral CQ predicted task performance in managers, and that motivational CQ and behavioral CQ predicted both supervisor-rated and self-reported cultural adaptation in all contexts. The four facets of cultural intelligence explained the variance in supervisor-rated task performance by 36 percent, interactional adjustment by 28 percent and work adjustment by 29 percent. At the same time, the four facets explained 26 percent of the variance of self-rated interactional adjustment, 19 percent of work adjustment, 20 percent of general adjustment and 29 percent of wellbeing.

Further, in a study with international students in New Zealand, Ward and colleagues (Ward et al. 2009) found that the only significant predictor of cultural adaptation was motivational CQ. However, none of the facets was a significant predictor of academic adaptation. Based on these results, the authors challenged the utility of CQ as a predictor of cultural adaptation. Later, Ward, Wilson and Fischer (2011) found that motivational CQ was related to fewer psychological symptoms and fewer socio-cultural difficulties, while metacognitive CQ was associated with improved socio-cultural outcomes.

In addition, Lee and Sukoco (2010) examined the impact of CQ and cultural effectiveness on the performance of employees working for a Taiwanese MNC. They found that CQ had a positive significant effect on cultural adjustment, but not on performance. Moreover, cultural adjustment mediated the relationship between CQ and performance. Cultural effectiveness also mediated the relationship between CQ and performance. Based on the above-mentioned empirical evidence, we expect that CQ will act as a predictor of performance.

EQ is another variable that we believe should influence performance. Emotions are responses to internal or external events that have a positive or negative meaning to the individual (Salovey and Mayer 1990) and that can be a signal of, and response to, changes in the relationship between the individual and the environment (Mayer et al. 2000). Besides, EQ is a set of mental abilities that allows monitoring one's own and others' emotions, to discern among these and to use the information to guide thinking and action (Salovey and Mayer 1990). EQ includes the capacity to accurately perceive, assess and express emotions. EQ also involves the capacity to understand emotions and to regulate them to promote development (Mayer and Salovey 1997). EQ has four branches (perception, appraisal and expression of emotions; emotional facilitation of thinking, understanding and analyzing emotions; employing emotional knowledge; and reflective regulation of emotions), ranging from more basic psychological processes to higher, more psychologically integrated ones (Mayer and Salovey 1997).

EQ also allows individuals to have better social interactions, as it lets them identify and understand emotions in themselves and in others, regulate and manage emotions to make better decisions leading to perform well in the social arena and to get effective results. Considering that cognitive ability accounts for almost 25 percent of the variance of job performance (Conte 2005; Mayer et al. 2008), EQ is likely to be related to performance.

Wong and Law (2002) found a positive relationship between EQ and job performance in a sample of non-teaching employees at a university. Furthermore, the correlation between job performance and EQ in emotionally loaded jobs was highly significant and positive. Van Rooy and Viswesvaran (2004) found a positive correlation between EQ and performance and also found that EQ predicted performance in various domains (employment, academic and life). Moreover, the analysis included different countries, allowing for generalizations of the results across populations. They finally concluded that EQ is a valuable predictor of performance and that it is a very relevant ability for expatriate managers, as this allowed them to be more prepared for facing new cultural contexts.

Law, Wong and Song (2004) also found that EQ was positively associated with task performance, independently of whether EQ was measured by self-report or peer-report, which led them to suggest that EQ might be a good predictor of job performance. Further, in a study with US Air Force recruiters, Bar-on (2006) found a significant correlation between EQ and occupational performance, suggesting that EQ might allow us to discriminate between high and low performers. Moreover, in a study of Korean flight attendants, the authors concluded that EQ was related to service recovery and organizational loyalty (Lee et al. 2013).

Besides, Côté and Miners (2006) obtained a correlation of 0.32 between EQ and task performance among full-time employees at a public university. However, they also found a significant interaction between cognitive and EQ in the prediction of task performance. They concluded that: "the relationship between EQ and task performance becomes more positive as IQ decreases" (Côté and Miners 2006, p. 15). EQ was a significant predictor of job performance in employees with a lower score on the IQ test. In contrast, Rojell et al. (2006) found a positive significant association between EQ and job performance, whereas Jadhav and Mulla (2010) found that among executives with a large degree of interpersonal interactions, EQ was significantly related to job performance, whereas no significant relationship was found among those with fewer interactions. Based on the empirical evidence discussed above, it is possible to postulate that EQ will be positively associated with individual performance of MNC employees. Considering the interaction that has been found between EQ and IQ to explain job performance in previous research (Côté and Miners 2006), it is not unreasonable to expect that some relationship between EQ and other types of intelligence can explain job performance. Hence, in this study we suggest a complementary enquiry: is there any relationship between the types of intelligence when predicting individual performance of MNC employees?

## Methods

The sample consisted of 260 participants who were contacted by e-mail and who received a link to an online questionnaire. Most of the respondents were male (63 percent). Their ages ranged from 20 to 60 and they had an average work experience of 14 years. Most of them had a university or technical degree and held managerial, professional/technical or analyst positions. The design of the questionnaire followed the recommendations of Aaker, Kumar and Day (2010), and the scales were displayed randomly. Furthermore, the order of the questions within each category was pre-tested to prevent any order bias. Finally, when a respondent answered a question, it was impossible to return to change previous answers, avoiding that respondents would edit previous answers to be consistent with latter ones. The questionnaire consisted of scales assessing CQ, ethnocentrism EQ and job performance. A number of control variables were also included and are detailed below.

CQ was measured using the CQS (Van Dyne et al. 2008), a questionnaire with four subscales that each represents a different facet of the model. CQS is a 20-item questionnaire with questions that are responded according to a Likert scale ranging from 1 (strongly disagree) to 7 (strongly agree). This is the most commonly used scale in studies examining cultural intelligence and adaptation, and its structure has been validated in previous research (Ang et al. 2007; Crowne 2006; Ward et al. 2009).

EQ was measured using the WLEIS scale (Wong and Law 2002; Law et al. 2004, Kafetsios and Zampetakis 2008; Jadhav and Mulla 2010). WLEIS is a 20-item questionnaire that is responded according to a Likert scale, ranging from 1 (strongly disagree) to 7 (strongly agree). This scale is based on Salovey and Mayer's work on EQ and describes four dimensions: oneself's emotions appraisal, others' emotions appraisal, use of emotions and regulation of emotions.

Ethnocentrism was measured using the Generalized Ethnocentrism Scale (GENE scale) developed by Neuliep and McCroskey (1997). The scale is a 22-item questionnaire answered according to a Likert scale ranging from 1 (strongly disagree) to 5 (strongly agree). This questionnaire has shown reliability and validity in different studies (Chen 2010; Dong et al. 2008; Neuliep 2002). For the purposes of this study, we only used the ten items with the highest factor loadings from the 15 used for scoring ethnocentrism in the revised scale (Neuliep and McCroskey 1997; Neuliep 2002).

Performance was measured according to employees' perception of their own performance (self-report measures). According to Giacobbe et al. (2006) and Law et al. (2004), we included three items about performance with a Likert scale ranging from 1 (poor) to 7 (outstanding). The respondents were asked to rate their global performance, their performance in comparison to their peers, and their performance in relation to their personal goals. In spite of the controversy about using self-report measures of performance, there are a number of studies supporting their use (Churchill et al. 1985; Román and Iacobucci 2010).

Control variables that we included in the analysis were: competitive intensity, economic situation faced by the company, job satisfaction, educational level, age, gender and the respondent's level within the company.

We incorporated a variable to control for the competitive characteristics of faced international markets (i.e. competitive intensity). This variable referred to the respondent's perception of the level of competition that the company faced in its international markets (Homburget al. 2002). Based on Jaworski and Kohli (1993) and Homburg et al. (2002), we developed a three-item scale answered according to a Likert scale ranging from 1 (strongly disagree) to 5 (strongly agree). The items were: "We face intense competition in our business", "Anything that we can offer to our customers, our competitors can match readily" and "Price competition is a hallmark of our industry". A higher score indicates a more competitive business environment. Additionally, we measured the employee's perception of the economic situation of the company in the past 12 months, according to a 9-point scale ranging from Very Bad (1) to Excellent (9).

In order to consider the internal environment of the company represented by the employees' attitudes about their jobs, we utilized the Minnesota Satisfaction Questionnaire (MSQ) (Weiss et al. 1967). The MSQ is a 22-item questionnaire with questions that are responded according to a Likert scale ranging from 1 (very dissatisfied) to 5 (very satisfied). This is the most commonly used scale in studies examining job satisfaction (Spector 1997; Hancer and George 2003; Wang and Hwang 2012).

Concerning internal consistency, all scales but one showed satisfactory alphas above 0.7 (Nunnally and Bernstein 1994). However, in the case of competitive intensity, the alpha obtained was only 0.46, possibly due to the fact that it only consisted of three items (Nunnally and Bernstein 1994). Another explanation for the lower internal consistency of this scale could be that it might be a formative one, with each item explaining a separate area of the concept, meaning that high correlations among the indicators are not to be expected (Christophersen and Konradt 2012).

Educational level was coded from 1 (elementary school) to 3 (university degree), whereas work experience was measured according to the total number of years working. The hierarchical level within the company was coded from 1 (operative) to 4 (senior manager). However, no respondent in the current study belonged to the lowest hierarchical level (i.e. level 1). Finally, the respondents were asked to register their birth year (to obtain the age of the respondent) and gender.

When analyzing data, we applied certain filters to the database. In the questionnaire, respondents were asked if they had had any contact with customers (internal or external) from a country of origin different from theirs. Following this procedure, the subsample consisted of 106 participants.

## Results

In order to assess the construct validity of the scales, we conducted a Harman one-factor test including all items from CQ, EQ and the GENE scales into a principal component factor analysis (Podsakoff and Organ 1986; Podsakoff et al. 2003). According to this analysis, we did not find a one-factor solution, as Factor 1 only accounted for 37.58 percent of the total variance. We therefore utilized a principal component analysis with quartimin rotation to assess the construct validity of CQS, WLEIS and the GENE scale. In the case of CQS, our results showed that the structure theorized by Van Dyne et al. (2008) of a four-factor correlated model did not appear. In spite of the findings in other studies (Crowne 2006; Van Dyne et al. 2008; Lee and Sukoco 2010; Moon 2010), the EFA showed a three-factor solution, with meta-cognitive and cognitive facets appearing as one factor, apart from the motivational and behavioral factors. For WLEIS, the analysis generated a four-factor model as described by Wong

**Table 9.1** Zero-order correlations and Cronbach's alpha

| Variables | 1 | 2 | 3 | 4 | C |
|---|---|---|---|---|---|
| 1. Performance | | | | | |
| | | | | | 0.90 |
| 2. CQ | 0.31* | | | | |
| | 0.00 | | | | 0.94 |
| 3. Ethno. | −0.19* | −0.15 | | | |
| | 0.03 | 0.08 | | | 0.90 |
| 4. EQ | 0.39* | 0.59* | −0.20* | | |
| | 0.00 | 0.00 | 0.03 | | 0.96 |
| 5. Job Satisf. | 0.20* | 0.59* | −0.10 | 0.59* | |
| | 0.03 | 0.00 | 0.16 | 0.00 | |

*Significant correlations, $p < 0.05$

and Law (2002). As a result, the four factors consisted of one factor with items associated to self-emotions appraisal; another with the others' emotions appraisal items; a third factor consisting of the use of emotion items; and a last factor that was comprised of regulation of emotions items. Finally, the ten selected items from the GENE scale (Neuliep and McCroskey 1997) were associated to one factor, as expected.

Analyzing Table 9.1, it is possible to see that ethnocentrism was negatively related to performance ($r = -0.19$, $p < 0.05$), whereas CQ and EQ were positively associated to performance ($r = 0.31$, $p < 0.01$, and $r = 0.39$, $p < 0.01$, respectively). However, although significant, the association between ethnocentrism and performance was not very high, with ethnocentrism only explaining 3.6 percent of the variance of the performance variable.

## Assessing the Proposed Model

A multiple regression analysis was conducted to examine the relationship between individual performance, CQ, EQ and ethnocentrism. We utilized the ordinary least-squares methodology where the dependent variable was individual performance and the independent variables were a set of control variables and CQ, EQ, ethnocentrism, job satisfaction and an interaction between CQ and EQ.

As we found that the initial models did not satisfy the OLS assumptions, with the Breutsch-Pagan test indicating heteroscedasticity ($Chi^2 = 6.48$; $p = 0.0109$) and high multicollinearity between CQ, EQ and the interaction between these two (VIF for CQ and EQ above 10 and VIF for the interaction above 30, Wooldridge 2009), all the variables were standardized (Balli and Sorensen 2013; Marquardt 1980), and after this all the OLS assumptions were supported. The two tests supported the homoscedasticity (Breutsch-Pagan test, $Chi^2 = 2.87$; $p = 0.09$; and White test $Chi^2 = 93$; $p = 0.4512$).

If we look at the multiple regression presented in Table 9.2, we can see that the only variable that is significantly related to performance in the second step of the regression analysis is EQ, $\beta = 0.378$ ($p < 0.01$). Based on this, we would have to reject H1, stating that ethnocentrism is negatively associated with performance and H2, stating that CQ is positively associated with individual performance of MNC employees. At this step of the analysis, the $\beta$ coefficient between CQ and performance is 0.144, not reaching significance ($p = 0.286$). At step 2, we only find support for H3, as the association between EQ and performance reaches significance ($\beta = 0.378$, $p < 0.01$).

In the third step of the multiple regression analysis, we entered the interaction between CQ and EQ into the analysis, and came up with our third model. This final model was significant ($F(9.83) = 4.151$, $p < 0.001$) and had an adjusted $R^2$ of 31 percent. According to this model, three of our independent variables significantly predict individual performance of employees in a MNC, namely CQ ($\beta = 0.258$, $p = 0.034$), EQ ($\beta = 0.489$, $p < 0.001$), and the interaction between CQ and EQ ($\beta = 0.491$, $p < 0.001$).

According to these findings, we can only partially confirm our H1, stating that ethnocentrism is negatively associated with individual performance. Although we found a significant negative correlation between these two variables, it was not strong enough to explain a significant proportion of the individual performance, and this association was not confirmed in our multiple regression analysis. On the other hand, we can confirm H2, stating that CQ is positively associated with individual performance of MNC employees and H3, stating that EQ is positively associated with individual performance of MNC employees. Interestingly,

**Table 9.2** Regression analysis

| Variable | *B* | *SE* $\beta$ | Β | *p* | $R^2$ | $\Delta R^2$ | $\Delta F$ | (*dfs*) |
|---|---|---|---|---|---|---|---|---|
| Step 1 | | | | | 0.035 | 0.035 | 0.798 | (4.88) |
| Age | −0.002 | 0.015 | −0.014 | 0.899 | | | | |
| Gender | −0.130 | 0.220 | −0.062 | 0.558 | | | | |
| Educational level | 0.007 | 0.335 | 0.002 | 0.983 | | | | |
| Company level | 0.477 | 0.286 | 0.178 | 0.099 | | | | |
| Step 2 | | | | | 0.208 | 0.173 | 4.602** | (4.84) |
| Ethnocentrism | −0.080 | 0.104 | −0.080 | 0.442 | | | | |
| CQ | 0.144 | 0.135 | 0.140 | 0.286 | | | | |
| EQ | 0.380 | 0.136 | 0.378 | 0.007 | | | | |
| Job satisfaction | −0.131 | 0.136 | −0.128 | 0.339 | | | | |
| Step 3 | | | | | 0.375 | 0.307 | 22.09** | (4.83) |
| *Model 3* | | | | | | | | |
| Age | 0.001 | 0.012 | 0.010 | 0.908 | | | | |
| Gender | −0.142 | 0.190 | −0.068 | 0.457 | | | | |
| Educational level | −0.355 | 0.283 | −0.115 | 0.214 | | | | |
| Company level | 0.344 | 0.243 | 0.128 | 0.160 | | | | |
| Ethnocentrism | −0.024 | 0.093 | −0.024 | 0.799 | | | | |
| CQ | 0.266 | 0.123 | 0.258 | 0.034 | | | | |
| EQ | 0.492 | 0.124 | 0.489 | 0.000 | | | | |
| Job satisfaction | −0.042 | 0.123 | −0.041 | 0.732 | | | | |

**Significant at 1 percent

the association between CQ and individual performance seems to be positively moderated by EQ, as the association between CQ and individual performance only emerges once the interaction between CQ and EQ is entered into the analysis.

## Discussion and Conclusions

The main purpose of this study was to examine the relationship between personal characteristics and the international service performance of employees from a MNC. We argued that given the international nature of their jobs, with intercultural interactions on a regular basis, employees' performance ought to be related to their personal characteristics. In this line, our first hypothesis posed that lower levels of ethnocentrism in respondents would be associated with a higher self-perceived performance. The results showed that although a statistically negative relationship was found between these two variables, this association was not replicated in the multiple regression analysis, once the other variables were entered into the analysis.

We also suggested that a higher level of cultural intelligence would be a good predictor of individual job performance in contexts with regular intercultural interactions. Our analyses showed that a significant positive correlation was found between cultural intelligence and perceived individual performance, but this association only became significant in the third model of the multiple regression analysis, when the interaction between cultural intelligence and emotional intelligence was included.

In addition, we predicted that higher levels of emotional intelligence across all branches would be a good predictor of performance. The analyses showed that emotional intelligence was in fact positively associated with perceived performance, and this association was significant both in the bivariate correlation analysis and the multiple regression analysis. Finally, we included a research question in order to assess a possible interaction between EQ and CQ in the prediction of individual performance of MNC employees, which was something that the current study confirmed. The interaction between CQ and EQ was found to significantly predict perceived performance of employees working for a multinational company. Hence, given high levels of CQ, higher levels of EQ would help to improve job performance. At the same time, employees scoring lower on CQ could show satisfactory levels of job performance, provided that they showed high levels of EQ. In all, this finding seems to indicate that EQ can boost the positive effects of CQ on job performance, with a moderation effect being present.

The use of a convenience sample does not provide us with a statistically representative sample in order to generalize to all kinds of MNC companies. The current sample only represents the IT industry, which is why it would be necessary to extend this study to include different industries in order to be able to generalize the findings. It would also be necessary to study larger samples of employees, in an attempt to extrapolate the results and improve the significance levels of some variables. As a next step of our project, this model will be tested with other methodologies, such as structural equation modeling, which would allow us to assess more sophisticated relationships among the variables. In this project we analyzed self-reported performance. In future research, more objective measures of performance like supervisors' evaluations should also be included.

For any MNC, the management of intercultural interactions is a way of life. These daily internal and/or external exchanges and interactions pose regular challenges for MNC employees and the company as a whole. Part of the success of a company depends on an effective management of these discrete interactions between employees, or between employees and customers, in order to accomplish their daily tasks and activities. By assessing and helping employees develop higher EQ and CQ, MNCs can guarantee that they have positive employees who enjoy these intercultural interactions, and who, in the end, can contribute to creating competitive advantages and capabilities. A secondary finding, not part of the purposes of the current study, was that important, significant, positive bivariate correlations were found between employees' job satisfaction and their cultural intelligence ($r = 0.59$, $p < 0.001$) and emotional intelligence ($r = 0.59$, $p < 0.001$). This might indicate that employees of a MNC with regular intercultural interactions are significantly more satisfied with their work if they have a higher degree of cultural and emotional intelligence, helping them deal with these interactions in an effective and constructive way. This is only a speculative conclusion that should be further explored in a future study.

On the one hand, it is possible to point out the necessity of measuring the CQ, EQ and ethnocentrism levels of employees and/or job candidates. These assessments might help companies evaluate who to hire for a position with cross-cultural relationships or who to promote. They can also help employers or managers understand which cultural environments would be most appropriate for different people, or what interventions to put in place. It might also help companies assess which staff members or candidates might have the best chance of adapting to new cross-cultural conditions (e.g. a new boss, position or international assignment). Companies need to create training and development policies with regard to creating a culture in which employees are capable of understanding different kinds of customers and co-workers, and in which they can work together efficiently. In the same vein, the evaluation process ought to include EQ, apart from CQ, as this variable seems to be very relevant in the sense that it moderates the effect of CQ on individual performance.

## References


Aaker, D.A., V. Kumar, and G.S. Day. 2010. *Marketing research*. 10th ed. Wiley: New York.

Adorno, T.W., E. Frenkel-Brunswik, D.J. Levinson, and R.N. Sanford. 1950. *The authoritarian personality*.

Ang, S., and L. Van Dyne. 2008. Conceptualization of cultural intelligence: Definition, distinctiveness, and nomological network. In *Handbook of cultural intelligence: Theory, measurement, and applications*, 3–15. Armonk: M.E. Sharpe.

Ang, S., L. Van Dyne, C. Koh, K.Y. Ng, K.J. Templer, C. Tay, and N.A. Chandrasekar. 2007. Cultural intelligence: Its measurement and effects on cultural judgment and decision making, cultural adaptation and task performance. *Management and Organization Review* 3 (3): 335–371.

Balli, H.O., and B.E. Sørensen. 2013. Interaction effects in econometrics. *Empirical Economics* 45 (1): 583–603. New York: Guilford Publications.

Bandura, A. 1999. Social cognitive theory of personality. *Handbook of personality: Theory and research*, 154–196.

Bar-On, R. 2006. The Bar-On model of emotional-social intelligence (ESI) 1. *Psicothema 18* (Suplemento): 13–25.
Brett, J., K. Behfar, and M.C. Kern. 2006. Managing multicultural teams. *Harvard Business Review* 84 (11): 85–91.
Caligiuri, P., and I. Tarique. 2011. Dynamic cross-cultural competencies and global leadership effectiveness. *Journal of World Business* 47 (4): 612–622.
Chen, G.M. 2010. The impact of intercultural sensitivity on ethnocentrism and intercultural communication apprehension. *Intercultural Communication Studies* 19 (1): 1–9.
Christophersen, T., and U. Konradt. 2012. Development and validation of a formative and a reflective measure for the assessment of online store usability. *Behaviour & Information Technology* 31 (9): 839–857.
Churchill, G.A., Jr., N.M. Ford, S.W. Hartley, and O.C. Walker Jr. 1985. The determinants of salesperson performance: A meta-analysis. *Journal of Marketing Research* 22: 103–118.
Conte, J.M. 2005. A review and critique of emotional intelligence measures. *Journal of Organizational Behavior 26* (4): 433–440.
Côté, S., and C.T. Miners. 2006. Emotional intelligence, cognitive intelligence, and job performance. *Administrative Science Quarterly* 51 (1): 1–28.
Crowne, K.A. 2006. Examining the antecedents of cultural intelligence. In *Widener University proceedings-AIB-Se (USA) annual meeting: Clearwater Beach, FL*, 127–138.
Dong, Q., K.D. Day, and C.M. Collaço. 2008. Overcoming ethnocentrism through developing intercultural communication sensitivity and multiculturalism. *Human Communication* 11 (1): 27–38.
Earley, P.C. 2002. Redefining interactions across cultures and organizations: Moving forward with cultural intelligence. *Research in Organizational Behavior* 24: 271–299.
Earley, P.C., and S. Ang. 2003. *Cultural intelligence: Individual interactions across cultures*. Stanford: Stanford University Press.
Giacobbe, R.W., D.W. Jackson Jr., L.A. Crosby, and C.M. Bridges. 2006. A contingency approach to adaptive selling behavior and sales performance: Selling situations and salesperson characteristics. *Journal of Personal Selling & Sales Management* 26 (2): 115–142.
Hancer, M., and R.T. George. 2003. Job satisfaction of restaurant employees: An empirical investigation using the Minnesota satisfaction questionnaire. *Journal of Hospitality & Tourism Research* 27 (1): 85–100.
Homburg, C., W.D. Hoyer, and M. Fassnacht. 2002. Service orientation of a retailer's business strategy: Dimensions, antecedents, and performance outcomes. *Journal of Marketing* 66 (4): 86–101.

Jadhav, S., and Z.R. Mulla. 2010. Do emotionally intelligent people do well in all jobs? Exploring the moderating role of inter-personal interaction. *Vision 14* (4): 247.

Jaworski, B.J., and A.K. Kohli. 1993. Market orientation: Antecedents and consequences. *The Journal of Marketing* 57: 53–70.

Kafetsios, K., and L.A. Zampetakis. 2008. Emotional intelligence and job satisfaction: Testing the mediatory role of positive and negative affect at work. *Personality and Individual Differences* 44 (3): 712–722.

Kayes, D.C., A.B. Kayes, and Y. Yamazaki. 2005. Essential competencies for cross-cultural knowledge absorption. *Journal of Managerial Psychology 20* (7): 578–589.

Kogut, B., and U. Zander. 1996. What firms do coordination, identity and learning. *Organization Science* 7 (5): 502–518.

Law, K.S., C.S. Wong, and L.J. Song. 2004. The construct and criterion validity of emotional intelligence and its potential utility for management studies. *Journal of Applied Psychology 89* (3): 483.

Lee, L.Y., and B.M. Sukoco. 2010. The effects of cultural intelligence on expatriate performance: The moderating effects of international experience. *The International Journal of Human Resource Management* 21 (7): 963–981.

Lee, J.H., M.S. Kim, and A. Jeon. 2013. The effects of emotional intelligence on service recovery and organizational loyalty: A case of flight attendants of South Korean airlines. *Service Business* 7 (4): 665–686.

Marquardt, D.W. 1980. Comment. *Journal of the American Statistical Association* 75 (369): 87–91.

Mayer, J.D., P. Salovey, and D. Caruso. 2000. Models of emotional intelligence. In *The handbook of intelligence*, ed. R.J. Sternberg, 396–420. New York: Cambridge University Press.

Mayer, J.D., P. Salovey, and D.R. Caruso. 2008. Emotional intelligence: New ability or eclectic traits? *American Psychologist 63* (6): 503.

Maznevski, M.L., and J.J. DiStefano. 2000. Global leaders are team players: Developing global leaders through membership on global teams. *Human Resource Management 39* (2, 3): 195.

Meyer, J.D., and P. Salovey. 1997. What is emotional intelligence? In *Emotional Development and Emotional Intelligence: Educational Implications*, 1. New York: Basic Books.

Moon, T. 2010. Emotional intelligence correlates of the four-factor model of cultural intelligence. *Journal of Managerial Psychology* 25 (8): 876–898.

Neuliep, J.W. 2002. Assessing the reliability and validity of the generalized ethnocentrism scale. *Journal of Intercultural Communication Research 31* (4): 201–215.

Neuliep, J.W., and J.C. McCroskey. 1997. The development of a US and generalized ethnocentrism scale. *Communication Research Reports* 14 (4): 385–398.

Neuliep, J.W., S.M. Hintz, and J.C. McCroskey. 2005. The influence of ethnocentrism in organizational contexts: Perceptions of interviewee and managerial attractiveness, credibility, and effectiveness. *Communication Quarterly* 53 (1): 41–56.

Nunnally, J.C., and I.H. Bernstein. 1994. *Psychometric theory*. Vol. 226. New York: McGraw-Hill.

Podsakoff, P.M., and D.W. Organ. 1986. Self-reports in organizational research: Problems and prospects. *Journal of Management* 12 (4): 531–544.

Podsakoff, P.M., S.B. MacKenzie, J.Y. Lee, and N.P. Podsakoff. 2003. Common method biases in behavioral research: A critical review of the literature and recommended remedies. *Journal of Applied Psychology 88* (5): 879.

Rojell, E.J., C.E. Pettijohn, and R.S. Parker. 2006. Emotional intelligence and dispositional affectivity as predictors of performance in sales people. *Journal of Marketing Theory and Practice* 14 (2): 113–124.

Román, S., and D. Iacobucci. 2010. Antecedents and consequences of adaptive selling confidence and behavior: A dyadic analysis of salespeople and their customers. *Journal of the Academy of Marketing Science* 38 (3): 363–382.

Salovey, P., and J.D. Mayer. 1990. Emotional intelligence. *Imagination, Cognition and Personality* 9 (3): 185–211.

Shaffer, M.A., D.A. Harrison, H. Gregersen, J.S. Black, and L.A. Ferzandi. 2006. You can take it with you: Individual differences and expatriate effectiveness. *Journal of Applied Psychology 91* (1): 109.

Spector, P.E. 1997. *Job satisfaction: Application, assessment, causes, and consequences*. Vol. 3. Thousand Oaks: Sage.

Sumner, W.G. 1906. *Folkways*. Boston: Ginn.

Templer, K.J., C. Tay, and N.A. Chandrasekar. 2006. Motivational cultural intelligence, realistic job preview, realistic living conditions preview, and cross-cultural adjustment. *Group & Organization Management* 31 (1): 154–173.

Teng, C.I., and T.W. Liu. 2014. How do personality interactions affect service quality? The perspective of processing efficiency theory. *Service Business 8* (2): 375–397.

Van Dyne, L., S. Ang, and C. Koh. 2008. Development and validation of the CQS. In *Handbook of cultural intelligence*, 16–40. Armonk: M.E. Sharpe.

Van Rooy, D.L., and C. Viswesvaran. 2004. Emotional intelligence: A meta-analytic investigation of predictive validity and nomological net. *Journal of Vocational Behavior* 65 (1): 71–95.

Wang, M.K., and K.P. Hwang. 2012. The impact of employee perceptions of human resource management systems on job satisfaction and organizational commitment during privatization the transformations of privatization: An empirical study of telecommunications corporations in Taiwan. *Asia Pacific Management Review* 17 (3): 321–342.

Ward, C., R. Fischer, F.S.Z. Lam, and L. Hall. 2009. The convergent, discriminant, and incremental validity of scores on a self-report measure of cultural intelligence. *Educational and Psychological Measurement* 69 (1): 85–105.

Ward, C., J. Wilson, and R. Fischer. 2011. Assessing the predictive validity of cultural intelligence over time. *Personality and Individual Differences 51* (2): 138–142.

Weiss, D.J., R.V. Dawis, and G.W. England. 1967. Manual for the Minnesota satisfaction questionnaire. In *Minnesota studies in vocational rehabilitation*. Minneapolis: University of Minnesota.

Wong, C.S., and K.S. Law. 2002. The effects of leader and follower emotional intelligence on performance and attitude: An exploratory study. *The Leadership Quarterly 13* (3): 243–274.

Wooldridge, J.M. 2009. *Introductory econometrics: A modern approach*. Mason, OH: South-Western Cengage Learning.

# 10

# Examining the Influence of Self-Efficacy, Optimism and Curiosity on the Performance of International Locals

Leonardo Liberman, David Kimber C., and Javier Pinto Garay

## Introduction

Firms with operations spanning national borders are characterized by a large number of interactions and exchanges among employees, customers and suppliers coming from multiple cultures. Given the development of international trade and the surge of connectivity over the past decade, intercultural interactions have become customary and taken for granted by most regular employees working within companies. International exchanges are no longer limited to the roles of expatriate assignees, but have become a part of most employees' roles within international companies.

L. Liberman (✉)
Libens Research and Development, Santiago, Chile

D. Kimber C. • J. Pinto Garay
Universidad de los Andes, Santiago, Chile
e-mail: dkimber@uandes.cl; jpinto@uandes.cl





W. Newburry et al. (eds.), *Contemporary Influences on International Business in Latin America*, AIB Latin America, https://doi.org/10.1007/978-3-319-98340-0_10

In spite of this shift, few studies have focused on the relationship between performance and character traits on domestic employees that regularly deal with customers, employees and suppliers from other countries and cultures. Much of the research has focused on expatriates (Caligiuri 1997; Caligiuri 2000a) and international assignees (Black et al. 1991, 1999). However, scientists have recently turned their attention to what have been called non-standard international experiences (Suutari et al. 2013), such as intercultural interactions, commuting and virtual collaboration. These are the "international locals", employees who, albeit not officially appointed to any international position, frequently engage with employees, clients, suppliers and other stakeholders from a different national-cultural background.

In this vein, we are interested in learning about the characteristics of international locals that might affect their performance in their interactions in their workplace. Personnel who, as part of their jobs, frequently engage with employees, clients, suppliers and other stakeholders from a different national-cultural background.

## Theoretical Development

There is a large body of research that has studied individual character and personality traits in general, and a large number of attributes, behaviors and taxonomies have been identified (Allport 1936; Cattell 1965; Eysenck 1992; McCrae and Costa 1997). There is also a growing interest in individual differences and the effectiveness of expatriate personnel (Shaffer et al. 1999, 2006).

Another recent area of study has emphasized the importance of positive character attributes for an individual's personal functioning (Seligman and Csikszentmihalyi 2000; Kelloway et al. 2012). Open-mindedness, modesty, self-control, curiosity, persistence, integrity and confidence are only some of these (Gillham and Seligman 1999; Gillham 2000; Shatte et al. 2000; Seligman 2002; Peterson and Seligman 2004). It has also been suggested that these character traits play an important role in an individual's motivation, problem solving, stress, resilience and even well-being (Seligman and Csikszentmihalyi 2000). Another recent theoretical perspective that underpins this field of study is positive organizational behavior (POB). This perspective endeavors to measure, develop and effectively manage positive strengths to improve performance in the workplace (Luthans 2002a, b; Bakker and Schaufeli 2008). It also studies how to attract and retain positive employees who make organizations grow. Yamazaki and Kayes (2004) found that employees who show higher levels of intercultural personality traits before starting their international assignments are more competent in terms of global management.

In all, both theory and research indicate these personal traits are related to positive outcomes such as job performance and problem-solving capacity (Avey et al. 2010). However, research still needs to systematically examine in which contexts employees' character traits are related to their performance. In this study, we draw concepts and evidence from positive psychology (Cameron 2008), psychological capital (Luthans et al. 2007) and the self-efficacy framework (Bandura 2000) and we focus on three main character traits: self-efficacy, optimism and curiosity. According to these frameworks, self-efficacy, optimism and curiosity improve the functioning and adaptability of individuals, and hence may play a role in the performance of local employees who are subject to intercultural interactions.

## Theoretical Framework

In the following subsections, we examine the constructs of self-efficacy, optimism and curiosity.

### Self-efficacy

Self-efficacy is a person's beliefs about his or her capabilities to produce designated levels of performance (Bandura 1986, 1997; Schwarzer 1994). These beliefs link cognitions, motivation and actions and allow a person to feel in control in certain situations while attaining defined goals (Wood and Bandura 1989). Therefore, self-efficacy plays an important role when it comes to the self-regulation of motivation and performance (Stajkovic and Luthans 1998). According to Bandura (1986), self-efficacy boosts motivation and improves problem-solving efforts (Wood and Bandura 1989).

In the context of the workplace, self-efficacy has been defined as "the employee's conviction about his or her abilities to mobilize the motivation, cognitive resources or courses of action needed to successfully execute a specific task within a given context" (Stajkovic and Luthans 1998, p. 66). Research has found that self-efficacy enables employees to attain positive outcomes (e.g. Avey et al. 2009, 2010) and influences a wide array of behaviors when coping with different types of challenging situations (Luthans 2007). When faced with difficulties, self-efficacy will influence how much effort a person puts in and how long she or he will persevere. Lower levels of self-efficacy are related to distress and despair that impair a person's level of performance. In the international management context, self-efficacy has been looked upon as confidence in terms of a person's own effectiveness when confronted with unfamiliar situations and difficulties in other cultures (Kim 1987). This construct is related to self-assurance (Javidan and Teagarden 2011) that entails attributes like resilience, coping capabilities and self-confidence when facing demanding or risky situations.

As such, self-efficacy is a central aspect when adjusting to cross-cultural encounters and transitions (Ward and Kennedy 1993).

Overall, self-efficacy is related to job effectiveness, productivity, satisfaction and the ability to cope with adjustment to new cultures and circumstances. Based on this previous literature, we suggest that the performance of employees who have regular intercultural contacts will be improved by a higher sense of self-efficacy. Hence, we pose that self-efficacy will be positively associated with the job performance of international locals.

## Optimism

Optimism entails thinking about the future and developing an expectation toward it. It is a disposition to believe that one will reach favorable outcomes in life (Scheier and Carver 1992) and takes the form of a broad expectation that the future is full of good things and holds a limited number of bad things (Scheier et al. 1994, 2001). Optimism has been found to facilitate adjustment (Scheier et al. 2001) to challenging situations and it has also been reported as being associated with morale, perseverance, problem-solving capacity and overall health (Peterson 2000; Peterson and Seligman 1987). According to Seligman (1998), optimism enables a person to make internal, stable and global attributions regarding positive events, and external, unstable and specific attributions regarding negative events.

Further, optimism has been considered a trait that people possess to varying degree, as it is thought to be relatively stable over time. People high in optimism tend to trust that their goals can be successfully achieved in spite of impediments, which would make them more resistant to giving up when faced with difficulties. Generally, optimism has been associated with an active and effective coping style (Scheier et al. 1986) and better coping strategies when faced with adversity (Scheier et al. 1994). According to Luthans et al. (2007) optimism is part of psychological capital and is related to an individual's strength, attitudes and perceptions toward work and a general outlook on life.

In the international management field, optimism is considered one of the essential personality factors for intercultural effectiveness (Mamman 1995) and it has also been considered as part of one of the composite variables of instruments that measure intercultural personality characteristics and effectiveness (Furuya et al. 2009). In our study, we suggest that higher levels of optimism will be related with better performance of local employees involved in daily intercultural interactions. Thus, based on the empirical evidence discussed above, we hypothesize that optimism will be positively associated with the performance of local employees involved in frequent international interactions.

## Curiosity

Curiosity is another important trait that has been methodically studied (Izard 1977; Peterson and Seligman 2004; Reiss 2000) and it has been considered as one of the most important motivators of human behavior throughout life (Loewenstein 1994). Curiosity is related to inquiry, search and learning, and was early thought to be a transitory state that stimulated information and knowledge seeking (Berlyne 1960).

Together with exploratory behavior, curiosity is one of the main enablers of learning since it is a way to cope with novelty and ambiguity (Berg and Sternberg 1985; Silvia 2008; Spielberger and Starr 1994). It allows individuals to explore their environments with a positive attitude, open to the challenges that uncertainty involves (Kashdan and Rottenberg 2010). According to Voss and Keller (1983), curiosity allows individuals to flexibly adapt to changing environmental conditions and it implies "a direction of development toward differentiated interaction patterns and more effective problem solving" (p. 156). Besides, according to Levy et al. (2007), curiosity is part of a global mindset (Srinivas 1995; Maznevski and Lane 2004; Javidan and Teagarden 2011) and it is understood as a concept closely associated with a "tendency to engage" and an "opportunity seeking" behavior, allowing employees to grasp multi-faceted and unforeseen cultural, business and geopolitical forces (Levy et al. 2007).

Hence, curiosity is a mental strength (Peterson and Seligman 2004) and has a significant evolutionary and adaptive function (Tomkins 1962, 1963). It allows people to embrace new uncertain situations without fear, helping to build knowledge, relations and expertise (Izard 1977; Kashdan and Rottenberg 2010). Curiosity has been associated with other constructs, such as sensation-seeking (Zuckerman et al. 1964), novelty-seeking (Pearson 1970), openness to experience (Krietler and Krietler 1994) and even creativity (Robinson and Stern 1997).

In the context of employees undertaking expatriate assignments, it is commonly understood that curiosity and a need for adventure play a central role in accepting international assignments (Brewster and Hegewisch 1994). A concept closely related to curiosity is "openness to experience" and it reflects an individual's willingness to try new ideas and tolerate uncertainty and dissonance; one who is generally eager to learn (Barrick and Mount 1991). Prior research has suggested that this construct is an important explanatory variable for the cultural adjustment of international assignees (Brewster and Hegewisch 1994; Ulanova 2014). It has been found that those with a higher score on curiosity scales tend to perform better in their tasks and in terms of their assignment-specific performance (Rose et al. 2010). Besides, curiosity has been found to be a critical factor for the successful adjustment of expatriates to new cultures as it positively predisposes them to learning and problem solving while facing novel events and uncertainty in their host countries (Ulanova 2014). Curiosity is closely related to "quest for adventure" and "passion for diversity" (Javidan and Bowen 2013; Javidan and Teagarden 2011). The first construct comprises a deep interest and willingness to deal with challenging and unpredictable situations, to take risks and the desire to test one's own abilities in different situations. The second concept, passion for diversity, is understood as a genuine strong interest in experiencing diverse countries, cultures and people.

Given the evidence, we suggest that this attribute would also help international locals when interacting with stakeholders from different cultures as these individuals may bring novelty and uncertainty to the workplace. It is because of this that we argue that higher self-reported levels of curiosity in international locals would be associated with more success in their tasks. Thus, based on the empirical evidence discussed above, we hypothesize that curiosity will be positively associated with the performance of international locals.

Individual job performance plays a central role in the functioning of a company as it reflects the contribution of its members to the achievement of the company's goals. Job performance is related to abilities, knowledge and motivation of employees with regard to their formal duties and tasks (Campbell, McHenry and Wise 1990). According to McCloy, Campbell and Cudeck (1994), individual differences have a pervasive effect on job performance. For instance, Barrick, Mount and Strauss (1993) found that highly conscientious individuals tend to perform better in their jobs.

Viswesvaran (1996) contended that these traits may take several expressions that would result in higher job knowledge and productivity. Others have suggested that character traits predict contextual performance better than other factors, such as skills and job-related habits. In general, it seems that job performance in its different dimensions is influenced by an array of factors, and it is difficult to define one single trait as the sole cause. Black (1990) suggested that the openness trait would improve the adjustment and performance of expatriates. Open individuals would tend to have more flexible views of right and wrong, ideas, norms and behaviors, and this trait would allow them to have more effective relations and interactions with host nationals. In general, individual differences are related to expatriate job performance (e.g. Parker and McEvoy 1993; Ones and Viswesvaran 1999; Shaffer et al. 1999, 2006; Caligiuri 2000b; Hechanova et al. 2003).

## Methods

A questionnaire was set up online and a mass e-mail was sent out to 900 employees of a company operating in Latin America, inviting them to take part in the study. All respondents were required to complete a consent form agreeing to participate in the study before they could move on to the questionnaire itself. The response rate for the online questionnaire was around 30%. As the purpose of the study was to learn more about international locals, we focused on international locals, those local employees who had frequent contact with customers, suppliers or other employees coming from a country different from their own. Respondents were asked to rate the time they spent dealing with people from countries different from theirs. At the end, we included 99 cases that had the highest frequency of international contact in their domestic positions. All the participants responded to a questionnaire composed of four scales: namely self-efficacy, optimism, curiosity and performance. These scales are briefly described below.

To assess self-efficacy, we used the General Self-efficacy Scale (Schwarzer and Jerusalem 1995; Schwarzer et al. 1997). This is a unidimensional scale developed to measure perceived self-efficacy in relation to coping and adaptation capabilities in both daily activities and stressful events. The General Self-efficacy Scale is a 10-item scale that is answered according to a 1–4 Likert-type scale, indicating how true (1 = not at all true to 4 = exactly true) the respondent considers each statement. This scale has been used in several research studies and it has been found to have acceptable levels of validity and reliability (Schwarzer 1997).

To assess optimism we used the Life Orientation Test-Revised (Lot-r) by Scheier et al. (1994). In this scale, respondents are asked to rate to what degree they agree with each of statements (1 = I agree a lot; to 5 = I disagree a lot). The original scale has ten items measuring both optimism and pessimism (Vautier et al. 2003). However, as four of the ten items of the original scale are "fillers", these items were not related to the dimension in study and were therefore eliminated. Hence, the final scale for optimism had six items.

To measure curiosity, we used the Curiosity and Exploration Inventory-II of Kashdan et al. (2009). This scale has 10 questions that are rated on a 1–5 scale and it has been used and tested in different samples and there is good evidence for its psychometric properties. It has also been found to have good discrimination capacity and construct validity (Kashdan et al. 2009).

Employees' performance was assessed by a self-report scale consisting of items rated on a scale ranging from 1 (poor) to 7 (outstanding). Employees were asked to rate their own general performance in relation to their individual goals and to their colleagues (Giaccobe et al. 2006). Although there is a debate about the validity of self-report measures, there are a number of studies supporting their use (Churchill et al. 1985; Román and Iacobucci 2010), arguing that these self-reports are a fairly valid and reliable estimate of employees' actual performance.

The control variables that we included in our analyses were educational level, age and gender of the respondents.

## Results

To analyze the data, we used a two-step approach. First, we explored the correlations and internal consistencies of the different scales used in this study and then we assessed the impact of the character traits on performance through a multiple linear regression analysis.

The bivariate correlations between the variables are presented in the correlation matrix in Table 10.1. We found significant correlations ($p < 0.05$) between the independent variables, but most of these were weak with the exception of self-efficacy and curiosity (0.716, $p < 0.01$).

**Table 10.1** Internal consistencies of the different subscales and correlations

| Variables | 1 | 2 | 3 | 4 | *Alpha* |
|---|---|---|---|---|---|
| 1. Performance | | | | | |
| | | | | | 0.90 |
| 2. Self-efficacy | 0.604* | | | | |
| | 0.00 | | | | 0.91 |
| 3. Optimism | 0.363* | 0.372* | | | |
| | 0.00 | 0.00 | | | 0.79 |
| 4. Curiosity | 0.627* | 0.716* | 0.493* | | |
| | 0.00 | 0.00 | 0.00 | | 0.83 |

*Significant correlations, $p < 0.05$

Given the correlation between self-efficacy and curiosity and ruling out multi-collinearity (Farrar and Glauber 1967), we tested the variance inflation factor (VIF). We calculated VIFs for each predictor and found that they were all in the range between 1 and 2, far below the maximum tolerance suggested in the literature (O'Brien 2007; Wooldridge 2009).

We also found that performance was positively related to self-efficacy, optimism and curiosity ($r = 0.604$, $p < 0.001$; $r = 0.363$, $p < 0.001$; and $r = 0.627$, $p < 0.001$, respectively).

Following this, we carried out a regression analysis to identify the best predictors of performance. We tested a model assessing the impact of self-efficacy, optimism and curiosity on job performance, considering age, gender and educational level. We entered gender, age and educational level in the first step and then we entered self-efficacy, optimism and curiosity in the second step.

If we look at the multiple regression model presented in Table 10.2, we can see that in the first step of the analysis, no control variable resulted as being a significant predictor of performance. In the second step, we entered self-efficacy, optimism and curiosity, resulting in only two variables being significant predictors, curiosity ($B = 0.630$, $p < 0.05$) and self-efficacy ($B = 0.560$, $p < 0.05$). According to these findings, we can state that curiosity and self-efficacy are significant predictors of performance in the sample.

**Table 10.2** A multiple regression analysis

| Variable | $B$ | $SE\ B$ | β | $p$ | $R^2$ | $\Delta R^2$ | $\Delta F$ | ($dfs$) |
|---|---|---|---|---|---|---|---|---|
| Step 1 | | | | | 0.110 | 0.110 | 2.909 | (4.94) |
| Age | 0.002 | 0.011 | 0.019 | 0.851 | | | | |
| Gender | 0.053 | 0.162 | 0.032 | 0.745 | | | | |
| Educational level | −0.040 | 0.245 | −0.016 | 0.872 | | | | |
| Step 2 | | | | | 0.450 | 0.340 | 18.779** | (3.91) |
| Age | −0.001 | 0.009 | −0.005 | 0.949 | | | | |
| Gender | 0.027 | 0.131 | 0.016 | 0.837 | | | | |
| Educational level | −0.136 | 0.197 | −0.056 | 0.490 | | | | |
| Self-efficacy | 0.560 | 0.192 | 0.332 | 0.004 | | | | |
| Optimism | 0.110 | 0.147 | 0.068 | 0.456 | | | | |
| Curiosity | 0.630 | 0.208 | 0.378 | 0.003 | | | | |

**Significant at 1%

Based on these results, we accept H1 stating that self-efficacy is positively associated with employees' performance and H3 predicting that curiosity is positively related to the performance of employees with frequent international contacts. Moreover, based on the bivariate correlations, we would partly accept H2 predicting a positive correlation between optimism and performance, even though optimism was not found to be a significant predictor of performance according to our linear regression analysis.

## Discussion and Conclusions

This exploratory study aimed at increasing our understanding of the relationship between character traits and the performance of international locals. In the context of growing intercultural contacts between international stakeholders within companies, we tested the effect of three traits—self-efficacy, optimism and curiosity—that were thought to influence performance. We contended that higher levels of self-efficacy, optimism and curiosity would be related to a higher performance of employees, helping them to better fulfill their roles.

Concerning our first hypothesis suggesting that international locals with a higher sense of personal efficacy would perform better than those with a lower sense of personal efficacy, this was accepted. In our study, those employees who showed a general positive perception about their capacity to perform their jobs exhibited higher performance in relation to their duties, individual goals and peers. According to the theory, these employees exhibit a better performance as their motivation and problem-solving efforts are positively affected by this general sense of being capable of successfully doing their jobs (Stajkovic and Luthans 1998).

Regarding our second hypothesis positing that more optimistic international locals would display higher performance in their work, this hypothesis could only be partially accepted. According to the bivariate correlation, optimism would explain 13% of the variance of performance. However, when included in the analysis together with self-efficacy and curiosity, optimism was not found to be a significant predictor of performance. Prior research suggests that optimism facilitates adjustment to challenging situations and it has been associated with morale, determination, problem solving and superior coping strategies when faced with adversity (Scheier et al. 1994, 2001). Nevertheless, our analyses did not show that effect.

Finally, concerning our third hypothesis suggesting that higher levels of curiosity in international locals would be associated with higher performance, this is also accepted. The studies mentioned above have identified curiosity as an essential trait in order to be successful when adjusting and coping with uncertainty and dealing with other cultures. It is part of the core properties of what has been called “a global mindset” (Srinivas 1995) and it predisposes employees to detect, learn, engage and grasp multi-layered and unexpected cultural dynamics in international contacts (Levy et al. 2007). A higher level of curiosity in international locals was associated with better performance in relation to their goals, to their own colleagues and to the functions that their positions imposed.

Our attention was drawn to the fact that optimism was not found to be a significant predictor of performance when included together with the other variables in the model. This is despite earlier findings within the field of expatriate management.

A potential explanation for this might be that due to a statistical artifact, the effect of optimism on performance was obscured by the effect of the other two variables. Still, as the correlation between optimism and the other two variables is not that high, this should not be the case. Another possibility is related to the construct and measurement used in this research. Optimism is a trait that reflects the extent to which individuals hold generalized favorable expectations about their future. It is related to higher levels of engagement and coping capacity. A fundamental difference is that perceived competence or self-efficacy is focused on the individual’s behavior in achieving success, whereas optimism has to do with an expected positive outcome that may not be behaviorally dependent: factors that are out of the control of the individual that can affect the development of a favorable outcome.

Like any other research study, this project also has some caveats. First, the data was drawn from a single source, which raises the possibility of common method bias effects having influenced the observed relationships (Podsakoff et al. 2003; Spector 1994). However, we tested the variance inflation factors and ruled out multi-collinearity given by a potential common method bias. Moreover, the performance assessment was based on self-reports, leaving room for social desirability issues and motif biases (Podsakoff and Organ 2003). Nevertheless, previous studies (Román and Iacobucci 2010) have contended that these reports are a fairly valid and reliable estimate of employees' performance. Moreover, due to the large scope of the current study, involving almost 100 employees, self-report measures were considered the most adequate instruments at the time. Finally, our study relies on cross-sectional data, meaning that we measured different variables in the sample of interest at a single point in time, indicating that our findings are just a snapshot of the respondent conditions and state. In a future study, it would be interesting to include additional variables such as cultural intelligence, job satisfaction or supervisor performance, and to carry out the assessment at least at two different points in time.

Taken together, examining the influence that character traits may exert on the performance of international locals adds to the field in several ways. First, it links a new, fast-developing theoretical perspective, character traits, to employee performance in an international setting. Additionally, this study contributes by focusing on international locals, those employees who are not necessarily appointed to an international position but who are subject to intercultural interactions and burdens and affected in other ways. Hence, we move the traditional focus toward the study of non-conventional international experiences (Suutari et al. 2013) shedding light on how character traits may contribute to the performance of international locals.

There has been a debate in the literature since the 1980s (Allen and Potkay 1981; Zuckerman 1983) about whether to consider certain characteristics as transient states or relatively stable traits. Based on this debate, Wright (2007) suggested distinguishing the relative temporal difference between states and traits when studying organizational behavior. In response to this proposition, Luthans, Avolio, Avey and Norman (2007) suggested a state-trait categorization according to a continuum of stability of positive constructs ranging from positive temporary states to character traits that are more stable and more difficult to change.

Nevertheless, irrespective of whether self-efficacy, optimism and curiosity are considered transient states or stable attributes, an important feature of these traits is that they are subject to development. For instance, training and coaching using cognitive and behavioral strategies can improve the sense of self-efficacy (Bandura 1997, 2000). Besides, Carver, and Scheier (2005) have developed a number of strategies to boost optimism and Seligman (1998) contends that optimism can be subject to the principle of learning. Besides, curiosity has also been studied as part of career adaptability and it has been deemed an attribute that can be enhanced (Koen et al. 2012).

The fact that these traits can be strengthened and developed indicates that managers and practitioners can actually support and enhance their employees' performance when facing intercultural exchanges. We believe that if these interactions are well managed and international locals show the appropriate character traits (already when they come to the company or through training or other interventions), then the overall quality and effectiveness of the intercultural interactions can be strengthened, as well as their performance and thus the performance of the firm.

Finally, it would be interesting to also analyze data considering the previous international experience of international locals. Earlier studies have shown that expatriates' past international working and travel experiences have a moderating effect on competencies that influence cultural adjustment and effectiveness (Lee and Sukoco 2010). Future research should therefore include this factor to further understand the effect of self-efficacy, optimism and curiosity, and other traits, on international locals.

## References

Allen, B.P., and C.R. Potkay. 1981. On the arbitrary distinction between states and traits. *Journal of Personality and Social Psychology* 41: 916–928.

Allport, G.W., and H.S. Odbert. 1936. Trait-names: A psycho-lexical study. *Psychological Monographs* 47 (211): 1–38.

Avey, J.B., F. Luthans, and S.M. Jensen. 2009. Psychological capital: A positive resource to combat employee stress and turnover. *Human Resource Management* 48 (5): 677–693.

Avey, J.B., F. Luthans, and C.M. Youssef. 2010. The additive value of positive psychological capital in predicting work attitudes. *Journal of Management* 36 (2): 430–452.

Bakker, A.B., and W.B. Schaufeli. 2008. Positive organizational behavior: Engaged employees in flourishing organizations. *Journal of Organizational Behavior* 29 (2): 147–154.

Bandura, A. 1986b. The explanatory and predictive scope of self-efficacy theory. *Journal of Clinical and Social Psychology* 4: 359–373.

———. (1997a). *Self-efficacy: The exercise of control*. New York: Freeman.

———. 2000. Exercise of human agency through collective efficacy. *Current Directions in Psychological Science* 9: 75–78.

Barrick, M.R., and M.K. Mount. 1991. The big five personality dimensions and job performance a meta-analysis. *Personnel Psychology* 44: 1–25.

Barrick, M.R., M.K. Mount, and J.P. Strauss. 1993. Conscientiousness and performance of sales representatives: Test of the mediating effects of goal setting. *Journal of Applied Psychology* (5): 715–722.

Berg, C.A., and R.J. Sternberg. 1985. A triarchic theory of intellectual development during adulthood. *Developmental Review* 5 (4): 334–370.

Black, J.S. 1990. Personal dimensions and work role transitions. *Management International Review* 30: 119–134.

Black, J.S., M. Mendenhall, and G. Oddou. 1991. Toward a comprehensive model of international adjustment: An integration of multiple theoretical perspectives. *Academy of Management Review* 16: 291–317.

Black, J.S., H.B. Gregersen, M. Mendenhall, and L. Stroh. 1999. *Globalizing people through international assignments*. Boston: Addison-Wesley.

Brewster, C., A. Hegewisch, and L. Mayne. 1994. Trends in HRM in Western Europe In. In *Human resource management in Europe: Perspectives for the 1990s*, ed. P.S. Kirkbride, 56–89. London/New York: Routledge.

Caligiuri, P.M. 1997. Assessing expatriate success: Beyond just 'being there'. In *Expatriate management: Theory and practice*, ed. Z. Aycan, vol. 4, 45–67. Greenwich: JAI Press.

———. 2000a. The big five personality characteristics as predictors of expatriate success. *Personnel Psychology* 53: 67–88.

———. 2000b. Selecting expatriates for personality characteristics: A moderating effect of personality on the relationship between host national contact and cross-cultural adjustment. *Management International Review* 40 (1): 61–80.

Cameron, K.S. 2008. Paradox in positive organizational change. *Journal of Applied Behavioral Science* 44: 7–24.

Campbell, J.P., J.J. McHenry, and L.L. Wise. 1990. Modeling job performance in a population of jobs. *Personnel Psychology* 43 (2): 313–333.

Carver, C.S., and M.F. Scheier. 2005. Optimism. In *Handbook of positive psychology*, ed. C.R. Snyder and S.J. Lopez, 231–256. Oxford: Oxford University Press.

Cattell, R.B. 1965. *The scientific analysis of personality*. Baltimore: Penguin Books.

Churchill, G.A., Jr., N.M. Ford, W.H. Steven, and O.C. Walker Jr. 1985. The determinants of salesperson performance: A meta-analysis. *Journal of Marketing Research* 22: 103–118.

Eysenck, H.J. 1992. Four ways five factors are not basic. *Personality and Individual Differences* 13: 667–673.

Farrar, D.E., and R.R. Glauber. 1967. Multicollinearity in regression analysis: The problem revisited. *Review of Economics and Statistics* 49: 92–107.

Furuya, N., M.J. Stevens, A. Bird, G. Oddou, and M. Mendenhall. 2009. Managing the learning and transfer of global management competence: Antecedents and outcomes of Japanese repatriation effectiveness. *Journal of International Business Studies* 40 (2): 200–215.

Giaccobe, R.W., D.W. Jackson Jr., L.A. Crosby, and C.M. Bridges. 2006. A contingency approach to adaptive selling behavior and sales performance: Selling situations and salesperson characteristics. *Journal of Personal Selling and Sales Management* 26 (2): 115–142.

Gillham, J.E., and M.E.P. Seligman. 1999. Footsteps on the road to a positive psychology. *Behavior Research and Therapy* 37: 163–173.

Gillham, B. 2000. *The research interview*. London: Continuum.

Hechanova, R., T.A. Beehr, and N.D. Christiansen. 2003. Antecedents and consequences of employees' adjustment to overseas assignment: a meta-analytic review. *Applied Psychology: An International Review* 52 (2): 213–236.

Izard, C.E. 1977. *Human emotions*. New York: Plenum.

Javidan, M., and M.B. Teagarden. 2011. Conceptualizing and measuring global mindset. *Advances in Global Leadership* 6: 13–39.

Javidan, M., and D. Bowen. 2013. The 'Global Mindset' of managers: What it is, why it matters, and how to develop it. *Organizational Dynamics* 42 (2): 145–155.

Kashdan, T.B., M.W. Gallagher, P.J. Silvia, B.P. Winterstein, W.E. Breen, D. Terhar, and M.F. Steger. 2009. The curiosity and exploration inventory-II: Development, factor structure, and initial psychometrics. *Journal of Research in Personality* 43: 987–998.

Kashdan, T.B., and J. Rottenberg. 2010. Psychological flexibility as a fundamental aspect of health. *Clinical Psychology Review* 30 (7): 865–878.

Kelloway, E.K., N. Turner, J. Barling, and C. Loughlin. 2012. Transformational leadership and employee psychological well-being: The mediating role of employee trust in leadership. *Work & Stress* 26 (1): 39–55.

Kim, Y.Y. 1987. Preface. In *Cross-cultural adaptation: Current approaches*, ed. Y.Y. Kim and W.B. Gudykunst, 7–17. Newbury Park: Sage.

Koen, J., U.-C. Klehe, and A.E.M. Van Vianen. 2012. Training career adaptability to facilitate a successful school-to-work transition. *Journal of Vocational Behavior* 81 (3): 395–408.

Krietler, S., and H. Krietler. 1994. Motivational and cognitive determinants of exploration. In *Curiosity and exploration*, ed. H. Keller, K. Schneider, and B. Henderson, 259–284. New York: Springer.

Lee, L.Y., and M. Sukoco. 2010. The effects of cultural intelligence on expatriate performance: The moderating effects of international experience. *The International Journal of Human Resource Management.* 21 (7/9): 963–981.

Levy, O., S. Beechler, S. Taylor, and N. Boyacigiller. 2007. What we talk about when we talk about global mindset: Managerial cognition in multinational corporations. *Journal of International Business Studies* 38 (2): 31–258.

Lowenstein, G. 1994. The psychology of curiosity: A review and reinterpretation. *Psychological Bulletin* 116: 75–98.

Luthans, F. 2002a. The need for and meaning of positive organizational behavior. *Journal of Organizational Behavior* 23: 695–706.

———. 2002b. Positive organizational behavior: Developing and managing psychological al strengths. *The Academy of Management Executive* 16: 57–73.

Luthans, F., B.J. Avolio, J.B. Avey, and S.M. Norman. 2007. Positive psychological capital: Measurement and relationship with performance and satisfaction. *Personnel Psychology* 60: 541–572.

Luthans, F., and C.M. Youssef. 2007a. Emerging positive organizational behavior. *Journal of Management* 33: 321–349.

Mamman, A. 1995. Expatriates' intercultural effectiveness: Relevant variables and implications. *Asia Pacific Journal of Human Resources* 33 (1): 40–49. https://doi.org/10.1177/103841119503300103.

Maznevski, M.L., and H.W. Lane. 2004. Shaping the global mindset: Designing educational experiences for effective global thinking and action. In *Crossing cultures: Insights from master teachers*, ed. M. Phillips, 171–184. London: Routledge.

McCloy, R.A., J.P. Campbell, and R. Cudeck. 1994. A confirmatory test of a model of performance determinants. *Journal of Applied Psychology* 79 (4): 493–505.

McCrae, R.R., and P.T. Costa. 1997. Personality trait structure as a human universal. *American Psychologist* 52: 509–516.

O'Brien, R.M. 2007. A caution regarding rules of thumb for variance inflation factors. *Quality & Quantity* 41 (5): 673–690.

Parker, B., and G.M. McEvoy. 1993. Initial examination of a model of intercultural adjustment. *International Journal of Intercultural Relations* 17: 355–379.

Pearson, P.H. 1970. Relationships between global and specified measures of novelty-seeking. *Journal of Consulting and Clinical Psychology* 37: 23–30.

Peterson, C. 2000. The future of optimism. *American Psychologist* 55 (1): 44–55.

Peterson, C., and M.E. Seligman. 1987. Explanatory style and illness. *Journal of Personality* 55 (2): 237–265.

Peterson, C., and M.E.P. Seligman. 2004. *Character strengths and virtues: A handbook and classification*. New York/Washington, DC: Oxford University Press/American Psychological Association.

Podsakoff, P., S.B. MacKenzie, J.-Y. Lee, and N. Podsakoff. 2003. Common method biases in behavioral research: A critical review of the literature and recommended remedies. *Journal of Applied Psychology* 88 (5): 879–903.

Reiss, S. (2000a). Human individuality, happiness, and flow. *American Psychologist* 55: 1161–1162.

Robinson, A.G., and S. Stern. 1997. *Corporative creativity how innovation and improvement actually happen*. San Francisco: Berrett-Koehler Publishers.

Román, S., and D. Iacobucci. 2010. Antecedents and consequences of adaptive selling confidence and behavior: A dyadic analysis of salespeople and their customers. *Journal of the Academy of Marketing Science* 38 (3): 363–382.

Rose, R.C., S.S. Ramalu, J. Uli, and N. Kumar. 2010. Expatriate performance in international assignments: The role of cultural intelligence as dynamic intercultural competency. *International Journal of Business and Management* 5 (8): 76–85.

Scheier, M.F., and C.S. Carver. 1992. Effects of optimism on psychological and physical well-being: Theoretical overview and empirical update. *Cognitive Therapy and Research* 16 (2): 201–228.

Scheier, M.F., C.S. Carver, and M.W. Bridges. 1994. Distinguishing optimism from neuroticism (and trait anxiety, self-mastery, and self-esteem): A re-evaluation of the Life Orientation Test. *Journal of Personality and Social Psychology* 67: 1063–1078.

———. 2001. Optimism, pessimism, and psychological well-being. In *Optimism and pessimism: Implications for theory, research, and practice*, ed. E.C. Chang, 189–216. Washington, DC: American Psychological Association.

Scheier, M.F., J.K. Weintraub, and C.S. Carver. 1986. Coping with stress: Divergent strategies of optimists and pessimists. *Journal of Personality and Social Psychology* 51 (6): 1257–1264.

Schwarzer, R. 1994. Optimism. Vulnerability, and self-beliefs as health-related cognitions: A systematic overview. *Psychology and Health: An International Journal* 9 (3): 161–180.

Schwarzer, R., and A. Born. 1997. Optimistic self-beliefs: Assessment of general perceived self-efficacy in thirteen cultures. *World Psychology* 3 (1–2): 177–190.

Schwarzer, R., and M. Jerusalem. 1995. Generalized self-efficacy scale. In *Measures in health psychology: A user's portfolio. Causal and control beliefs*, ed. J. Weinman, S. Wright, and M. Johnston, 35–37. Windsor: Nfer-Nelson.

Schwarzer, R., J. Bäßler, P. Kwiatek, K. Schröder, and J.X. Zhang. 1997. The assessment of optimistic self-beliefs: Comparison of the German, Spanish, and Chinese versions of the General Self-efficacy Scale. *Applied Psychology: An International Review* 46 (1): 69–88.

Seligman, M.E.P. 1998. Positive social science. *APA monitor* 29 (4): 2–5.

———. 2002. Positive psychology, positive prevention and positive therapy. In *Handbook of positive psychology*, ed. C.R. Snyder and S.J. López, 3–9. New York: Oxford University Press.

Seligman, M., and M. Csikszentmihalyi. 2000. Positive psychology: An introduction. *American Psychologist* 55: 5–14.

Shaffer, M.A., D.A. Harrison, and K.M. Gilley. 1999. Dimensions, determinants, and differences in the expatriate adjustment process. *Journal of International Business Studies* 30: 557–581.

Shaffer, M.A., D.A. Harrison, H. Gregersen, J.S. Black, and L.A. Ferzandi. 2006. You can take it with you: Individual differences and expatriate effectiveness. *Journal of Applied Psychology* 91: 109–125.

Shatte, A.J., K. Reivich, and M.E.P. Seligman. 2000. Promoting human strengths and corporate competencies. *Psychologist* 4 (2): 183–196.

Silvia, P.J. 2008. Appraisal components and emotion traits: Examining the appraisal basis of trait curiosity. *Cognition and Emotion* 22 (1): 94–113.

Spector, P.E. 1994. Using self-report questionnaires in OB research: A comment on the use of a controversial method. *Journal of Organizational Behavior* 15: 385–392.

Spielberger, C.D., and L.M. Starr. 1994. Curiosity and exploratory behavior. In *Motivation: Theory and research*, ed. H.F. O'Neil Jr. and M. Drillings, 221–243. Hillsdale: Lawrence Erlbaum Associates, Inc.

Srinivas, K.M. 1995. Globalization of business and the third world: Challenge of expanding the mindsets. *Journal of Management Development* 14 (3): 26–49.

Stajkovic, A.D., and F. Luthans. 1998. Self-efficacy and work related performance: A meta-analysis. *Psychological Bulletin* 124: 240–261.

Suutari, V., C. Brewster, K. Riusala, and S. Syrjäkari. 2013. Managing non-standard international experience: Evidence from a Finnish company. *Journal of Global Mobility* 1 (2): 118–138.

Tomkins, S.S. 1962. *Affect, imagery, consciousness. Vol. I.* New York: Springer.

———. 1963. *Affect, imagery, consciousness. Vol. II.* New York: Springer.

Ulanova, A. 2014. *Norwegian expatriates in the U.S.: What skills are important for successful adjustment?* Masteroppgave, University of Stavanger, Norway. http://hdl.handle.net/11250/221291

Vautier, S., E. Raufaste, and M. Cariou. 2003. Dimensionality of the revised life orientation test and the status of the filler items. *International Journal of Psychology* 38: 390–400.

Viswesvaran, C., D.S. Ones, and F.L. Schmidt. 1996. Comparative analysis of the reliability of job performance ratings. *Journal of Applied Psychology* 81 (5): 557–574.

Viswesvaran, C., and D.S. Ones. 1999. Meta-analyses of fakability estimates: Implications for personality measurement. *Educational and Psychological Measurement* 59: 197–210.

Voss, H.-G., and H. Keller. 1983. *Curiosity and exploration: Theories and results.* New York: Academic Press.

Ward, C., and A. Kennedy. 1993. Psychological and socio-cultural adjustment during cross-cultural transitions: A comparison of secondary students overseas and at home. *International Journal of Psychology* 28: 129–147.

Wood, R.E., and A. Bandura. 1989. Social cognitive theory of organizational management. *Academy of Management Review* 14: 361–384.

Wooldridge, J.M. 2009. *Introductory econometrics: A modern approach.* Mason: South-Western CENGAGE Learning.

Wright, T.A. 2007. A look at two methodological challenges for scholars interesting in positive organizational behavior. In *Positive organizational behavior*, ed. D.L. Nelson and C.L. Cooper, 177–190. Thousand Oaks: Sage.

Yamazaki, Y., and D.C. Kayes. 2004. An experiential approach to cross-cultural learning: A review and integration of competencies for successful expatriate adaptation. *Academy of Management Learning and Education* 3 (4): 362–379.

Zuckerman, M., E.A. Kolin, L. Price, and I. Zoob. 1964. Development of a sensation seeking scale. *Journal of Consulting and Clinical Psychology* 28: 477–482.

Zuckerman, M. 1983. The distinction between trait and state scales is not arbitrary: Comment on Allen and Potkay's "On the arbitrary distinction between traits and states". *Journal of Personality and Social Psychology* 44 (5): 1083–1086.

# Index[1]



[1] Note: Page numbers followed by 'n' refer to notes.


W. Newburry et al. (eds.), *Contemporary Influences on International Business in Latin America*, AIB Latin America, https://doi.org/10.1007/978-3-319-98340-0

Printed by Printforce, the Netherlands